Current Perspectives on Consumer Psychology

Hatice Aydın & Aysel Kurnaz (Eds.)

Current Perspectives on Consumer Psychology

PETER LANG

Bibliographic Information published by the Deutsche Nationalbibliothek
The Deutsche Nationalbibliothek lists this publication in the Deutsche Nationalbibliografie; detailed bibliographic data is available online at http://dnb.d-nb.de.

Library of Congress Cataloging-in-Publication Data
A CIP catalog record for this book has been applied for at the Library of Congress.

Cover Illustration: @iStock.com / Quarta

ISBN 978-3-631-81634-9 (Print)
E-ISBN 978-3-631-83223-3 (E-PDF)
E-ISBN 978-3-631-83224-0 (EPUB)
E-ISBN 978-3-631-83225-7 (MOBI)
DOI 10.3726/b17423

Peter Lang – Berlin · Bern · Bruxelles · New York · Oxford · Warszawa · Wien

This publication has been peer reviewed.

www.peterlang.com

Preface and Acknowledgements

*If you want to understand what a consumer wants,
you must first understand their psychology.*

Consumer psychology explains why and how people buy things. Consumer psychology is an important area that studies how our thoughts, beliefs, feelings, and perceptions influence our buying behaviors. Business and marketing experts should try to understand consumer psychology because many consumers do not behave in rational ways. To understand consumer psychology, it is necessary to understand the perspectives of consumer psychology, know the theories of consumer psychology, and have knowledge of practices about consumer psychology. The concept of consumer psychology, which constitutes a new agenda in discussions on marketing, includes some theory and research. Before elaborating on research and theory we should know some important perspectives about consumer psychology. This book aims to clarify these points in three sections and twenty chapters. To this end, this book covers in-depth studies from marketing discipline that evaluate consumer psychology, theories, and practices. The first section includes the following chapters:

Section 1 Perspectives of Consumer Psychology

1 The Effect of the Brain on Consumer Behavior: Placebo Effect
2 Post-modern Truth of Consumerism: Hyperreal Consumption
3 Investor Tendencies within the Framework of Behavioral Finance: Herd Behavior
4 Brand Identity and Narcissism
5 The Importance of Slow Food Consumption for Tourism Marketing
6 Different Approaches to the Concept of Consumption
7 Spiritual Consumption as a Rising Trend in Consumer Psychology
8 Thorstein Veblen and Conspicuous Consumption
9 Minimalism in Consumption
10 Consumer Regret
11 The Relationship between Consumer Guilt and Shame and Impulse Buying
12 The Relationship between Subjective Well-Being and Consumer Well-Being
13 Consumer Wisdom

In the second section, there are four chapters that explain the theory of consumer psychology. All chapters present some important theoretical psychological approaches to understanding consumer's behaviors. These chapters contribute theoretically to our understanding of the psychology of consumer behaviors. Chapters in this section are as follows:

Section 2 Theories of Consumer Psychology

14 Customer Evangelism and its Theoretical Bases
15 Self-Identity Theory in Consumer Psychology and Behavior
16 Evaluation of Cognitive Dissonance Theory
17 Socioemotional Selectivity Theory

The third section contains three chapters. These chapters contribute empirically to our understanding of the psychology of consumer behavior. Consumer psychology research deals with the processes that individuals are engaged in when they select, purchase, use, or dispose of products, services, ideas, or experiences to satisfy their needs and desires. These chapters are as follows:

Section 3 Practices of Consumer Psychology

18 Metaphoric Analysis of Consumption Concept in Digital Natives
19 Does the Principle of Least Effort Affect the Intention to Continue Using a Mobile Shopping Application?
20 Bibliometric Analysis of the Journal of Consumer Psychology

In the pages that follow, we will explain the world of consumer psychology. This book will:

- Explain some perspectives on consumer psychology that help us understand consumer behavior,
- Help you and your business to evaluate some of the major perspectives on consumer psychology,
- Help you understand consumer behavior by some theory and research,
- Provide practical, real-world examples of consumer psychology success,
- Offer insight through interviews, analyses, and contributions from consumer psychology experts,
- Explain processes behind consumer decisions.

Consumer psychology is being explained by researchers who are expert in their field. This book aims to be one of the new reliable sources on consumer psychology research. We would like to thank all the authors and researchers who have contributed to this book. We would also like to thank our external reviewers for their expertise and contribution to our book. Furthermore, we appreciate the families and children who are the source of motivation for our authors with their patience. Last but not least, we would like to thank Professor Süleyman ÖZDEMİR, Rector of Bandırma Onyedi Eylül University for his support.

Best regards,

Editors; Hatice AYDIN & Aysel KURNAZ

Contents

List of Contributors

Selay ILGAZ SÜMER
Assistant Prof. Dr., Başkent University, Ankara, Turkey silgaz@baskent.edu.tr

Hülya ER
Lecturer, Bolu Abant İzzet Baysal University, Bolu, Turkey hulyaer@ibu.edu.tr

Evrim ERDOĞAN YAZAR
Assistant Prof. Dr., Ondokuz Mayıs University, Samsun, Turkey evrim.erdogan@omu.edu.tr

Yalçın KAHYA
Assistant Prof. Dr., Bandırma Onyedi Eylül University, Balıkesir, Turkey ykahya@bandirma.edu.tr

Ebru GÜNER
Graduate Assist., Aksaray University, Aksaray, Turkey ebruguner@aksaray.edu.tr

Mehmet Said KÖSE
Assistant Prof. Dr., Bartın Üniversity, Bartın, Turkey
mskose@bartin.edu.tr

Sezen GÜLEÇ
Dr., Sivas Science and Art Center, Sivas, Turkey gulecsezen@gmail.com

Melih BAŞKOL
Assistant Prof. Dr., Bartın University, Bartın, Turkey
mbaskol@bartin.edu.tr

Orhan DUMAN
Assistant Prof. Dr., Bandırma Onyedi Eylül University, Balıkesir, Turkey oduman@bandirma.edu.tr

Murat ER
Graduate Std., Bolu Abant İzzet Baysal University, Bolu, Turkey murat14er@gmail.com

Didem DEMİR
Dr., Toros University, Mersin, Turkey didem.demir@toros.edu.tr

Mutlu UYGUN
Associate Prof. Dr., Aksaray University, Aksaray, Turkey mutluuygun@aksaray.edu.tr

Özlem AKBULUT DURSUN
Assistant Prof. Dr., Sivas Cumhuriyet University, Sivas, Turkey oakbulut@cumhuriyet.edu.tr

Selçuk Yasin YILDIZ
Assistant Prof. Dr, Sivas Cumhuriyet University, Sivas, Turkey
selcukyasinyil@cumhuriyet.edu.tr

İlknur TÜFEKÇİ
Lecturer, Hitit University, Çorum, Turkey
ilknurtufekci@hitit.edu.tr

Elif KARA
Assistant Prof. Dr., Kahramanmaraş Sütçü İmam University, Kahramanmaraş, Turkey elifkara@ksu.edu.tr

Hayrettin ZENGİN
Associate Prof. Dr., Sakarya University, Sakarya, Turkey hzengin@sakarya.edu.tr

Ümit BAŞARAN
Assistant Prof. Dr., Zonguldak Bülent Ecevit University, Zonguldak, Turkey umitbasaran@beun.edu.tr

Somayyeh BIKARI
Dr., İstanbul, Turkey somaye_be@yahoo.com

Volkan TEMİZKAN
Assistant Prof. Dr., Karabük University, Karabük, Turkey vtemizkan@karabuk.edu.tr

Eda KUTLU
Graduate Std., Sakarya University, Sakarya,Turkey edaakutlu@gmail.com

Hatice AYDIN
Associate Prof. Dr., Bandırma Onyedi Eylül University, Balıkesir, Turkey, haydin@bandirma.edu.tr

Emre HARORLI
Dr., Atatürk University, Erzurum, Turkey eharorli@atauni.edu.tr

Aysel KURNAZ
Assistant Prof. Dr., Bandırma Onyedi Eylül University, Balıkesir, Turkey akurnaz@bandirma.edu.tr

Section 1 Perspectives of Consumer Psychology

Selay ILGAZ SÜMER

1 The Effect of the Brain on Consumer Behavior: Placebo Effect

Introduction

Marketing has an interdisciplinary aspect as it can draw from many other scientific disciplines. At this juncture, the task of marketing managers is to analyze the relationship between marketing and other closely related scientific disciplines accurately. Such an analysis would contribute to the formulation of more effective strategic marketing plans. Economics, mathematics, political science, international relations, history, statistics, law, geography, medicine, and psychology can be given as examples of other scientific disciplines to which marketing is related. Consumer-centric marketing activities are incontrovertibly and closely related to psychology.

Psychology can be defined as "the behavioral science focusing on the research of events occurring within one's inner life and in one's mind" (Ecer & Canıtez, 2004: 32). It is crucial for marketing managers to observe the changes in the consumer's mental life and inner world closely, interpret these changes, and reach certain conclusions based on his observations and interpretations. Consumers are regarded to be a driving force for the planning of marketing activities. Therefore, not understanding the consumer correctly harms the sustainability of the business and might decrease, or even eliminate in some cases, the chances of success in today's competitive conditions.

The reasons why consumers buy a certain good or service cannot always be explained with rationality. In such cases, the close interdisciplinary collaboration between marketing and psychology would contribute to the formation of the causal relationship. Furthermore, persuasive skills, regarded to be a concrete indicator of the success of sales forces in marketing activities, are obtained through a proper understanding of consumer psychology.

An argument put forward within the scope of sensory branding, an extensively studied concept in marketing literature, is that consumers might display a wide range of reactions due to the psychological meanings they assign to products during decision-making and purchasing processes. In other words, the five senses play a vital role in the consumer decision-making process. The visual, olfactory, auditory, gustatory, and tactile senses of consumers govern their perceptions and perceptual processes, leading them to make comments about certain goods and services. At this point, the concept of placebo and the placebo effect come into play. There are some marketing studies on placebo and the placebo effect in the academic literature. These studies aim to examine the impact of the placebo effect on consumer behavior.

This chapter will deal with the psychological factors affecting consumer behavior, the concept of "placebo", the placebo effect, the mechanisms related to the placebo effect, and the links between marketing and the placebo effect.

1 Psychological Factors Affecting Consumer Behavior

The key to success in marketing is to understand consumer behavior. However, even though considerable efforts are devoted to understanding the consumer, the reasons underlying consumer behavior are yet to be deciphered completely. Factors affecting consumer behavior can be categorized as cultural, social, personal, and psychological. Psychological factors consist of 'motivation, perception, learning, beliefs, and attitudes' (Kotler & Armstrong, 2012: 137).

Motivation refers to the mobilization of individuals through certain stimuli (Yükselen, 2012). Consumers particularly take action to meet certain unsatisfied needs (Berkman et al., 2001).

Perception can be defined as the process in which the individual gathers, selects, organizes, and interprets information to make sense of their world (Çağlayan, Korkmaz, & Öktem, 2014: 162).

Learning signifies the permanent change in behavior due to experience (Solomon, 2007). As for beliefs and attitudes, they are among the factors used to explain consumer behavior. Beliefs are the definitive thoughts of the individual regarding objects and ideas while attitudes denote the tendencies, emotions, and evaluations of the individual concerning certain objects and ideas (Yükselen, 2012: 133). Consumers might hold positive, negative, or neutral beliefs about a certain object. In fact, these assessments made by consumers might differ in each case and for each individual. For example, the consumer might dream of a hot cup of coffee on a cold day whereas the same beverage may not seem as appealing on a hot summer day (Pandit, 2015). While assessing consumer attitudes towards goods and services, marketing managers must take the effects of attitude components, categorized as cognitive, affective, and behavioral responses, on consumer behavior into account (Odabaşı & Barış, 2002).

2 The Concept of Placebo and the Placebo Effect

Psychological factors have profound impacts on consumer behavior. One of the essential ways of comprehending the reasons behind consumer behavior is trying to detect how psychological factors affect one's behavior. In this respect, marketing managers must take the potential effects of placebo on consumer behavior into consideration. An assessment in this regard would provide substantial benefits.

The use of the concept of placebo and the placebo effect dates back a long time in the history of medicine. A placebo can be defined as 'a way of medical treatment believed to have no specific effects on the treated condition and used for its symbolic impact or as an initiative aiming to accelerate medical treatment' (Göka, 2002: 59–60). The placebo effect is a concept denoting the outcome of a treatment that has no pharmacodynamic effect nor a specific feature for the treatment, yet that patient believes to be effective (Erdem, Akarsu, & Gülsün, 2013: 300). It is used for cases in which a patient recovers even though they were given a substance with no therapeutic effect or prescribed a "treatment" with no medical benefits. Research on the placebo effect shows that behavioral reactions are affected by one's expectations (Gerrig & Zimbardo, 2012).

The term "placebo" is the future tense conjugation of the Latin verb "placeo" in the first person singular, meaning "I will please" (Hedges & Burchfield, 2005: 161). The word "placebo" was first used in the Latin translation of a biblical prayer originally written in Hebrew. In the 14th century, the meaning of the word changes as it was used in the phrase "to sing placebo" to denote people who were hired to mourn after the passing of an important person. This period of history is significant for the meaning of this concept as it was used as "replacing something" for the first time. In the medical sense, the concept was first used in the 18th century (Göker, Yılmaz, & Kumbasar, 2009: 184). In 1811, a definition of the concept was included in Hopper's Medical Dictionary. In this dictionary, it was described as a treatment with pleasing effects for the patient rather than an actual therapeutic impact (Ertaş & Tuğlular, 1991: 11). In fact, one of the most prominent physicians of Ancient Rome, Galen associated the symptoms of therapeutic success with their psychological nature with a rate of 60% rather than their organic nature. Paracelsus, a Swiss physician, believed that the shapes and colors of plants are correlated with their therapeutic effects. For instance, he believed lungworts could be used to treat tuberculosis due to its shape resembling a lung (Göker, Yılmaz, & Kumbasar, 2009). In 1932, a clinical pharmacologist named Paul Martini clearly stated that simulated pills were used to control active treatments without using the term "placebo", 'taking one of the first steps in the development of these double-blind techniques'. Martini believed in 'the importance of mixing an active treatment with a controlled substance, a turning point in the history of clinical pharmacology' (Göker, Yılmaz, & Kumbasar, 2009: 184; Macedo, Farré, & Baños, 2003: 340). Various research studies published in 1964 and 1968 continued to focus on the concept of placebo and the placebo effect. A definition made in the 1990s describes a placebo as a medication affecting the person due to mental factors rather than showing therapeutic effects through regular organic mechanisms. In 2001, The Columbia Encyclopedia defined the concept as a non-active substance given in place of a strong medicine (Macedo, Farré, & Baños, 2003: 338).

3 Mechanisms Related to the Placebo Effect

The placebo effect is one of the subjects drawing considerable attention from psychologists. Researchers increasingly focus on and question the mechanisms underlying the placebo effect. A literature review reveals that research studies generally use expectancy theory and classical conditioning to explain the placebo effect (Ling, Shieh, & Liao, 2012). It can be argued that these two theoretical frameworks complement each other as far as the placebo effect is concerned (Williams & Podd, 2004). Understanding the relationship between the placebo effect and the expectancy theory and classical conditioning is considered to be crucial to make sense of the placebo effect in the marketing context.

3.1 The Expectancy Theory

The expectancy theory was proposed by Victor H. Vroom. Vroom stated that motivation stems from two main factors. According to his approach, one's expectations of achieving an end as a result of a certain action and the level of attractiveness of the result to be obtained by adopting a behavior in the eyes of the individual affect motivation (Şimşek, Akgemci, & Çelik, 2003).

The expectancy theory is frequently cited to explain the placebo effect. From the perspective of the theory in question, the placebo effect clearly acts as an intermediary for certain expectations (Williams & Podd, 2004). In other words, "placebo effects arise because beliefs about a substance/procedure serving as a placebo activate expectations that a particular effect will occur" (Ling, Shieh, & Liao, 2012: 265). The expectations in question are observed to arise in the forms of faith and hope (Makasi & Govender, 2014). The placebo exerts the effect expected by the individual and creates expectations for a certain effect. Therefore, it would be reasonable to claim that placebos are expectation manipulations (Williams & Podd, 2004).

3.2 Classical Conditioning

Classical conditioning is based on studies by Ivan Pavlov. Pavlov conducted various studies on dogs. His studies revealed that learning occurs as a result of the reactions to stimuli and that no reaction is displayed in the absence of stimuli. In addition to these findings, it was also indicated that three main principles, namely repetition, stimulus generalization, and stimulus discrimination, are crucial in classical conditioning (Koç, 2007; Odabaşı & Barış, 2002).

Studies in the academic literature underline that classical conditioning processes can be taken into account while explaining the placebo effect. In this context, placebo reactions are indicated to be based on classical conditioning (Voudouris, Peck, & Coleman, 1990). Within the framework of classical conditioning, expectations are considered to be conditioned responses (Williams & Podd, 2004).

4 The Placebo Effect in Marketing

There is a plethora of research studies on placebos and the placebo effect within the medical and psychiatric literatures. Owing to the intriguing nature of the subject, the number and variety of studies taking placebos into account have increased. Thus, similar studies have found a place in the marketing literature as well.

It is possible to make use of the placebo effect to make sense of consumer behavior, which has been studied for many years but yet to be deciphered completely. Within the context of marketing, the placebo effect can be briefly defined as the impact of consumers' beliefs and expectations shaped by their daily experiences on their judgments about products (Shiv, Carmon, & Ariely, 2005a). The placebo effect would shed light on consumer mentality, benefiting marketing managers.

In order for goods and services produced by businesses to meet consumer desires and needs, they need to have certain characteristics. One of them is product quality. However, consumers' beliefs and expectations regarding products play a crucial role in their experience concerning these goods and services. Based on various particles of information, consumers create their own realities and follow the beliefs in the subconscious rather than their objective observations (Zaltman, 2003). In other words, from time to time, consumers deceive their minds by not acting consciously (Akıllıbaş, 2019).

Marketing managers may create powerful perceptual effects in consumers' minds through their activities (Shiv, Carmon, & Ariely, 2005a). At this point, they can use the placebo effect while formulating their marketing strategies in a way that would govern consumer beliefs and expectations. However, this might occasionally contradict traditional economic models. Traditional models state that consumers initially question the benefits of the good or service while purchasing it. Furthermore, they also claim that they buy the product if the sales price is below the base price in the consumer's mind. Yet studies show that consumers occasionally consider a product's price as an indicator of its quality. In other words, they might perceive the price as a cue of the benefit to be enjoyed (Rao & Monroe, 1989). Therefore, the non-conscious beliefs of consumers regarding the correlation between the product and quality might affect their overall experience with the said product. Pursuant to this, the ability of the price to raise the expected value of the product would affect the perceptions regarding the real performance of the product in question (Irmak, Block, & Fitzsimons, 2005; Shiv, Carmon, & Ariely, 2005a). This shows that the price, one of the elements of the marketing mix, can create a placebo effect (Ling, Shieh, & Liao, 2012).

Thorstein Veblen stated that associating consumption solely with biological needs is inadequate. He also considered consumption as an indicator of social status. In other words, goods and services purchased by consumers might be associated with their efforts to imitate higher social classes. There are some efforts to use consumption as a means of obtaining status and prestige in one's society. For this reason, consumers prefer buying expensive and luxurious products (Güleç, 2015). In short, certain products are desired due to their emotional values rather than their functional benefits. This can be explained with the concept of hedonic consumption. In hedonic consumption, the symbolic benefits of products are foregrounded (Açıkalın & Yaşar, 2017). It can be stated that pricing produces a placebo effect in hedonic consumption. In this case, the phenomenon of high prices is the junction point of hedonic consumption and the placebo effect (Kim & Jang, 2013).

The country of origin has the potential of creating a positive or negative placebo effect within the scope of marketing activities. In this respect, goods and services produced in countries associated with negative stereotypes exert a negative placebo effect. Consumers are not satisfied with the products originating from such countries. The placebo effect is a subject that needs to be handled carefully by businesses for their success in international marketing activities. In fact, studies show that consumers assess the products they intend to purchase based on their country of origin in addition to features such as shape, design, or color. Occasionally, the country of origin can affect the perceptions of consumers regarding the quality of goods and services produced in the country in question. Statements like "American products are better than Chinese ones" or "imported goods are superior to local goods" can be given as examples to this situation (Lazzari & Slongo, 2015).

One of the elements of the promotional mix, advertising also has the potential of producing the placebo effect. With their advertisements, businesses stimulate consumer expectations and might alter the real impact of the advertised products (Shiv, Carmon, & Ariely, 2005b). Celebrity endorsements for a product might also affect the evocation of certain effects in consumers' minds. This can be explained with the placebo effect created in marketing activities. Consumers might have a more hospitable attitude towards products endorsed by celebrity figures they like. The reason behind this attitude is that the advertised products are confirmed by celebrity figures admired by the target market (Bhandari, 2014).

Marketing managers can change consumer perceptions, expectations, and beliefs by manipulating various factors such as product features or distribution channels (Pilat, 2014). Brand awareness might be used by businesses as a placebo to increase the perceived quality of the product in question (Hsiao et al., 2014). Research studies show that the scarcity, taste, and packaging of the said product are among the characteristics with the potential of producing the placebo effect in marketing. Within this scope, consumers relate the scarcity of certain products with quality, believe that tasteless products are healthy, and have their expectations regarding product uniqueness influenced by its packaging. It is also possible to explain the increase in positive expectations regarding the product correlated with its decreased taste with classical conditioning, one of the mechanisms related to the placebo effect (Wright et al., 2012; Wright et al., 2013).

Conclusion

A wide range of scientific disciplines contributes significantly to marketing studies. Psychology is the leading domain among such disciplines. The close relationship between marketing and psychology requires managers to take psychological concepts into consideration while formulating marketing plans. Placebos and the placebo effect are among such concepts.

A state that can be related to the fact that the brain steers consumers, the placebo effect particularly occurs within the context of pricing, promotion, and branding. In order to succeed, businesses operating in the highly competitive market conditions must determine what kind of emotions they want to evoke in consumers' minds and develop marketing plans and strategies taking the psychological impact they want to create into consideration.

While determining marketing strategies, marketing managers should make use of the placebo effect in a way that would steer consumer beliefs and expectations. Marketing scholars ought to conduct more qualitative and quantitative studies evaluating the placebo effect within the scope of consumer psychology.

References

Açıkalın, S. & Yaşar, M. (2017). A research on investigation of the consumer behaviours in the context of hedonic and utilitarian consumption: Determining the hedonic consumption tendency of youth. *The Journal of International Social Research*, 10(48), pp. 570–585.

Akıllıbaş, E. (2019). The power of five senses in the perception of marketing. *Bitlis Eren University Journal of Academic Projection*, 4(1), pp. 97–124.

Berkman, Ü., Can, H., Güngör Ergan, N., Paksoy, M., Yüksel, Ö., Altınışık, S., Aydın, A. H., Güney, S., Murat, G., Ulusoy, D., Bacacı Varoğlu, D., Arıkan, S., Arslan, M., Aşan, Ö., Çevik, H., Göksu, T., Kılıç, M., Minibaş, J. & Zel, U. (2001). *Yönetim ve Organizasyon*. Ankara: Nobel Yayın Dağıtım.

Bhandari, V. (2014). *The Placebo Effect-Marketing*. Retrieved February 13, 2020 from http://financetipoff.com/the-placebo-effect-marketing/.

Çağlayan, S., Korkmaz, M. & Öktem, G. (2014). Evaluation of visual perception in art in terms of literature. *Journal of Research in Education and Teaching*, 3(1), pp. 160–173.

Ecer, H. F. & Canıtez, M. (2004). *Pazarlama Ilkeleri Teoriler ve Yaklaşımlar*. Ankara: Gazi Kitabevi.

Erdem, M., Akarsu, S. & Gülsün, M. (2013). Neurobiology of placebo effect. *Current Approaches in Psychiatry*, 5(3), pp. 299–312.

Ertaş, M. & Tuğlular, I. (1991). Placebo-Nocebo. *Bull. Cli. Psychopharmacol*, 1(3), pp. 11–15.

Gerrig, R. J. & Zimbardo, P. G. (2012). *Psychology and Life*. New Jersey: Pearson Education.

Göka, E. (2002). The concept of placebo and the effect of placebo. *Turkish Journal of Psychiatry*, 13(1), pp. 58–64.

Göker, C., Yılmaz, A. & Kumbasar, H. (2009). Is placebo efficacious? Ethical? *Bulletin of Clinical Psychopharmacology*, 19, pp. 183–192.

Güleç, C. (2015). Thorstein Veblen ve gösterişçi tüketim kavramı. *Sosyal Bilimler Enstitüsü Dergisi*, 38, pp. 62–82.

Hedges, D. & Burchfield, C. (2005). The placebo effect and its implications. *The Journal of Mind and Behavior*, 26(3), pp. 161–180.

Hsiao, Y. H., Hsu, Y. H., Chu, S. Y. & Fang, W. (2014). Discussion of whether brand awareness is a form of marketing placebo. *International Journal of Business and Information*, 9(1), pp. 29–60.

Irmak, C., Block, L. G. & Fitzsimons, G. J. (2005). The placebo effect in marketing: Sometimes you just have to want it to work. *Journal of Marketing Research*, 42(4), pp. 406–409.

Kim, D. & Jang, S. (2013). Price placebo effect in hedonic consumption. *International Journal of Hospitality Management*, 35, pp. 306–315.

Koç, E. (2007). *Tüketici davranışı ve pazarlama stratejileri: global ve yerel yaklaşım*. Ankara: Seçkin Yayıncılık.

Kotler, P. & Armstrong, G. (2012). *Principles of Marketing*. U.S.A.: Pearson Education.

Lazzari, F. & Slongo, L. A. (2015). The placebo effect in marketing: The ability of country of origin to modify product performance. *Brazilian Business Review*, 12(5), pp. 39–56.

Ling, I. L., Shieh, C. H. & Liao, J. F. (2012). The higher the price the better the result? The placebo-like effects of price and brand on consumer judgments. *Theoretical Economics Letters*, 2, pp. 264–269.

Macedo, A., Farré, M. & Baños, J. E. (2003). Placebo effect and placebos: What are we talking about? Some conceptual and historical considerations. *European Journal of Clinical Pharmacology*, 59, pp. 337–342.

Makasi, A. & Govender, K. (2014). Price as a proxy of quality: Achieving something out of nothing through the placebo effect. *Journal of Economics*, 5(3), pp. 239–246.

Odabaşı, Y. & Barış, G. (2002). *Tüketici Davranışı*. İstanbul: MediaCat Akademi.

Pandit, A. (2015). Beliefs, attitudes and motivation that affect marketing of forest honey (A case study of honey marketing in west Bengal). *IOSR Journal of Business and Management*, 17(6), pp. 1–13.

Pilat, V. J. (2014). Qualitative research of placebo effect on marketing toward product pricing. *Journal EMBA*, 2(4), pp. 621–625.

Rao, A. R. & Monroe, K. B. (1989). The effect of price, brand name, and store name on buyers' perceptions of product quality: An integrative review. *Journal of Marketing Research*, 26(3), pp. 351–357.

Shiv, B., Carmon, Z. & Ariely, D. (2005a). Placebo effects of marketing actions: Consumers may get what they pay for. *Journal of Marketing Research*, 42(4), pp. 383–393.

Shiv, B., Carmon, Z. & Ariely, D. (2005b). Ruminating about placebo effects of marketing actions. *Journal of Marketing Research*, 42(4), pp. 410–414.

Solomon, M. R. (2007). *Consumer Behavior*. New Jersey: Pearson Education.

Şimşek, M. Ş., Akgemci, T. & Çelik, A. (2003). *Davranış Bilimlerine Giriş Ve Örgütlerde Davranış*. Konya: Adım Matbaacılık.

Voudouris, N. J., Peck, C. L. & Coleman, C. (1990). The role of conditioning and verbal expectancy in the placebo response. *Pain*, 43, pp. 121–128.

Williams, S. S. & Podd, J. (2004). The placebo effect: Dissolving the expectancy versus conditioning debate. *Psychological Bulletin*, 130(2), pp. 324–340.

Wright, S., Hernandez, J. M. C., Sundar, A., Dinsmore, J. & Kardes, F. (2012). Effects of set size, scarcity, packaging, and taste on the marketing placebo effect. *Advances in Consumer Research*, 40, pp. 917–919.

Wright, S., Hernandez, J. M. C., Sundar, A., Dinsmore, J. & Kardes, F. (2013). If it tastes bad it must be good: Consumer naïve theories and the marketing placebo effect. *International Journal of Research in Marketing*, 30, pp. 197–198.

Yükselen, C. (2012). *Pazarlama Ilkeler-Yönetim-Örnek Olaylar*. Ankara: Detay Yayıncılık.

Zaltman, G. (2003). *How Customers Think: Essential Insights into The Mind of the Market*. U.S.A.: Harvard Business School Press.

Orhan DUMAN

2 Post-Modern Truth of Consumerism: Hyperreal Consumption

Introduction

Hyperreality is a post-modern concept. The development and proliferation of technology and the Internet have started to reshape consumer mentality, triggering an evolution from the rigid identity structure of modernity to a constantly renewing identity structure owing to consumption. Augmented reality and virtual reality contributed to the existing consumer perceptions of reality, various artificial worlds like theme parks were created owing to the advancement of computer technologies and structural developments, and simulated spaces were constructed. Consequently, simulated and imaginary goods, services, and media that do not exist in the real world have emerged. By providing people with the opportunity to experience a wide range of emotions and thrilling sensations in artificial spaces such as computer games, technological advancements have narrowed the gap between reality and virtuality. These virtual worlds offered consumers the chance to experience various roles they are curious about as if they were real. Hyperreality allows contemporary consumers to experience identities they want to obtain and imitate, carrying them to virtual worlds as, for instance, a firefighter or an astronaut. In addition to every economic, social, political, and cultural assumption imposed by the modern lifestyle, the post-modern lifestyle also affects authority, information sources, and all disciplines including marketing. As for hyperreality, it is the most prevalent reflection of post-modernism upon consumption (Parsons & Maclaran, 2009).

Before dealing with hyperreal consumption, one needs to define the concepts of "real" and "reality". The concept of "real" denotes the formation and interpretation of one's perceptions regarding one's surroundings through their senses. The perception of reality signifies everything that can be related to the real. Today, the development of computer-mediated simulations and social structures blurs the difference between what is real and what is virtual (Rheingold, 1991). Reality is experienced by one's senses through computer systems; it is a simulation almost strong enough to imitate reality in one's mind (MacKinnon, 1998). Computer simulations are so realistic that they make people perceive the virtual as real and vice versa (Rheingold, 1991). In hyperreality, the real and meanings are produced multiple times. The production of goods and services in the modernist sense has little significance in the hyperreal realm. Today, material production has taken on a hyperreal aspect, transforming into a larger-scale entity while retaining certain features of traditional production. Even as a mere simulation of the real, the hyperreal leads to its convergence with the real in many aspects. In this sense, hyperreality can be defined as the recreation of reality with models through simulations without any foundation. It denotes the disappearance of the border between reality and fiction, reality becoming a simulation (Baudrillard, 1994).

Considering the present-day significance of post-modernism and hyperreality, this chapter will first explain these concepts, dealing with related issues. At this juncture, the issues of hyperreal consumption, being a consumer in the hyperreal realm, experiences of hyperreal consumption, and, ultimately, meaning and values in hyperreal consumption.

1 Post-Modernism and Hyperreality

Post-modernism has emerged with the proliferation of industrialization, technology, and capitalism, becoming evident with the rapid expansion of mass communication tools. While the concept of "consistency" is central in the modern period, "openness" is the key concept of the post-modern period. With post-modernism, tools of communication provided access to different perspectives, styles, and opinions from around the world and the consequent cosmopolitan attitude brought about increased ease of acceptance of variety. Therefore, based on one's point of view, all concepts can either be accepted or be approached with suspicion and rejected. This fragmented structure with no commitment, rejecting loyalty and confidence, in which anything can be tried and given up, has started to put pressure on modern social patterns. For post-modern consumers, no emotional or cognitive attachment beyond the purchase and trial of a good or service is necessary (Firat, 1991). Through cultural forms through marketing and advertising, the post-modern consumption culture systematically creates a culture of hypersignification (Goldman & Sapson, 1994). Since signs, unlike other works, cannot erode, contemporary culture denotes a continuous process of reappropriation and resignification of past signs. In this respect, the post-modern culture is the constant arrangement of trends, images, and styles. Thus, within the context of consumption, meanings are created, multiplied, manipulated, and restructured in places where signs are more important through continuous rearrangement (Barthes, 1983). The main idea of post-modernism is the fragmentation of culture and the increase of the significance of symbolism over the substance. As a symbolic activity rather than an instrumental one, consumption consists of meanings and emancipated signs with no constant meanings, not goods and services consumed by users. In the post-modern society, hyperreality means that any given object can bear any kind of meaning (Williams, 1998).

Post-modern consumption is comprised of five categories: hyperreality, fragmentation, reversal of production and consumption, decentering of the subject, and juxtapositions of opposites. The primary reasons for post-modern change are social and technical. While social change can be described as individualization and subsequent paradoxical series, technical change occurs in the form of hyperreality, chaos, and value actualization. The use of the product is more important than its production. Therefore, products are not significant and valuable for consumers until actual use; purchasing the product is not sufficient in this sense. In post-modernism, this is considered to be the reversal of production and consumption (Firat, 1992). From another perspective, it is possible to identify seven fundamental features of post-modernism: fragmentation, de-differentiation, hyperreality, chronology, pastiche, anti-foundationalism, and pluralism (Williams, 1998). With post-modernism, the lines separating production and consumption become blurry and consumers become producers of symbolic significance through their consumption. Post-modern advances in consumption processes offer consumers different identities and form independent of traditional constraints and roles like race, class, or gender. Using digital avatars, consumers are able to conduct many activities ranging from shopping and trading to socialization. In this sense, virtual consumption manifests an aspect of hyperrealism that members of the culture in question simulate, construct, and experience (Firat & Venkatesh, 1995).

2 Hyperreal Consumption

Consumption is a constant activity aiming to overcome material and immaterial deficiencies occurring due to human nature and to satisfy one's needs, like any other living beings, maintained until the end of life. The senses of depletion, spending, and waste are foregrounded in the concept of consumption (Williams, 1998). While other living beings consume to satisfy biological needs in nature, human beings also reflect their psychological and social needs to their consumption. While consumption is a physiological and social behavior, it also shows an institutional structure as a reflection of the social values system. In a post-modern society, in addition to material objects, ideas and signs are also consumed. In civilized and industrialized societies, it signifies the tangible and relational dialectic of wealth within the relationship between infinite needs and finite resources from the perspective of the differentiation of and competition between individuals. While each relationship increases wealth in primitive exchanges, every possession increases individual deprivation in our "differentiating" societies as possessions are relativized. Today, aiming values rather than objects, our needs obliges one to embrace values before satisfaction (Baudrillard, 2016).

3 Being a Consumer in the Hyperreal Context

Instead of having a single real self, post-modern consumers have multiple selves adapted to the necessities brought about by circumstances. If that single real self still exists, it is hidden behind the multiple selves in which it plays a situational role. This hyperrealistic compilation of selves paves the way for a wide range of experiences and excitements, yet these experiences are hollow. In many tourist destinations, particularly the historical and cultural elements are eviscerated for the sake of temporary entertainment venues for tourists. Detached from the lives and symbols of their past, tourists wander around these destinations to have a good yet idle time, disconnected from religious, national, cultural, and historical realities (Kundera, 1984).

In the modern age, an economy of scale was a significant concept attained by producing more of everything. Denoting the increased production of all goods and services, mass production signified the perpetual repetition of the same products. However, in the post-modern age, with the contribution of technological advancements, mass production has started to signify the production of different varieties and personalized versions of a product rather than the repeated production of the same product. Consequently, post-modern consumers have started to opt for unique products, all of their characteristics determined by the said consumers, rather than buying a previously-produced good or service. Today, from the screens of their computers or using tools like VR glasses, consumers can both experience finalized versions of products before their production and determine their preferences simultaneously (Belk et al., 1989).

Above all, the post-modern period eliminates the functionality of traditional structures of social inequality such as family, social class, or unions individualized by inequality. Various roles representing social roles and contracts such as paternity or maternity. Individuals can govern their identities regarding all lifestyle decisions related to professional life, marriage, and parenthood. While traditional values and norms rely on contracts made with God, post-modern values are based on variety, the lack of commitment, pragmatism, eclecticism, and tolerance (Harvey, 1990).

4 Experiences in Hyperreal Consumption

The concept of hyperreality creates an experience through a simulated reality. Consumption is an exchange between images and signs. Created through usage, images and signs replace significance and values while functionality becomes merely one of the signs. This simulation experience consists of four stages. The first stage reflects direct reality, the second denotes the representations of reality, the third signifies the images of reality, and the fourth marks the attainment of hyperreality in which these images are directly considered to be the reality (Baudrillard, 1994). In consumption experiences, imagination plays a crucial role. These hyperreal objects and symbols fill every space reflecting the contemporary consumer culture such as malls, various commercial venues, or theme parks. In such spaces, consumers are trapped in a perpetual chain of indicators such as images. The interaction of a consumer with a hyperreal service might bring about a more definite experience of reality when compared with conventional reality. In daily life, individuals constantly experience the multiplication of roles, relationships, and characteristics simulated through televised series. The belief that one's favorite television shows are the reality arising through signs and symbols and actors who play the antagonists being attacked in the streets might be given as examples (Venkatesh, 1999). With this aspect, consumer experiences affect the way one defines consumer behavior with its multi-sensory, fantasy and emotive facets (Hirschman & Holbrook, 1982).

Hyperreal experiences are the (partially) simulated versions of a service experience affecting consumer perceptions and behavior (Baudrillard, 1994). They provide a space in which impacts on the individual are carefully designated and managed while being directed by signs and symbols. In this respect, before buying a good or service, consumers might experience post-purchase satisfaction related to the product in a hyperrealistic way by testing is as if it exists in a real setting (Edvardsson et al., 2005). Real traffic or household conditions can be simulated with virtual reality in order to allow consumers to try, for instance, a car or a vacuum cleaner. Therefore, consumers get the chance to try the product and make a decision accordingly before purchasing it. Similarly, to the possibility of using a simulator to test a car, physical products can also be experienced through virtual reality. As far as testing services are concerned, only certain elements of the service in question should be tested; simulating the service in its entirety must be avoided. If the whole service is simulated, the consumer can experience the service with the simulation, obviating the necessity to purchase the service (Edvardsson et al., 2007). In general, it is difficult to detect the differences between authentic products and fake ones; this differentiation bears little significance for the consumer. In fact, imitation products might create a distortion in the idea of the hyperreal and simulation. If consumption is defined as a simulation, imitation products may be regarded as simulations of the simulation (Henningsen, 2010).

Consumer experiences regarding goods and services increasingly become significant within the scope of post-modernism as far as symbolic meaning is concerned. Brands aspire to maintain their existing customers by creating values and presenting various offers in the market and to maximize their profit by attracting new customers (Bendapudi & Leone, 2003). Today, what makes one brand superior to others is customer experiences rather than monetary outcomes or the cognitive assessments of a given service (Johnston & Clark, 2008). Within the scope of such experiences, evoking emotive reactions rather than focusing on functional qualities would make the experiences in question more striking (Cronin, 2003). Values are now created with customers no longer embedded in goods and services; their development relies on customer experiences. In product development, the customer might be integrated into the design process of the product to transform the product in question to a personalized experience; they can also participate in a pre-purchase experience (Prahalad & Ramaswamy, 2004). Therefore, through the creation of total customer experience, consumers are included in the production process (Berry et al., 2002).

5 Meaning and Value in Hyperreal Consumption

Realities experienced intensively through media and advertising and the construction of this situation comprises hyperreality. In hyperreality, advertising is a vital element of the product. By providing the consumer with a potential experience as a part of the product in question, advertising paves the way for the augmented product. The correspondence of the advertisement with reality can only be assessed after the experience with the product, an integral part of the consumer experience. If the consumer believes in the reality of the advertisement, they will attain the reality proposed by the advertisement while perceiving the proposition in it as real (Postman, 1985). This aspect of hyperrealism reveals the tendency of constructing and experiencing the simulation by creating a simulated environment between the members of a culture. This simulation can be described as the process in which a sign within a fictional game is changed constantly while producing a chain of endless meanings (Baudrillard, 1983: 113). When these simulations are embraced by the members of a social structure, they become the social reality of that community and members start to display identity behavior confirming the simulation. Consumer groups can participate in such simulations with great enthusiasm in several ways. Through the use of structures aiming to simulate the reality that would be experienced in a place where one has never been to such as theme parks or virtual reality technologies with computer simulations, consumers are given the opportunity to experience these situations. Scenes, sensations, and opinions are either presented or stimulated in such simulations (Kaplan, 1987). An integral part of the digital culture, computers represent a significant social transformation brought about by information and telecommunication technologies. While modern technologies are fundamentally perceived as production machines through instrumental terms, post-modern technologies are seen as communicative tools allowing one to navigate in cyberspaces, virtual realities, and computer-mediated domains. These advancements result in new identities and new communicative and consumption symbols for consumers (Poster, 1995).

Pre-purchase experiences become more significant for consumers. These experiences function as a kind of simulation for consumers. The novel experiential nature of consumption denotes the assessment of consumers as beings with social connections rather than potential buyers of a good or service. It underlines the significance of emotions and experiences instead of traditional marketing assumptions expecting consumers to reach rational decisions by processing the information they have obtained. In hyperreality, user experiences play a crucial role in consumers' lives along with hedonic consumption and fantasies (Holbrook, 1995). Contemporary consumers seek relational value rather than focusing on the usage value of goods and services. Consumers look for different and significant connections through goods and services and the value of the time spent on this search becomes more important than the money spent on the said product. As a part of their preferences, consumers try to experience more with the brands they purchase. As an indicator of social relationships, they form closer bonds with consumer groups similar to theirs, associating their experiences with a sense of belonging to a group (Cova, 1996).

Brands might create certain meanings through their goods and services, but if they fail to reflect these meanings upon consumers, they will not be considered original, leading to their rejection. In this respect, rather than adopting the value perception created by marketers, consumers will come up with their own personal and social meanings. The efforts of brands to shape consumers by creating social structures for their goods and services, brand promises, and values do not seem to be feasible in a post-modern market. Consumers pay high amounts to companies and, at the same time, do certain tasks in terms of experiences and hedonism. From the rationalist perspective of modernism, such an absurdity might only an outcome of the meanings created with hyperreal consumption (Parsons & Maclaran, 2009).

Conclusion

Meanings carried by today's reality might differ substantially from the reality of the past. We can define this reality as a sum of virtual or augmented realities through computer simulations. These simulations may appeal to all senses of the contemporary individual, directing them to perceptions and emotions through their effects. Present-day reality allows consumers to have real experiences that they are not at all familiar with, or even that they will never be familiar with, by creating a hyperreal space through simulations. These experiences are not only about reaching the most unattainable places but also about bringing the contemporary consumer to different realities, statuses, and wealth that their social and economic standing cannot afford socially and psychologically. By adopting certain consumption patterns, consumers become able to attain their realities by simulating wealth through imitation. Hyperreal consumption is about the adoption of the indicators related to the identity the consumer desires rather than having an authentic identity. Instead of a consistent linear path of one's past, present or future; individual's consumers strive to be, identities they attempt to experience, and innocent individual realities they just want to experience are foregrounded. With the advancement of technology and the development of social life in digital spaces, the individual presents themselves as they want to be seen and to the extent they want to be perceived, adopting different images through separate identity presentations for each addressee. This brings about a sense of liberty to the contemporary consumer beyond its control, potentially harming the dependability and consistency of their relationships significantly. An exceptionally large amount of fake content and imitations produced in this hyperreal realm in which one does and consumes as he pleases causes increased difficulties in finding reality and facts. The scope of hyperrealism has expanded through different meanings to the extent of transforming brands, goods, and services into concepts beyond mere commodities, making fundamental values like identities, lifestyles, genders, and religion a part of this consumption. Cut from their roots and disregarding their past, the contemporary consumer sacrifices the reality, a path that would allow them to take concrete steps for its future, for pleasures in a hyperreal world. These conveniences and unlimited opportunities offered by technology eradicate concerns about one's future, showing the contemporary consumer multiple ways. The contemporary consumer is free to choose one of these ways with the emancipation brought about by hyperreality.

References

Barthes, R. (1983). *Myth Today*. In S. Sontag (Ed.). New York: Hill and Wang.

Baudrillard, J. (1983). *Simulations*. New York: Semiotexte.

Baudrillard, J. (1994). *Simulacra and Simulation*. Ann Arbor: The University of Michigan Press.

Baudrillard, J. (2016). *The Consumer Society: Myths and Structures*. London: Sage.

Belk, R. W., Wallendorf, M., & Sherry, J. F. Jr. (1989). The sacred and the profane in consumer behavior: Theodicy on the Odyssey. *Journal of Consumer Research*, 16 (June), pp. 1–38.

Bendapudi, N. & Leone, R. P. (2003). Psychological implications of customer participation in co-production. *Journal of Marketing*, 67(1), pp. 14–28.

Berry, L. L., Carbone, L. P., & Haeckel, S. H. (2002). Managing the total customer experience. *MIT Sloan Management Review*, 43(3), pp. 85–89.

Cova, B. (1996). The postmodern explained to managers: Implications for marketing. *Business Horizons*, Nov/Dec, pp. 15–23.

Cronin, J. J. (2003). Looking back to see forward in services marketing: Some ideas to consider. *Managing Service Quality: An International Journal*.

Edvardsson, B., Enquist, B., & Johnston, R. (2005). Co-creating customer value through hyperreality in the prepurchase service experience. *Journal of Service Research*, 8(2), pp. 149–161.

Edvardsson, B., Enquist, B., & Johnston, B. (2007). *Creating test-drives for service experiences prior to purchase and consumption–case studies in three different service contexts*. In 10th QMOD Conference, Quality Management and Organizational Development, in Helsinborg, Sweden, No. 26.

Firat, A. F. (1991). The consumer in postmodernity. *Advances in Consumer Research*, 18, pp. 70–76.

Firat, A. F. (1992). Postmodernism and the marketing organization. *Journal of Organizational Change*, 5(1), pp. 79–83.

Firat, A. F. & Venkatesh, A. (1995). Liberatory postmodernism and the reenchantment of consumption. *Journal of Consumer Research*, 22(3), pp. 239–267.

Goldman, R. & Sapson, S. (1994). Advertising in the age of hypersignification. *Theory, Culture and Society*, 11 (August), pp. 23–54.

Harvey, D. (1990). *The condition of postmodernity*. Oxford: Basil Blackwell.

Henningsen, L. (2010). *Copyright matters, imitation, creativity and authenticity in contemporary Chinese literature*. Berlin: Berliner Wissenschafts-Verlag.

Hirschman, E. C. & Holbrook, M. B. (1982). Hedonic consumption: Emerging concepts, methods and propositions. *Journal of Marketing*, 46(3), pp. 92–101.

Holbrook, M. B. (1995). *Consumer Research.* New York: Sage.

Johnston, R. & Clark, G. (2008). *Service Operations Management: Improving Service Delivery*. London: Pearson Education.

Kaplan, E. A. (1987). *Rocking around the Clock: Music Television, Postmodernism and Consumer Culture*. London and New York: Methuen.

Kundera, M. (1984). *The Unbearable Lightness of Being*. London: Faber and Faber, 1990.

MacKinnon, R. C. (1998). *The Social Construction of Rape in Cyberspace, in Network and Netplay: Virtual Groups on the Internet*. In F. Sudweeks, S. Rafaeli & M. McLaughlinn (Eds.). California: AAAI Press.

Parsons, E. & Maclaran, P. (2009). *Contemporary Issues in Marketing and Consumer Behaviour.* London: Routledge.

Poster, M. (1995). *Cyber Democracy. Internet and the Public Sphere*. Working paper. University of California. Irvine.

Postman, N. (1985). *Amusing Ourselves to Death: Public Discourse in the Age of Show Business.* New York: Penguin Books.

Prahalad, C. K. & Ramaswamy, V. (2004). *The Future of Competition – Co-Creating Unique Value with Customers*. Boston: Harvard Business School Press.

Rheingold, H. (1991). *Virtual Reality: Exploring the Brave New Technologies.* New York: Simon & Schuster Adult Publishing Group.

Venkatesh, V. (1999). Creation of favorable user perceptions: Exploring the role of intrinsic motivation. *MIS Quarterly*, 23(2), pp. 239–260.

Williams, A. (1998). The postmodern consumer and hyperreal pubs. *International Journal of Hospitality Management*, 17(3), pp. 221–232.

Hülya ER and Murat ER

3 Investor Tendencies within the Framework of Behavioral Finance: Herd Behavior

Introduction

Consumer psychology is defined as "the study of processes in which individuals or groups choose, purchase, use, and then discard goods, services and/or ideas" (Solomon, 2004: 484). The approach of consumer psychology attempts to make sense of the decision-making processes of consumers and to examine factors affecting consumer behavior. Emerging as a sub-discipline of marketing in the 1900s, consumer psychology has become a common point of reference in other disciplines such as economics and finance.

Using theories of consumer psychology and becoming an increasingly significant research subject, the concept of behavioral finance is based on the assumption that investors do not behave rationally while making decisions and are influenced by psychological factors. Many models built upon the theory of behavioral finance have been proposed in recent years. These assumed models aim to analyze investor behavior and the impact of markets in which they make investment decisions. Affecting investment decisions and causing investors to behave irrationally, herd behavior is an important topic within behavioral finance that draws significant attention from economic experts. Herd behavior is defined as the situation in which investors and individuals place more trust in the knowledge of a group of other investors, follow their transactions, and make similar decisions instead of relying on market conditions and their knowledge on financial instruments. The present study attempts to inform individuals and organizations about behavioral finance and investor tendencies, examines herd behavior as well as its different types and makes an in-depth analysis of herd behavior on investment decisions.

1 Behavioral Finance

Traditional finance theories assuming that the individual behaves rationally have been questioned for a long time (Gazel, 2016: 4). Traditional finance presumes that humans are rational beings and that investors have an equal amount of knowledge in alignment with others around them. Furthermore, advocates of traditional finance seem to disregard human psychology. In recent years, human psychology and factors influencing investor behavior have come into the forefront and, in this respect, the concept of behavioral finance has gradually obtained significance (Tufan, 2008: 12–13). Adam Smith's "The Wealth of Nations" published in 1776 referred to this concept by stating that human behavior can be related to selfishness or self-interest. Then, Gabriel Tarde, the first person to link the science of psychology with the science of economics, advocated for the necessity of interpreting and analyzing economic behavior through the lens of psychology (Gazel, 2016: 4). Regarded as the roots of behavioral finance, the study of Kahneman and Tversky in 1979 built a new bridge between finance and psychology (Kıyılar & Akkaya, 2016: 111). In contrast to the "expected utility theory" defended by traditional finance, "the prospect theory" formulated in this study puts forward the behavior displayed during decision-making processes and underlines the importance of human psychology (Gazel, 2016: 4).

Behavioral finance indicates that individuals and markets are not rational; it explains decision-making processes using cause-effect and the way the decision is made (Çitilci, 2015: 23) while endeavoring to detect to what extent individuals are affected by psychological biases. The studies in this field draw from psychology and many researchers have put forward models and theories regarding investment decisions (Küçük, 2014: 105). In 1913, John D. Watson proposed a behaviorist approach as a new concept in psychology. In his studies, Watson stated that internal factors rather than external ones influence human behavior. B. F. Skinner, another researcher dealing with the behaviorist approach, argued that internal factors are not significant. In other words, apart from factors shaping human behavior such as emotions, attitudes, thoughts, and motivation, the environment of the individual is also a determinative element. Furthermore, based on his research on mice and pigeons, he claimed that all human behavior can be explained by classical conditioning (Daniel, Hirshleifer, & Teoh, 2002: 140).

1.1 Investor Tendencies

Psychology can be defined as "a system allowing one to obtain, record, analyze, and interpret rationally the optimal benefit in line with the information gathered". Additionally, it assumes that behavior displayed during decision-making is affected by both internal motives and external factors. According to economists, investor tendencies in the market stem from the senses of satisfying needs, tangible motivation, and self-interest. In this process, the claim is that no investor in the market digresses from rationality. In this respect, investor rationality can be defined as the situation in which the investor evaluates every alternative and makes a decision accordingly to invest and reach their goals (Barak, 2008: 68).

However, research studies revealed that even though investors want to maximize their earnings, diversify their portfolio, and avoid risks by making rational decisions, they cannot attain these objectives through rational decision-making. Investors were observed to keep stocks that make them lose profit instead of preserving profitable stocks and, therefore, tend to opt for stocks with which they are familiar while investing. The underlying reason here is cognitive flaws. In other words, it can be said that investors make decisions based on intuitions, their emotional state, and overall mood while straying further from rationality (Döm, 2003: 19).

Many studies on finance analyze herd behavior, a sub-field of behavioral finance and, thus, of social tendencies of investors, due to these behavioral impacts (Kurtoğlu, 2013: 78).

2 Herd Behavior

Psychology as a scientific discipline has a crucial place in the purchasing behavior of consumers because while it focuses on the emotions and reactions of consumers and their influence over other consumers, it also attempts to reveal the reasons why consumers buy goods or services. Psychology is used in many aspects of marketing, such as shaping perceptions through logo designs, colorful patterns, and prices. Individuals need motivation in their purchasing decisions and psychological elements stimulate the cognitive and emotional mechanisms within individuals (Jamaluddin, Hanafiah, & Zulkifly, 2013: 774). Developed by Leibenstein, the consumer demand theory classifies demand tendencies of consumers for goods or services into two categories based on motivation, i.e. the impetus behind customer's actions: Functional and non-functional demands. Functional demands are defined as the case in which the reason behind the demand is the quality of the good or service in question. As for non-functional demands, they signify external demands unrelated to the quality of the said goods or services. These external factors can be listed as the bandwagon effect, the snob effect, and the Veblen effect (Leibenstein, 1950: 188–189).

Also known as "the bandwagon effect", herd behavior has been an important topic of research since the 1800s. The frequently-used name derives from a clown making electoral propaganda from a bandwagon and inviting people to attend a political rally (Morton & Ou, 2015: 225). As the bandwagon creating a lot of noise leaves an impression among people and gathers a crowd around it, the word is a good signifier of the way the phenomenon works. In this regard, it can be said that people are influenced by the behavior of a certain group. Herd behavior is frequently utilized on many occasions within social sciences. The superior electoral popularity of candidates declared to be successful in the context of politics or the increased sales of a firm with a high market share in the context of business can be given as an example of the bandwagon effect. As far as communication is concerned, the popularity of cell phones and social media outlets can be considered as an example (Wang & Zhu, 2019: 37).

It can be stated that imitating others is one of the fundamental instincts of a human being. In consumer psychology, herd behavior is demonstrated as a trend or a fad. Furthermore, it is also frequently observed in economics (Gazel, 2016: 67). The discipline of economics argues that it is an element of imitation that increases the demand for a good or service among consumers (Wang & Zhu, 2019: 37). One of the investor tendencies examined within the framework of behavioral finance, herd behavior is defined as the situation whereby a group of investors, influenced by other investors, buy or sell the same financial instrument at the same time with the investors in question (Nofsinger & Sias, 1999: 2263). Some factors leading to the bandwagon effect are listed as follows (McMahon, 2005: 21);

- People want to make cautious decisions.
- People want to focus on the latest trends while making investment decisions.
- People want to avoid information collection costs while making investment decisions.

In herd behavior, investors tend to imitate the knowledge and activities of other investors rather than collecting information about the market themselves. In addition, in order to talk about the presence of the bandwagon effect, investors need to alter their decisions taken with their own knowledge on the basis of the influence of other individuals and investors (Decamps & Lovo, 2002: 3).

The concept of herd behavior can be divided into two forms: rational and irrational. Rational herd behavior focuses on external factors negatively affecting the decision-making process due to informational difficulties while irrational herd behavior focuses on investor psychology (Devenow & Welch, 1996: 604).

2.1 Rational Herd Behavior

Rational herd behavior occurs when analysts follow other fund managers rather than making decisions based on their knowledge to defend the interests of fund managers and to maintain their reputation (Bikhchandani & Sharma, 2001: 283). Many scientific studies indicate that investors use estimations by analysts while making investment decisions. The reason behind the use of expert estimations is the belief that they are unbiased, accurate and include sectoral knowledge that is hard to reach. However, this opinion does not seem to be entirely applicable since expert analysts are also influenced by the bandwagon effect (Gazel, 2016: 69).

Rational herd behavior is observed more frequently than the irrational one because the effect is more common among corporate investors. There are several reasons leading to this. The first reason is that corporate investors endeavor to get information among themselves about the quality of their transactions, leading to the bandwagon effect. The second one is that corporate investors are evaluated among themselves through comparison, on the basis of their sectors. Therefore, corporate investors tend to keep the same stocks as others in their group by following a unique investment strategy in order not to be left behind. The third reason is that upon encountering similar external signals such as changes in profits or analyst recommendations, corporate investors are more likely to display herd behavior when compared with individual investors (Lakonishok, Shleifer, & Vishny, 1992: 25–26).

If investors are not able to access the necessary information before making investment decisions, they tend to behave rationally by imitating other investors instead of basing their decisions on their thoughts (Gazel, 2016: 70). In financial markets, there are three approaches regarding rational herd behavior: Information-based (informational), reputation-based, and compensation-based herd behavior (Bikhchandani & Sharma, 2001: 283).

In informational herd behavior, investors need to evaluate and analyze different alternatives to reach an investment decision. This means additional costs and time spent on the process for the investor. Therefore, investors follow other investors, particularly successful ones, and use their knowledge while making decisions (Bikhchandani, Hirshleifer, & Welch, 1998: 152). An example of information-based herd behavior would be an investor disregarding their own knowledge and invest based on the decisions of other investors, imitating them in their investment decisions. In this case, it is possible to say that the investor in question believes that the decisions and knowledge of other investors are superior to their own knowledge (Devenow & Welch, 1996: 609).

Reputation-based herd behavior is another rational approach developed by Scharfstein and Stein (1990). In this theory of herd behavior, investors are not aware of the level of ability of managers. Managers with higher skills receive informational signals as they observe the facts on investments while those with lower skills receive different and insignificant signals concerning investments. Thus, by comparing a manager they certainly perceive as successful to another manager, investors make a decision regarding the level of skills of managers. Unskilled managers would try to preserve their reputation by imitating skilled managers. Even though a particular decision made by a skilled manager might be wrong, the investor would not think that both managers are incompetent and believe that this faulty decision can be explained by a lack of chance (Scharfstein & Stein, 1990: 466).

The third type to be examined here is compensation-based herd behavior. It arises from the evaluation of the performances of investment experts and comparing them with other experts (Borensztein & Gelos, 2000: 5). This can be explained as the effort of investment experts to improve their experts and to avoid the risk of reduction in their financial compensations due to their performances by imitating each other while making decisions (Altay, 2008: 31). Creating similar investment portfolios in order to prevent losses in financial compensations would result in compensation-based herd behavior among investment experts (Maug & Naik, 1995: 2).

2.2 Irrational Herd Behavior

While rational herd behavior explains investment decisions through informational effects, irrational herd behavior makes associations with societal pressure, social consensus, and trends. A general consensus is formed as investors find out about the thoughts of other investors regarding various stocks. Herd behavior might develop with investors and other individuals with a potential for investment acting based on this consensus (Döm, 2003: 148). Societal pressure also influences investment decisions of individuals. If investors fail after following a strategy independent of other investors, they regret not following other investors. To avoid this sense of regret, they tend to imitate other investors, leading to the emergence of irrational herd behavior. Investors displaying such behavior make investment decisions based on psychological prejudices rather than systematic analyses (Nofsinger, 2001: 70).

3 Evaluating Herd Behavior within the Framework of Behavioral Finance

Behavioral finance is a discipline dealing with the impact of psychology on investor behavior and markets (Çitilci, 2015: 23). Based on the assumption that people are not rational, behavioral finance attempts to explain decision-making processes and investor behavior using the knowledge of social sciences such as economics, finance, psychology, business administration, and sociology. Research studies show that behavioral finance obtained many results indicating the existence of irrational situations and their influence on the changes in investment preferences, associating these outcomes with psychological factors

(Gazel, 2016: 12). Furthermore, the irrationality of investor behavior during decision-making processes has been proved with research studies; this has led to the rise of the significance of behavioral finance in finance theory (Sefil & Çilingiroğlu, 2011: 263). Upon examining different studies in the academic literature, one can see that Kahneman & Tversky (1979), Taner & Akkaya (2005), Phan & Zhou (2014), Aydın & Ağan (2016), and Yürekli (2019) indicated that investors are influenced by behavioral factors while making investment decisions and that they display irrational behavior. Furthermore, investors were also found to be affected by psychological factors while making investment decisions.

An inspection of studies concerning herd behavior, one of the investor tendencies within the scope of behavioral finance literature reveals that Lakonishok, Shleifer, & Vishny (1992), Cajueiro & Tabak (2009), Akın (2009), & Özsu (2015) concluded that investors are not rational and while making investment decisions, they are influenced by psychological factors and the bandwagon effect. However, studies made by, for example, Amirat & Bouri (2009) and Ergün & Doğukanlı (2015) did not find herd behavior to be influential on investment decisions.

Upon evaluating the examples of research studies provided above, one can reach the conclusion that psychological factors underlying the behavioral financial approach are crucial in investment decisions along with the bandwagon effect. In a general sense, within the scope of behavioral finance, herd behavior or the bandwagon effect can be regarded as a significant concept for explaining investor tendencies and consumer psychology.

Conclusion

Today, consumer psychology is an emerging field of study benefiting from many other disciplines such as marketing, sociology, and finance. Included in consumer psychology as a concept, herd behavior can be generally defined as the actions and moods of people generated by imitation based on a certain belief. Herd behavior is frequently observed in various domains such as fashion, the music industry, social media, politics, and finance.

Recently, the importance of this concept emerging within finance and, in particular, behavioral finance literature seems to increase each day. The herd behavior approach concretizes the extent to which investors are influenced by psychological factors as well as the way in which they act while making investment decisions. In this respect, the concept of herd behavior put forward by different researchers in various studies is crucial in determining to what extent investors influence one another while making investment decisions.

The present study first examined the behavioral finance theory and investor tendencies. Then, it discussed the concept of herd behavior (the bandwagon effect) and different types of herd behavior; it also makes a general evaluation within the scope of behavioral finance and consumer psychology based on research studies on herd behavior. The knowledge provided in this study is thought to contribute to the comprehension and analysis of psychological factors affecting purchasing decisions of individuals or investment decisions of investors. Many research studies showed tendencies towards and examples of herd behavior. It was also observed that investors tend to be influenced by others' ideas and imitate others within their social circles in their investment decisions rather than focusing on their own thoughts. In this context, it might be a good idea to train investors in order for them to make more accurate decisions in their investments. Such training might help investors mitigate the effects of such factors upon encountering them while preventing negative influences in the stock market stemming from wrong decisions made because of the bandwagon effect.

References

Akın, H. (2009). *Menkul kıymet portföy yatırımlarında davranışsal finans yönteminin kullanılması ve bir uygulama örneği.* Master Thesis, Selçuk University, Konya.

Altay, E. (2008). Sermaye piyasasında sürü davranışı: İMKB'de piyasa yönünde sürü davranışının analizi. *BDDK Bankacılık ve Finansal Piyasalar, 2* (1), pp. 27–58.

Amirat, A. M. I. N. A., & Bouri, A. (2009). Modeling informational cascade via behavior biases. *Global Economy and Finance Journal, 2* (2), pp. 81–103.

Aydın, Ü., & Ağan, B. (2016). Rasyonel olmayan kararların finansal yatırım tercihleri üzerindeki etkisi: Davranışsal finans çerçevesinde bir uygulama. *Ekonomik ve Sosyal Araştırmalar Dergisi, 12* (2), pp. 95–112.

Barak, O. (2008). *Davranışsal Finans Teori ve Uygulama.* Ankara: Gazi Kitabevi.

Bikhchandani, S., Hirshleifer, D., & Welch, I. (1998). Learning from the behavior of others: Conformity, fads, and informational cascades. *Journal of Economic Perspectives, 12* (3), pp. 151–170.

Bikhchandani, S., & Sharma, S. (2001). Herd behavior in financial markets. *International Monetary Fund, 47* (3), pp. 229–310.

Borensztein, E., & Gelos, R. G. (2000). *A panic-prone pack? The behavior of emerging market mutual funds.*

Cajueiro, D. O., & Tabak, B. M. (2009). Multifractality and herding behavior in the Japanese stock market. *Chaos, Solitons and Fractals, 40* (1), pp. 497–504.

Çitilci, T. (2015). *Para ve psikoloji*. İstanbul: Beta Yayınları.

Daniel, K., Hirshleifer, D., & Teoh, S. H. (2002). Investor psychology in capital markets: Evidence and policy implications. *Journal of Monetary Economics, 49*, pp. 139–209.

Decamps, J.-P., & Lovo, S. (2002). Risk aversion and herd behavior in financial markets. *HEC Paris, 758*, pp. 1–36.

Devenow, A., & Welch, I. (1996). Rational herding in financial economics. *European Economic Review, 40* (3–5), pp. 603–615.

Döm, S. (2003). *Yatırımcı psikolojisi*. İstanbul: Değişim Yayınları.

Ergün, B., & Doğukanlı, H. (2015). Hisse senedi piyasalarında sürü davranışı: BİST'te bir araştırma. *Uluslararası Sosyal Araştırmalar Dergisi, 8* (40), pp. 690–699.

Gazel, S. (2016). *Davranışsal finans psikolojik eşik ve önyargılar*. Ankara: Detay Yayıncılık.

Jamaluddin, M. R., Hanafiah, M. H., & Zulkifly, M. I. (2013). Customer-based psychology branding. *Procedia - Social and Behavioral Sciences, 105*, pp. 772–780.

Kahneman, D., & Tversky, A. (1979). Prospect theory: An analysis of decision under risk. *Econometrica, 47* (2), pp. 263–291.

Kıyılar, M., & Akkaya, M. (2016). *Davranışsal Finans*. İstanbul: Literatür Yayınları.

Kurtoğlu, R. (2013). *Küresel para savaşları ve davranış ekonomisi nörofinans*. Ankara: Orion Kitapevi.

Küçük, A. (2014). Bireysel yatırımcıları finansal yatırım kararına yönlendiren faktörlerin davranışsal finans açısından ele alınması: Osmaniye önreği. *Akademik Araştırmalar ve Çalışmalar Dergisi, 6* (11), pp. 104–122.

Lakonishok, J., Shleifer, A., & Vishny, R. W. (1992). The impact of institutional trading on stock prices. *Journal of Financial Economics, 32* (1), pp. 23–43.

Leibenstein, H. (1950). Bandwagon, snob and Veblen effects in the theory of consumers' demand. *The Quarterly Journal of Economics, 64* (2), pp. 183–207.

Maug, E., & Naik, N. (1995). Herding and delegated portfolio management: The impact of relative performance evaluation on asset allocation. *The Quarterly Journal of Finance, 1* (2), pp. 265–292.

McMahon, R. (2005). Behavioural finance: A backround briefing. *Journal of Accounting and Finance, 4*, pp. 45–64.

Morton, R. B., & Ou, K. (2015). What motivates bandwagon voting behavior: Altruism or a desire to win? *European Journal of Political Economy, 40*, pp. 224–241.

Nofsinger, J. R. (2001). *Investment madness: How psychology affects your investing and what to do about it?*. New Jersey: Financial Times Prentice Hall Books.

Nofsinger, J. R., & Sias, R. W. (1999). Herding and feedback trading by institutional and individual investors. *The Journal of Finance, LIV* (6), pp. 2263–2295.

Özsu, H. H. (2015). *Herd behavior on Borsa İstanbul (BİST): An Empirical Analysis*. PhD Thesis, Dokuz Eylül University, İzmir.

Phan, C. K., & Zhou, J. (2014). Factors influencing individual investors' behavior: An empirical study of the Vietnamese stock market. *American Journal of Business and Management, 3* (2), pp. 77–94.

Scharfstein, D. S., & Stein, J. C. (1990). Herd behavior and investment. *The American Economic Review, 80* (3), pp. 465–479.

Sefil, S., & Çilingiroğlu, H. K. (2011). Davranışsal finansın temelleri: karar vermenin bilişsel ve duygusal eğilimleri. *İstanbul Ticaret Üniversitesi Sosyal Bilimler Dergisi*, (19), pp. 247–268.

Solomon, M. R. (2004). Consumer psychology. *Encyclopedia of Applied Psychology, 1*, pp. 483–492.

Taner, B., & Akkaya, C. (2005). Yatırımcı psikolojisi ve davranışsal finans yaklaşımı. *Muhasebe ve Finansman Dergisi*, (27), pp. 47–54.

Tufan, E. (2008). *Davranışsal finans*. Ankara: İmaj Yayıncılık.

Wang, C. J., & Zhu, J. J. H. (2019). Jumping onto the bandwagon of collective gatekeepers: Testing the bandwagon effect of information diffusion on social news website. *Telematics and Informatics, 41*, pp. 34–45.

Yürekli, A. (2019). *Bireysel yatırımcıların davranışlarına etki eden faktörlerin davranışsal finans kapsamında incelenmesi: Hizmet ve üretim sektörü çalışanları üzerine bir araştırma*. Master Thesis. İstanbul Gelişim University, İstanbul.

Evrim ERDOĞAN YAZAR

4 Brand Identity and Narcissism

Introduction

Under the present-day competitive conditions, strong brands form bonds between their clients and products through their brand identity. Giving the product a personal, cultural, relational and reputational aspect, brand identity aims to make clients see the brand as a reflection of their ego (Belk, 1988). Globally popular brands such as Starbucks, Nike or Harley Davidson emphasize their identity so strongly that it has become one of the complementary factors for their ego, bearing significance for their clients and utilized as a means of communicating with the outside world. The admiration with "self" among contemporary consumers has increased undeniably for brands, becoming a part of brand identity. Therefore, brands aiming for success endeavor to increase the value of their products for their consumers by building brands that consumers would associate with their own identities.

Even though personality traits associated with a brand have been the subject for numerous research studies throughout the years, the study of the relationship between narcissism, defined as an excessive attachment to and admiration for one's own mental and physical ego or identity (MacDonald, 2014; Twenge & Campell, 2009), and brand identity is relatively a novel one in the existing academic literature. From the 2000s to the 2020s, there has been a global surge in narcissistic tendencies. The new understanding of consumption, use of social media outlets, increasing prevalence of personal branding, frequent use of "you" discourse directly targeting the consumer and other ways of communication by brands seem to nurture the narcissism of consumers. The relationship of this increasingly common personality type with consumption and branding has become one of the new areas of study for consumer psychology. This chapter will first define the concepts of identity and brand identity; then, it will elaborate on narcissism and its role in consumer behavior. Ultimately, it will examine the relationship between brand identity and narcissism.

1 Identity and Brand Identity

Social interaction and existence depend on the knowledge of individuals regarding their self-identities and identities of others. Identity and ego help individuals make sense of the world (Aaker & Akutsu, 2009; Hogg & Vaughan, 2014). Rather than emotional, behavioral or committal, identity is a cognitive dimension of the congruence between the individual and existence (Carlson et.al, 2009). As stated by Baudrillard (2016), consumption has obtained a central position within post-modern society and products have become objects consumed for their symbolic significance rather than functional benefits. Consumption for the sake of significance is a part of the endeavor of the individual for self-knowledge. The individual uses consumption goods as a means of building and maintaining their self-identity as well as forming relationships (Lunt & Livingstone, 1992). As a part of the consumer's social and individual identity, consumption is both a tool of social competition providing them social status, position, and vanity and a means of differentiating themselves from the lower class and imitating the upper class. From this point of view, as far as today's society is concerned, consumption is "a self-strategy [sic] in which a unique identity is expressed and at the same time constructed as something distinct from all others" (Falk, 1994:38).

As for brand identity, it represents the characteristics that managers want to see in their brands (Aaker & Joachimsthaler, 2000). Brand identity facilitates the purchase of products for consumers by increasing the recognition of companies and providing them with a distinctive professional image. A strong brand identity would help companies create a brand value through increased recognition, awareness and customer loyalty (Wheeler, 2013).

Even though the general belief is that brand identity is governed by managers, both brand managers and consumers play an active role in creating the brand identity of a business (Silveira et al., 2013). Brand is a sum of consumer experiences concerning the brand (Kapferer, 2008: 327). This point of view clarifies the relationship between consumers and brand identity and underlies the argument put forward by Silveira et al. (2013: 35) claiming that "consumers' identities transfer to the identity of the brands they use". The common ground of identity conceptions about branding is that identity is not exclusively about signs showing visual elements. An effective identity consists of features such as the physical properties of a good or service, a memorable name or a distinctive packaging design, a symbol, a slogan, auditory aspects, and the country of origin. Furthermore, the vision and aim of the brand, its uniqueness, the needs it fulfills, its features and values also define brand identity (Kapferer, 2008). More simply put, the concrete and abstract elements constituting the brand are reflected in the brand identity.

2 Being in Love with Oneself: Narcissism

Used to denote self-admiration, self-esteem or self-love in everyday language, narcissism was first defined by Freud within the literature of psychoanalysis (MacDonald, 2014). Freud conceptualized narcissism as a normal developmental stage preceded by the auto-erotic stage and followed by the more mature stage of object-love; however, subsequent research studies defined narcissism as a psychiatric personality disorder. While narcissism is observed in 2% to 16% of our society and primarily among men in the clinical sense (APA, 2013; Beck et al., 2004), the prevalence rate of narcissism is considerable in modern society (Twenge & Campell, 2009).

The roots of the term "narcissism" date back to an ancient Greek myth with several versions. One of the descriptions in Ovidius (2005: 70–72)'s *Metamorphoses*[1] is as follows: Born with a prophecy suggesting that he would live a long and happy life as long as he did not see himself, Narcissus, as a young man, did not care for the young girls and nymphs falling in love with him. One day, a nymph named Echo fell in love with Narcissus. Yet as her love was not reciprocated, she waned and was reduced to a wailing sound. Having seen Echo's state, other nymphs complained to the Gods about Narcissus. After a hunt, when Narcissus came to a riverbank and leaned towards the stream to drink water, he saw his reflection and falls in love with it. He could not leave the riverbank; he was not able to take his eyes off of his reflection until he died of exhaustion. This story represents the harms of self-admiration against the individual and the people around them. Even though a positive attitude towards one's self and others is considered to be healthy and normal, a narcissistic individual inherently believes that they are special and superior (Beck et al., 2004). Vanity, pride, ostentatiousness, and egocentrism are also among other common names for narcissism (Twenge & Campell, 2009).

As a psychological phenomenon, narcissism can be either healthy or unhealthy (MacDonald, 2014). Unhealthy narcissism is a personality disorder. This form of narcissism is distinguished by the sense of superiority, lack of empathy and need for admiration. The individual imagines that they have infinite success, power, intelligence, and beauty. As far as interpersonal relationships are concerned, they act based on self-interests, lack empathy, and display behaviors like jealousy and arrogance (Beck et al., 2004). Such behaviors increase one's self-respect, yet they are excessive at the pathological level. Unhealthy narcissism leads to

1 Taken from the original version translated into French in the 1806 version by G. T. Villenave as "Les Métamorphoses".

the inability of forming warm and loving relationships with others, lack of flexibility, sense of superiority, lack of empathy, and reactions causing adjustment disorder (Köroğlu & Bayraktar, 2011; MacDonald, 2014). On the other hand, social psychology discusses the positive features of narcissism visible among normal individuals (Rosenthal & Hooley, 2010). Individuals with healthy narcissism are self-aware and know about their strengths as well as weaknesses. They possess the courage and ability to withstand self-critical thoughts questioning their actions and identity. They are capable of self-reflection (Wardetzki, 2017). As their imagination is unproblematic, they are usually in a good mood in their daily lives, do not generally feel despair, and have optimistic outlooks on life. They mainly remember their positive behavior (Gosling et al., 1998; Köroğlu & Bayraktar, 2011). Furthermore, different forms of narcissism like grandiose and vulnerable narcissism as well as overt and covert narcissism were clinically defined. Such forms of this personality disorder lead to individuals having different senses of self and behavioral patterns and developing different behavioral outputs (Dickinson & Pincus, 2003; Fossati et al., 2010).

In social psychology, narcissism is considered to be a dimensional temperament without distinct points in which the individual typically shifts from "normal" to "narcissist" (Foster & Campbell, 2007). Although narcissism as a personality disorder is a serious case rarely diagnosed clinically, narcissistic characteristics have surged critically in society. Increasing on a daily basis, its negative effects like greed, self-obsession, superficial relationships and vanity are becoming apparent (MacDonald, 2014).

3 Narcissism and Consumption

Humans are social beings and they need steady and fulfilling relationships to increase and maintain their identity and self-value (Wardetzki, 2017). Individuals are in a constant quest for establishing their self-identities. As consumers, they associate themselves with the status, lifestyle or social identity represented by the product they purchase (Falk, 1994). This quest is also visible as far as narcissism is concerned, but the discomfort arising from the void narcissistic individuals want to fill is a manifestation of the narcissistic absorption rather than a genuine pursuit (Giddens, 1991). Individuals experiencing negative emotions (anxiety, apprehension, self-doubt) and feeling insufficient regarding a certain issue tend to consume materialistic manifestations improving their sense of self-value and strengthening particularly issue-specific identity (e.g. branded items) (Braun & Wicklund, 1989; Dittmar, 2001). A narcissistic temperament concerns the way one looks rather than what one is (Wardetzki, 2017).

Related to self-love, self-care, and self-esteem, narcissism usually occurs within the context of relationships with society (Sedikides et al., 2007). As stated by Swann (2005), identities cannot be formulated by individuals alone. Everyone needs to be approved and appreciated by society. Therefore, it can be said that each individual has a certain degree of narcissism. In a society in which consumer goods are considered as a material symbol of who an individual is or might be and as a manifestation of an individual's self-identity (Dittmar, 2001), narcissists perceive the purchase of consumer goods as an opportunity to maintain and increase their positivity and attach greater importance to the symbolic value of objects than functional properties (Sedikides et al., 2007).

There is a positive correlation between narcissism and subjective well-being (Sedikides & Brewer, 2015). A distinct indicator of narcissism is an excessive need for admiration. Their self-respect is generally very fragile. The need for admiration in narcissism is nurtured by image. In other words, narcissistic individuals believe that image is everything. Their primary concern is to control and preserve their image. Therefore, the image of the individuals themselves and even that of their spouse and children are crucial (Beck et al., 2004). The need for admiration urges such individuals to buy products providing elevated social status and reputation (e.g. expensive automobiles, jewelry) (Twenge & Campell, 2009). The lack of self-esteem underlying narcissism, instability within the self-value system, and fragility of self-respect (Wardetzki, 2017) make them addicted to social sources of affirmation (Morf & Rhodewalt, 2001). The will of narcissists to control and maintain their images also affects the selection of their social environment. The thought of making others understand how special the narcissistic individual is inclines the narcissist to social interactions apart from their inner circles suitable for their image and allowing them to realize themselves. Having power in social contexts, looking attractive and being needed are ways to develop and maintain relationships for narcissists (Vangelisti et al., 1990).

Narcissism is not exclusive to individuals. It can also be observed in organizations, families, and societies (Wardetzki, 2017). Narcissistic tendencies within society can be reinforced through advertisements, creating demand, and the hedonistic consumer culture. Along with symbolic and hedonic consumption brought about by post-modernism, a society based on mass consumption saliently endorses self-indulgence and conceives the narcissistic culture (Lash, 1979). The narcissistic tendencies of the present-day society have been strengthened due to the aspect of marketing activities increasing the inclination of individuals to be self-centered and to own (Lambert et al., 2013) As indicated by Twenge and Campbell (2009), personality cannot exist separately from others. Thus, the increase of narcissism is a result of self-directed focus within the culture. Substantially governed by the accumulation and consumption of material goods, "the consumer society" (Shaughnessy & Shaughnessy, 2002) gave rise to an understanding of narcissism popularizing the will to obtain everything one wants (Twenge & Campell, 2009).

4 Narcissism within the Scope of Brand Identity

Efforts to standardize consumption and shaping one's desires through marketing communication tools play an important role in the proliferation of narcissism. Consuming the right products supposedly granting their consumers attractiveness, beauty, and personal popularity promises the obtainment of a socially valuable individuality (Giddens, 1991), thus making narcissism a part of the identity of consumer society. While consumption is a self-strategy in which a unique identity is expressed and structured as something different than the rest (Falk, 1994), brands are the focus of the self-strategy of the consumer. Products remain as objects creating functional benefits for consumers, yet brands, status symbols, have become an integral part of their identities.

In materialistic societies, owning expensive products is a way of drawing attention, obtaining social status and getting affirmed by status groups (Richins & Dawson, 1992). As far as consumer preferences are concerned, the relationship between materialism and narcissism emerges in certain preferences, e.g. the preferences of individuals with narcissistic tendencies related to their physical appearance stemming from their concerns about their image (Sedikides et al., 2007). Sedikides et al. (2018) indicate that narcissists opt for luxury brands due to the desire of creating positive differences, materialism, the will to increase the significance of their lives, and to wish to improve their sexual attractiveness. According to Kang and Park (2016), buying products of luxury brands provides psychological superiority for narcissists; they make direct associations between the general impressions and meanings of luxury brands and their images.

Narcissists focus on the image, reputation, tradition, and uniqueness of brands. In other words, they focus on the brand identity of luxury brands. Furthermore, narcissistic individuals tend to buy products to increase personal uniqueness (Lee et al., 2013). Ultimately, one of the motivations behind the brand identity activities of companies is to be differentiated from their competitors and to be unique. Therefore, the preference of narcissistic consumers for branded products might help them differentiate themselves from ordinary people and give them a unique character.

Personalization and customization services offered by brands create new opportunities for the narcissist to use brands as a means of communication with the outside world. By giving the client to create their own brand or providing them with a system of symbols to convey their identities, personalization and customization help clients develop positive attitudes (Fox & Rooney, 2015). Lee et al. (2013) revealed that narcissism leads to an increase in the interest in personalizable and customizable products. Many popular brands offer their clients customizable options on various occasions, from design to packaging. The ease of product personalization and customization has created the optimal setting as far as the desire of narcissistic individuals for uniqueness is concerned. However, de Bellis et al. (2016) states that even though real automobile buyers with higher levels of narcissism create different automobiles, this cannot be explained with varying levels of self-respect or the need for uniqueness. Nevertheless, customization applications in mass-scale brands might allow consumers with narcissistic tendencies, using their creativity, to formulate brand identities reflecting their desires of superiority and uniqueness.

Another issue that can be evaluated within the context of the relationship between narcissism and brand identity is the use of social media. The number of research studies on social media posts and selfies posted on social media seems to have increased recently. Consumers with narcissistic tendencies have positive attitudes towards a selfie marketing campaign and they are willing to participate in the said campaign (Fox et al., 2018). McCain and Campbell (2018) suggest that narcissism (grandiose) is related to the frequency of sending selfies. A study by Sung et al. (2018) reported that narcissism is one of the estimators of the act of publishing selfies on social media. Consumers associate themselves with brands by sharing brand logos and products in their selfies to express the real and ideal self, affluence or social status. These posts are a result of the drive for self-expression through brands that consumers associate with their identities.

Conclusion

Although the number of individuals with a narcissistic personality disorder is limited, the prevalence of narcissism as a personality type within society seems to increase. Understanding consumer behavior has always been the focus of marketing thought. The increase in the narcissistic tendencies of modern-day consumers is estimated to affect the marketing activities of companies. In this respect, the relationship between brands and narcissism is an interesting one. While advertisements and other communicative messages conveyed by brands are considered to be among the factors fostering narcissistic tendencies, brands design their identities taking into account the characteristics (ego, personality, experience, expectations, etc.) of their target audiences. Therefore, brands must consider narcissistic tendencies among their consumers. Communicative activities aimed to serve this purpose also increase narcissistic tendencies among individuals.

Aiming to put forward the relationship between narcissism and brand identity in a conceptual way, the present study concludes that the role and significance of narcissism in brand identity will increase. The promotion of products symbolizing social status through television, series, and advertisements and the increasing interest in such products, conspicuous consumption, customization offers by companies, heavy use of social media, and the increasing number of personal posts strengthens narcissistic tendencies among consumers. Even though the spread of narcissism is negative from a societal point of view, brands should not overlook this tendency and consider the impacts of narcissism on consumer psychology while designing new brands. In fact, luxury brands currently use some of the features associated with narcissism in their brand identities. The question here is that if companies targeting consumers apart from users of luxury products can increase brand awareness among consumers using certain brand identity features associated with narcissistic individuals in their brand identities.

References

Aaker, J. L., & Akutsu, S. (2009). Why do people give? The role of identity in giving. *Journal of Consumer Psychology*, *19*(3), pp. 267–270.

Aaker, D. A., & Joachimsthaler, E. (2000). The brand relationship spectrum: The key to the brand architecture challenge. *California Management Review*, *42*(4), pp. 8–23.

APA (2013). *Diagnostic and Statistical Manual of Mental Disorders*. Washington, DC: American Psychiatric Publishing.

Baudrillard, J. (2016). *The Consumer Society: Myths and Structures*. London: Sage.

Beck, A. T., Davis, D. D., & Freeman, A. (2004). *Cognitive Therapy of Personality Disorders*. New York: Guilford Press.

Belk, R. W. (1988). Possessions and the extended self. *Journal of Consumer Research*, *15*(2), pp. 139–168.

Braun, O. L., & Wicklund, R. A. (1989). Psychological antecedents of conspicuous consumption. *Journal of Economic psychology*, *10*(2), pp. 161–187.

Carlson, B., Todd Donavan, D., & Cumiskey, K. (2009). Consumer-brand relationships in sport: Brand personality and identification. *International Journal of Retail & Distribution Management*, *37*(4), pp. 370–384.

De Bellis, E., Sprott, D. E., Herrmann, A., Bierhoff, H. W., & Rohmann, E. (2016). The influence of trait and state narcissism on the uniqueness of mass-customized products. *Journal of Retailing*, *92*(2), pp. 162–172.

Dickinson, K. A., & Pincus, A. L. (2003). Interpersonal analysis of grandiose and vulnerable narcissism. *Journal of Personality Disorders*, *17*(3), pp. 188–207.

Dittmar, H. (2001). Impulse buying in ordinary and "compulsive" consumers. *Conflict and Tradeoffs in Decision Making*. Cambridge: Cambridge University Press, pp. 110–135.

Falk, P. (1994). *The Consuming Body*. London: Sage.

Fossati, A., Borroni, S., Eisenberg, N., & Maffei, C. (2010). Relations of proactive and reactive dimensions of aggression to overt and covert narcissism in nonclinical adolescents. *Aggressive Behavior: Official Journal of the International Society for Research on Aggression*, *36*(1), pp. 21–27.

Foster, J. D., & Campbell, W. K. (2007). Are there such things as "narcissists" in social psychology? A taxometric analysis of the narcissistic personality inventory. *Personality and Individual Differences*, *43*(6), pp. 1321–1332.

Fox, A. K., Bacile, T. J., Nakhata, C., & Weible, A. (2018). Selfie-marketing: Exploring narcissism and self-concept in visual user-generated content on social media. *Journal of Consumer Marketing*, *35*(1), pp. 11–21.

Fox, J., & Rooney, M. C. (2015). The Dark Triad and trait self-objectification as predictors of men's use and self-presentation behaviors on social networking sites. *Personality and Individual Differences*, *76*, pp. 161–165.

Giddens, A. (1991). *Modernity and Self-Identity: Self and Society in the Late Modern Age*. Stanford, CA: Stanford University Press.

Gosling, S. D., John, O. P., Craik, K. H., & Robins, R. W. (1998). Do people know how they behave? Self-reported act frequencies compared with on-line codings by observers. *Journal of Personality and Social Psychology*, *74*(5), p. 1337.

Hogg, M. A., & Vaughan, G. M. (2014). *Social Psychology: An Introduction*. London: Harvester Wheatsheaf.

Kang, Y. J., & Park, S. Y. (2016). The perfection of the narcissistic self: A qualitative study on luxury consumption and customer equity. *Journal of Business Research*, *69*(9), pp. 3813–3819.

Kapferer, J. N. (2008). *The New Strategic Brand Management: Creating and Sustaining Brand Equity Long Term*. Philadelphia: Kogan Page Publishers.

Köroğlu, E., & Bayraktar, S. (2011). *Personality Disorders*. Ankara: HYB Publishing (In Turkish).

Lambert, A., Desmond, J., & O'Donohoe, S. (2013). Narcissism and the consuming self: An exploration of consumer identity projects and narcissistic tendencies. *Consumer Culture Theory, Research in Consumer Behaviour, 16*, pp. 35–57.

Lash, C. (1979). *The Culture of Narcissism: American Life in an Age of Diminishing Expectations*. Skopelos: Nisides.

Lee, S. Y., Gregg, A. P., & Park, S. H. (2013). The person in the purchase: Narcissistic consumers prefer products that positively distinguish them. *Journal of Personality and Social Psychology, 105*(2), p.335.

Lunt, P. K., & Livingstone, S. (1992). *Mass Consumption and Personal İdentity: Everyday Economic Experience*. Buckingham: Open University Press.

MacDonald, P. (2014). Narcissism in the modern world. *Psychodynamic Practice, 20*(2), pp. 144–153.

McCain, J. L., & Campbell, W. K. (2018). Narcissism and social media use: A meta-analytic review. *Psychology of Popular Media Culture, 7*(3), pp. 308–327.

Morf, C. C., & Rhodewalt, F. (2001). Unraveling the paradoxes of narcissism: A dynamic self-regulatory processing model. *Psychological Inquiry, 12*(4), pp. 177–196.

Ovidius, P. N. (2005). Les Métamorphoses (Translator: G.T. Villenave). *Ebooks libres et gratuits.*

Richins, M. L., & Dawson, S. (1992). A consumer values orientation for materialism and its measurement: Scale development and validation. *Journal of Consumer Research, 19*(3), pp. 303–316.

Rosenthal, S. A., & Hooley, J. M. (2010). Narcissism assessment in social–personality research: Does the association between narcissism and psychological health result from a confound with self-esteem? *Journal of Research in Personality, 44*(4), pp. 453–465.

Sedikides, C., & Brewer, M. B. (2015). *Individual Self, Relational Self, Collective Self.* New York: Psychology Press.

Sedikides, C., Gregg, A. P., Cisek, S., & Hart, C. M. (2007). The I that buys: Narcissists as consumers. *Journal of Consumer Psychology, 17*(4), pp. 254–257.

Sedikides, C., Hart, C. M., & Cisek, S. Z. (2018). Narcissistic consumption. Hermann, Anthony D., Brunell, Amy B., & Foster, Joshua D. (Eds.), *Handbook of Trait Narcissis,* Springer, Cham. pp. 291–298.

Shaughnessy, J., & Shaughnessy, N. J. (2002). Marketing, the consumer society and hedonism. *European Journal of Marketing, 36*(5–6), 524–547.

Silveira, C., Lages, C., & Simões, C. (2013). Reconceptualizing brand identity in a dynamic environment. *Journal of Business Research*, *66*(1), pp. 28–36.

Sung, Y., Kim, E., & Choi, S. M. (2018). Me and brands: Understanding brand-selfie posters on social media. *International Journal of Advertising*, *37*(1), pp. 14–28.

Swann Jr, W. B. (2005). The self and identity negotiation. *Interaction Studies*, *6*(1), pp. 69–83.

Twenge, J. M., & Campbell, W. K. (2009). *The Narcissism Epidemic: Living in the Age of Entitlement*. Simon and New York: Schuster.

Vangelisti, A. L., Knapp, M. L., & Daly, J. A. (1990). Conversational narcissism. *Communications Monographs*, *57*(4), pp. 251–274.

Wardetzki, B. (2017). *Narzissmus, Verführung und Macht in Politik und Gesellschaft*. Munchen: Europa Verlag GmbH.

Wheeler, A. (2013). *Designing Brand Identity: An Essential Guide for the Whole Branding Team*. New Jersey: John Wiley & Sons.

Didem DEMİR

5 The Importance of Slow Food Consumption for Tourism Marketing

Introduction

With the advance of globalism and the development of technology, countries have gone through both economic and cultural changes (Yurtseven et al., 2010: 2). This process of change has allowed people to move from one place to another faster and to make swifter decisions (Tosun, 2013: 234). Greater mobility of consumers also affects consumer behavior and alternatives. Consumers might make impulse purchases, a behavioral pattern that can be described as more casual. Apart from their shopping habits, their food consumption has also been influenced by the change mentioned above. An indication of this would be the proliferation of fast food consumption, a type of fast-moving consumption.

During this process in which fast food consumption increases, the movement of slow food against fast food was initiated especially in Europe. The primary reason behind the rise of slow food may be the scarcity of resources. Considering that our resources are limited, slow food particularly encompasses ethical production methods along with the concepts of "eco-gastronomy" and "virtuous globalization". The slow food movement champions the cause of good, clean, and fair food. Furthermore, it is significant for the maintenance of originality of the culinary culture to be transferred to future generations (Pajo & Uğurlu, 2015: 65). In this respect, slow food can also be associated with sustainable consumption. Additionally, it can be supported by sustainable agriculture owing to the variety of organic local foods and cooking techniques of local masters (Williams, Germov, Fuller, & Freij, 2015:1). Related to a wide range of issues, paradigms on which the Slow Food Movement will focus on can be listed as protecting food biodiversity, establishing connections between producers and consumers, and to raise awareness on issues affecting the food system (Preserve Biodiversity, n.d.).

Connected to many paradigms, the slow food movement has recently become significant in marketing literature as a psychological phenomenon. Taking the importance of the issue into account, this chapter will examine slow consumption from the perspective of consumer psychology.

1 Slow Food

Slow food helps consumers discover the taste of local food and decrease or eliminate the adverse effects of fast food. The slow food movement is included in slow tourism. Slow tourism primarily anticipates changes in the traveling behavior of consumers as well as their choices of transportation. Slow food is also included in the sustainable tourism movement. In slow tourism, the good or service in question must be labeled as "slow" (Fullagar, Markwell, & Wilson, 2012: 53). To develop culinary tourism, local foods and beverages, as well as sustainable agriculture practices, must be encouraged. Furthermore, local businesses must be supported to attract more visitors and investors. This would particularly enable rural communities to enhance environmental sustainability (Sims, 2009: 322). Distinction brought about by local foods and beverages within the Slow Food network would benefit farmer's markets and trade fairs. This would increase the sales of goods produced in local farms, paving the way for localization strategies (Brunori, 2007: 3).

The adaptation of tourism activities such as culinary festivals and farmer's markets based on ethical and collaborative production with an aim to develop the slow food philosophy and to attract prospective tourists into daily life is crucial. The transformation of this adaptation into a lifestyle would benefit societies as a whole (Williams et al., 2015: 1). The appreciation and popularity of an aliment among consumers are mostly determined through the sensorial perceptions induced by the aliment in question in the consumer's mind (Nosi & Zanni, 2004). The impact of the sensorial perception in the consumers' mind on purchasing behavior has become even more significant as they are offered an ever-widening product range and have their purchasing power increased. Especially, the taste of the food product in question must be perceived as tasty in order for the consumer to buy it again. As a result, for food companies to be successful in the market, they need, at the very least, to be able to observe the sensorial features evoked by the product among consumers during production and product development (de Graaf & Kok, 2010). Companies with competitive advantage would be the ones that can manipulate and control consumer perceptions. These companies must be able to control active and sensorial features. Such a control mechanism would only arise only if one comprehends the relationship between food structure and sensorial features (Wilkinson, Dijksterhuis, & Minekus, 2000: 442). When compared with their non-organic counterparts, organic foods produced within the scope of the slow food movement might be less attractive for consumers in terms of both texture and mouthfeel. Therefore, companies need to redesign their products to produce aliments especially with appealing textures (Lillford & Norton, 1994: 196).

The application of the slow food concept into production has many objectives. The primary aims of this concept can be listed as follows (Simonetti, 2012:169):

1. Raising awareness about places of production within the scope of the slow food movement, drawing the attention of consumers with different recipes each season, and appealing to different tastes,
2. Disallowing low quality and taking precautions against potential food frauds,
3. Protection of the resources of local food and beverages which are under risk of extinction,
4. Increasing the variety of food and beverage resources to help local people increase the productivity.

Since tourists need to eat at least twice or three times a day, gastronomy is vital for tourism. As a component of the target marketing mix, food is crucial because it allows consumers to experience the place they are at while giving tourists the chance to literally taste and directly experience the local culture. Culinary cultures in different touristic destinations vary depending on geographical conditions (Fullagar, Markwell, & Wilson, 2012: 227).

2 Slow Food Consumption and Consumer Psychology

This section will discuss the impacts of motivation and lifestyle on slow food consumption and consumer psychology.

2.1 Motivation

Finding out tourists' motivations behind their preferences for choosing a destination is crucial for tourism marketing. For example, visitors of the Namyangju Slow Life Festival (NSLF) in South Korea participated in this festival to perceive the value of "slowness", including slow food and an authentic experience (Chung, Kim, Lee, & Kim, 2018: 1). Culinary festivals offering locally-produced slow food are a motivating factor for tourists to opt for such destinations. Furthermore, Oh, Assaf and Baloglu (2016: 4) determined the motivations of slow tourism as 'relaxation, self-reflection, escape, novelty-seeking, engagement, and discovery'. These motivations correspond considerably with general motivations for traveling.

The motivational theory, described by Gnoth (1997) as internal and external motivations, is based on a "push and pull" approach. Push factors refer to the decision whether to take a vacation whereas pull factors refer to the selection of a destination (Klenosky, 2002: 385). To attract tourists with sufficient internal motivation, destinations attempt to draw attention by promoting their centers of attraction, facilities, and experiences. Substantial benefits and values can be, at least in the initial stage, can be one of the push factors leading to the decision to travel (Özdemir & Çelebi, 2018: 2). For instance, taking the value of self-respect into account, if the destination is promoted with the statement "I feel good after tasting the food in this destination" instead of "The destination has good food" within the context of slow food, the destination in question would draw more attention. For tourists who want to experience slow tourism, their access to information about the destination and the authenticity of the food in that destination will increase their interest and intentions (Meng & Choi, 2016: 407). Furthermore, the concretization of abstract experiences to increase the sensorial experiences of tourists would create added value for consumers. Concretizing the slow tourism and slow food concept of tourists would strengthen their motivations. Photographs, souvenirs crafted with natural materials, cookbooks including visuals and recipes of local dishes, or food festivals might be listed as examples to such concretization. The slow food movement also aims to increase the aesthetic value of products. The aesthetic appearance of restaurants and foods and the setting in which food is presented is vital for consumer motivation (Miele & Murdoch, 2002: 312).

2.2 Lifestyle

Food is an important component of the lifestyles of individuals espousing the slow food philosophy; these people put the values of the movement into daily practice. Therefore, slow food can be, in fact, considered as a part of the habits of these people. The slow food movement is also associated with slow travel. The relation of travels to ethical consumption is about relocalization, 'local food systems, and the carbon footprint of food' (Hall, 2012: 70). Individuals participating in the slow food movement expand its values through other consumer behaviors such as transport, traveling, and vacationing (Nevison, 2008:27).

Lee et al. (2015) examined how and why people travel and how their lifestyles affect their choice of destination. Their research revealed that those embracing the slow food movement are more interested in new and local cultures whereas others seek familiarity and comfort in their travels. Furthermore, it was shown that slow food enthusiasts interact more with locals (Arslan, Yılmaz, & Boz, 2018: 31). Ensuring local participation in decision-making is an initiative not only for increasing the benefits of tourism for the local economy but also providing a higher-quality experience for tourists, protecting the environment, and increasing the quality of life for host societies (Jung, Ineson, & Miller, 2014: 432).

In Italy, France, Spain, and other Mediterranean countries, traditional food consumption patterns and the dominance of regional cuisines still prevail. In contemporary Western societies, the rise of "lifestyle" marketing particularly in catering services stems from the desire of consumers to experience things (Miele & Murdoch, 2002: 313).

The differences between individuals who embrace slow food within their lifestyle preferences and those who do not are listed below (Lee, Packer, Scott, 2015: 2).

1. Slow food enthusiasts have different lifestyles and preferences in terms of traveling than those who do not adopt the philosophy.
2. The touristic objectives of the members of the slow food movement are different. They are more consistent in the selection of activities during their travels than those who do not care for the movement (e.g. activities during vacation).
3. Lifestyles of slow food enthusiasts affect the preference of destination throughout their journey.

3 Slow Food and Tourism Marketing

Tourism is one of the key economic activities for states in terms of profit generation. Innovation and locality are crucial in tourism services; 30% of tourists generally opt for local businesses. In this case, for utilizing food and tourism experiences as growth strategies, encouraging incoming tourists to stay longer, and spending more, local governments need to support local businesses (OECD, 2012: 21). Keeping the culinary culture alive in touristic destinations can be an important advantage for marketing, because the branding of local foods and beverages, preserving the origins of food and cooking techniques, presenting of food and the sensory features of slow foods in humans are important factors in tourism marketing (Richards, 2015: 1).

Culinary tourism can be defined as traveling "for the purpose of exploring and enjoying the destination's food and beverage" (Kivela & Crotts, 2005: 42). The motivation of slow food enthusiasts through local food especially in their travels with the purpose of vacation would be beneficial (Lee, Scott, & Packer, 2014: 271). In gastronomy tourism, various local food, recipes, tastes reflecting different cultures curated by chefs, and the cultural backdrop that makes gastronomy an ideal product are integral parts of the vacation experience (Kivela & Crotts, 2005: 42–43). The development and promotion of slow food provide economic benefits for societies. Therefore, tourism incentives supporting slow food must be increased in order to increase the demand for tourism in certain regions (Kivela & Crotts, 2005: 52).

The motivation for traveling of slow food enthusiasts is generally different tastes in the destination. Tourists caring about different culinary cultures might travel to expand continuously their gastronomical knowledge or to taste different food. This may become a suitable alternative, particularly for regions without natural or cultural centers of attraction. In slow food tourism, there are various ways to offer tourists different food-related experiences. First of all, local culture must be supported. While conducting traditional tourism activities, especially experts on culinary tourism must be sensitive about the protection of natural and cultural resources as well as the integration of these resources into the local cuisine. Many associations of slow food advocates aim to preserve food variety and food heritage. Furthermore, it is possible to protect natural resources and to improve the quality of life of societies within the region in question through culinary tourism. This is vital for both economic development and the preservation of local food and production methods at risk of extinction due to globalization (Buiatti, 2011: 92). Additionally, the integration and presentation of local products within the local heritage of the region are invaluable for slow tourism (Heitmann, Robinson, & Povey, 2011: 117).

Slow life is an inclination denoting the preference of being more harmonious with the environment, along with being closer to anything traditional, local, fair, organic, and authentic (Meng & Choi, 2016). It is about participating in sustainable production and consumption and behaving in an environmentally sensitive way. The idea of slow life emerged for the first time in 1999 in Italy. The recent increase in disposable income in the West has led to high levels of food quality and a wide range of food products. This placed spending time outside and eating out among the most remarkable features of urban life (Heitmann, Robinson, & Povey, 2011:114). However, perceived to be of high quality yet also to be highly expensive, slow tourism and slow food products must be priced reasonably. Furthermore, prices must be formulated clearly for consumers willing to opt for slow food products. This would allow consumers to estimate costs, reducing the psychological pressure created by price uncertainty.

Conclusion

Slow food is particularly crucial for a healthy and sustainable life. While making consumption decisions, consumers must be aware of the benefits of slow food and transfer this knowledge to future generations. Fast food consumption might cause both physical and psychological problems for the consumer in the long term.

Research studies in academic literature underline the importance of applying slow food strategies to protect and maintain local cultures. Arguing that consumer motivation for slow food and slow tourism during decision-making as well as the transformation of these concepts into lifestyle preferences can be reinforced particularly by attaching due importance to sensorial perception, the present study is expected to contribute to the existing literature in the theoretical sense. The study is intended to encourage qualitative and quantitative studies for the assessment of consumer attitudes, motivations, intentions, and behavior regarding the issue in question. Factors affecting the purchasing decision-making processes of consumers might be explained through similar studies.

As for sectoral practices, the study suggests the establishment of a rewards system enabling active tourists motivated with slow food to encourage prospective tourists. Furthermore, the private sector must create synergies with public institutions and civil society organizations through localization strategies. A holistic approach to slow food and slow tourism practices is considered to be beneficial.

References

Arslan, A., Yılmaz, Ö., & Boz, H. (2018). Destinasyon seçiminde yenilik arama davranişi. *Pamukkale University Journal of Social Sciences Institute*, (30).

Brunori, G. (2007). Local food and alternative food networks: A communication perspective. *Anthropology of Food*, (S2).

Buiatti, S. (2011). Food and tourism: The role of the "Slow Food" association. Sidali, Katia Laura, Spiller, Achim, & Schulze, Birgit (Eds.), *Food, Agri-Culture and Tourism* (pp. 92–101). Springer, Berlin, Heidelberg.

Chung, J. Y., Kim, J. S., Lee, C. K., & Kim, M. J. (2018). Slow-food-seeking behaviour, authentic experience, and perceived slow value of a slow-life festival. *Current Issues in Tourism*, *21*(2), pp. 123–127.

De Graaf, C., & Kok, F. J. (2010). Slow food, fast food and the control of food intake. *Nature Reviews Endocrinology*, *6*(5), p. 290.

Fullagar, S., Markwell, K., & Wilson, E. (Eds.). (2012). *Slow tourism: Experiences and mobilities,* (Vol. 54). New York: Channel View Publications.

Gnoth, J. (1997). Tourism motivation and expectation formation. *Annals of Tourism Research, 24*(2), pp. 283–304.

Hall, C. M. (2012). The contradictions and paradoxes of slow food: Environmental change, sustainability and the conservation of taste. Simone Fullagar, Kevin Markwell, & Erica Wilson, *Slow Tourism: Experiences and Mobilities* (pp. 53–68). New York: Channel View Publications.

Heitmann, S., Robinson, P., & Povey, G. (2011). Slow food, slow cities and slow tourism. *Research Themes for Tourism* (pp. 114–127). Wallingford: CAB International.

Jung, T. H., Ineson, E. M., & Miller, A. (2014). The slow food movement and sustainable tourism development: A case study of Mold, Wales. *International Journal of Culture, Tourism and Hospitality Research, 8*(4), pp. 432–445.

Kivela, J., & Crotts, J. C. (2005). Gastronomy tourism: A meaningful travel market segment. *Journal of Culinary Science & Technology, 4*(2–3), pp. 39–55.

Klenosky, D. B. (2002). The "pull" of tourism destinations: A means-end investigation. *Journal of Travel Research, 40*(4), pp. 396–403.

Lee, K. H., Scott, N., & Packer, J. (2014). Where does food fit in tourism? *Tourism Recreation Research, 39*(2), pp. 269–274.

Lee, K. H., Packer, J., & Scott, N. (2015). Travel lifestyle preferences and destination activity choices of Slow Food members and non-members. *Tourism Management, 46*, pp. 1–10.

Lillford, P. J., & Norton, I. T. (1994). High molecular weight food additives: Where are we going? *Trends in Food Science & Technology, 5*(6), pp. 196–198.

Meng, B., & Choi, K. (2016). The role of authenticity in forming slow tourists' intentions: Developing an extended model of goal-directed behavior. *Tourism Management, 57*, pp. 397–410.

Nevison, J. H. (2008). *Impacts of sustainable consumption choices on quality of life: The Slow Food example.* Doctoral dissertation, Simon Fraser University.

Nosi, C., & Zanni, L. (2004). Moving from "typical products" to "food-related services". *British Food Journal, 106*(10/11), pp. 779–792.

OECD. (2012). Food and the tourism experience. The OECD-Korea workshop. *OECD Studies on Tourism.* Paris: OECD Publishing, https://doi.org/10.1787/9789264171923-en. Accessed Date: 15.04.2020

Oh, H., Assaf, A. G., & Baloglu, S. (2016). Motivations and goals of slow tourism. *Journal of Travel Research, 55*(2), pp. 205–219.

Özdemir, G., & Çelebi, D. (2018). Exploring dimensions of slow tourism motivation. *Anatolia, 29*(4), pp. 540–552.

Pajo, A., & Uğurlu, K. (2015). Cittaslow kentleri için slow food çalışmalarının önemi. *EJOVOC (Electronic Journal of Vocational Colleges), 5*(6), pp. 65–73.

Preserve Biodiversity. (n.d.). Slow Food. https://www.slowfood.com/what-we-do/preserve-biodiversity/ Accessed on: 15.03.2020.

Richards, G. (2015). Food experience as integrated destination marketing strategy. *World Food Tourism Summit in Estoril, Portugal, 10*, 2015.

Simonetti, L. (2012). The ideology of slow food. *Journal of European Studies, 42*(2), pp. 168–189.

Sims, R. (2009). Food, place and authenticity: Local food and the sustainable tourism experience. *Journal of Sustainable Tourism, 17*(3), pp. 321–336.

Tosun, E. K. (2013). Yaşam kalitesi ekseninde şekillenen alternatif bir kentsel yaşam modeli: yavaş kentleşme hareketi. *Uludağ Üniversitesi İktisadi ve İdari Bilimler Fakültesi Dergisi, 32*(1), pp. 215–237.

Williams, L. T., Germov, J., Fuller, S., & Freij, M. (2015). A taste of ethical consumption at a slow food festival. *Appetite, 91*, pp. 321–328.

Wilkinson, C., Dijksterhuis, G. B., & Minekus, M. (2000). From food structure to texture. *Trends in Food Science & Technology, 11*(12), pp. 442–450.

Yurtseven, H. R., Kaya, O. & Harman, S. (2010). *Yavaş Hareketi*. Ankara: Detay Yayıncılık.

Yalçın KAHYA

6 Different Approaches to the Concept of Consumption

Introduction

An in-depth examination of consumption reveals a social dimension in addition to its economic aspect. Consumption exhibits the tastes, habits, behavior, and social class of an individual. While individuals used to consume for subsistence, the industrial revolution has engendered a novel pursuit of pleasure and luxury consumption.

These changes have created new needs, encouraging the replacement of all possessions with new ones. In this sense, consumption has turned into a machine going in circles indefinitely. From this perspective, each period in history has different definitions of needs (Ginsborg, 2010: 106–107). In this context, as pointed out by Gaines, does consumption signify buying, owning, or using goods or services? (cited in McRobbie, 2013: 57). The purpose of the present study is to analyze the shifts in the concept of consumption and consumer behavior from the modern age to the present day based on the opinions of Zygmunt Bauman, Jean Baudrillard, Richard Sennett and Erich Fromm.

1 Consumption and Consumer Behavior

Encompassing an interdisciplinary approach, the concept of consumption is examined in sociology, psychology, social psychology, economics, and cultural anthropology. At this point, varying approaches of scientific disciplines to consumption reflect their specific perspectives regarding consumer behavior. In this context, psychology attempts to understand consumer behavior by studying issues such as personality, motivation, attitudes, and learning. Psychology contributes to the understanding of the designation of consumer needs, consumer reactions to various products and messages, or the way personality or past experiences affect product selection (Odabaşı & Barış, 2010: 43). Related to economic development, consumption makes references to goods, services, energy, and resources used by individuals. Rising consumption levels indicate that people live in better, more comfortable conditions when compared with past circumstances (Giddens, 2008: 995). According to Bocock (1993), consumption is a socially-constructed historical process of change. The changes in production styles have led to the development of international markets and the replacement of the feudal structure by urban social classes, bringing about a transformation of the societal structure (cited in Chaney, 1999: 25–26).

The examination of consumption from the point of view proposed by Karl Marx and Max Weber, prominent thinkers of classical sociology, underlines that classes retaining the means of production regulate and exploit consumers. Weber explains this through the concepts of rationalization and disenchantment. Rationalization transforms cathedrals of consumption into efficient sales machines, giving rise to the increased monitoring and exploitation of consumers (Ritzer, 2016: 93–94). Intrinsically, this can be described as an ideological process of supervision (Çağlayan & Bayrakcı, 2016: 269). Wiswede defines the concept of consumption as behaviors aiming for the acquisition and private use of economic goods. However, consumption is not merely an economic behavior; it also has a personal significance for the individual. Modern consumption is characterized by usage values inferior to the promises of happiness and it generally acts as a means of social rewarding for working people (Institut für Gesellschaftspolitik, 1987: 18; Wiswede, 1989: 359 cited in Meyer, 2008).

2 Evolution of Consumption Culture from the Modern Age to the Present Day

Contemporary studies on consumption draw attention from social theorists and social psychologists. Needs-based consumption of the modern age is superseded by consumption focusing on dreams, images, tastes, and pleasure with the objective of obtaining an elevated identity, status, and reputation. At this point, consumer psychology research is used frequently in marketing and product development. In the aftermath of the Second World War, scientists started to defined consumers as entities aiming to maximize their benefits rationally. In this respect, consumer psychology underlies the modern market economy by narrowing the gap between the consumer's willingness to buy a product and the offer of the seller. Consumer psychology is able to decipher the motivations behind a purchasing decision by analyzing the behavior displayed by different consumers. Many studies in this field manifested that individuals make around 70% of their decisions unconsciously while only 30% of the decisions affecting daily life are taken consciously. However, this does not mean that decisions, even the conscious ones, are not solely determined by free will. A plethora of external factors might change a decision and shape the process in which one makes a decision fundamentally (Zum Kaufen verführt, 15.03.2020; Hausel, 2007). Based on this impact, this chapter presents the opinions of certain thinkers on the concept of consumption changing from the modern age to the present day, as well as its role and basic characteristics.

2.1 Zygmunt Bauman

Bauman argues that today's society has become a consumer society. As a matter of fact, all living beings have been consuming since the very beginning. Therefore, while people sought to answer the question of whether people worked to live or vice versa in the past, whereas today the question discussed is whether one consumes to live or vice versa. The second part of the question concerning the present day requires the market to seduce consumers using marketing strategies to sell products. To do so, the market needs consumers willing to be seduced. However, a shift in the factors affecting the purchasing behavior of these consumers is observed. Nowadays, consumers go from one attractive product to another, from one seduction to another, just for the sake of change. Associating consumption with fashion and citing Simmel who claimed that fashion is not a fait accompli and that it develops incessantly, Bauman examines fashion within the cultural context and analyzes it through the concept of consumption. He interprets the concept as the endeavor of an individual to transform into any other being during their search for identity as they act as themselves, appear to do so, or become someone else with the powerful effect of consumer markets (Bauman, 2015: 23–29).

The primary factor in the development of the consumer society is the shift from the fulfillment of real needs to the creation of needs transforming into the stimulation of desire. Even though demand creation is costly, service providers monitor, classify, and provide feedback about consumer data or their electronic traces by materializing their surveillance practices through the use of the Internet. In this sense, Bauman believes that consumption forms a connection between societal divisions, social identity, and common lifestyles. However, while consumption seems to be a pleasing concept for consumers, it has an underlying system of supervision on a mass scale. This brings the data-based marketing system into question. In this context, service providers know about the preferences and hobbies of consumers better than themselves (Bauman & Lyon, 2013: 24, 124). To sum up, Bauman emphasizes the fact that as long as the trajectory of consumption stays the same, based on the prediction by Rosa Luxemburg stating that capitalism will die of malnutrition, the waste and poison accumulating as a result of the increase in global production capacity will disrupt the ecological balance of the world, enhancing the possibility of humanity coming to an end as a result of the waste of its production (Bauman, 2018: 85–86).

2.2 Jean Baudrillard

In addition to the Marxist dichotomy of use-value (utility of objects) and exchange value (financial costs, commercial value), Baudrillard proposes the concept of "sign-value", denoting the capacity of commodities to grant reputation and represent social status and dominance (Best & Kellner, 2016: 166). In other words, the individual is reduced to a mere consumer and consumption objects do not have a real function nor cater to a defined need; instead, they only comply with the logic of desires (Yanıklar, 2006: 196). Today, humanity faces a reality of consumption and abundance created as a result of the increased accumulation of objects, services, and material goods, transforming the ecological balance of the world. Individuals are now surrounded by objects (Baudrillard, 2018: 15).

He believes the phenomenon of consumption to be the primary foundation of social order. By creating a system of classification, consumption objects affect the way behavior is structured. When they are consumed, their significance is transferred to the individual. With the illusion of a sense of liberation, an endless game of signs maintaining order in society is set into motion. In this respect, the concept is not about the consumption of use-values but of signs. This leads to a situation in which the function of products for sale is not only to satisfy individual needs but to allow the individual to establish a relationship with the social order (Sarup, 2014: 227–228). Within the scope of "garbage-can civilization", Baudrillard makes a moral emphasis by discussing the disregard of the use-value and moral codes, i.e. life expectancy, of the object by the individual who throws away their possessions or replaces them with new ones as demanded by their economic and social standing or fashion trends, in addition to the mention of the extravagance at the national and international level. In this sense, extravagance is considered a malfunction regardless of the circumstances (Baudrillard, 2018: 40–41). In brief, one might talk about the presence of unhealthy growth and saturity. One lives within a system in which everyone owns more than what they need. Furthermore, the ubiquitous nature of surplus causes the system to disintegrate (Baudrillard, 2015: 186). In other words, the bond between one individual and another is severed, reducing the individual to a commodity. In short, human and societal relationships are deconstructed. This deconstruction demotes the individual from a subject to an object, making commodity fetishism the principal factor.

2.3 Richard Sennett

Sennett argues that a new mentality emerged in the retail sector in the 19th century according to which buyers assess goods not based on use-value but in reference to stimuli creating personal meanings. The investment in personal emotions made the products displayed in shop windows more appealing. Therefore, the inherent mystery, significance, and connotations unrelated to the use-value of commodities divert one's attention to the object itself rather than the societal conditions in which it is produced. As explained within the context of the Marxist concept of "commodity fetishism", such practices hide the inequality between the worker producing the commodity and the owner in the modern capitalist order (Sennett, 2010: 194–195).

In this respect, while changing society and the new capitalistic culture subject individuals to a fear of redundancy under the concept of a skills society, they also inspire the formulation of new skills and abilities through advanced technology, global finance, and the new tertiary sectors (Sennett, 2015:16). According to Sennett, Wal-Mart gathers every product appealing to consumers under a single roof with low prices. However, what is worthy of attention here is that salespeople at Wal-Mart are excluded from the process of consumption. There is no face-to-face mediation and persuasion in this context. The individual decides which discounted products to buy based on constructed global images and marketing (Sennett, 2015: 97–98). This also brings about certain changes in advertising and marketing activities. Producers now hope to market the connotations of the object rather than the information about the object itself. In this respect, as indicated by Erving Goffman, advertising put forward an opinion with the participation of the consumer. The most sophisticated definitions are half-completed outlooks inviting the consumer to complete the whole picture. Ironic advertisements accomplish this task. Establishing connotations now falls to the consumer's imagination (cited in Sennett, 2015: 102–107).

2.4 Erich Fromm

Unlimited development, the capacity to attain all desires, and the promise of unlimited wealth sustaining humanity as a source of hope and trust in the industrial age have gradually given way to disappointment. Even though the reason why the industrial age was unable to keep these promises is economic, there are two inherent psychological sources of the system. The first source is the perception of the single objective of living as happiness or the maximization of pleasure. The second source is the personality traits the system has been obliged to nurture to survive such as selfishness, self-interest, greed, and the urge to possess

(Fromm, 2003: 19–21). Taking the concept of welfare society into consideration, Fromm argues that everyone needs food, water, clothing, and a place to live in. In other words, people have to use and consume many things. This is called consumption. However, Fromm claims that what is wrong here is the psychological problem stemming from the consumer behavior within the scope of which one desires to eat more, buy more, possess more, and use more (Fromm, 2004: 22).

On the other hand, changes in the ways of production result in shifts in the ways of consumption while the question of what is good for a person that had contributed to the development of the economic system has been supplanted by the question of what is good for the further development of the system. The more individuals are attached to material possession; the more significance commodities have in relation to the subject whose importance diminishes. In other words, if a person feels close to a certain principle, that principle will affect their entire life. This means that if the individual's world view is focused on possessing material goods, they will behave in a way that allows them to possess, obtain, and dominate. If one acts according to the principle of being, this will manifest itself as the ability to see the essence beyond the deceptive appearance, vitality, and the establishment of a proper relationship with the world (Fromm, 2003: 27, 48, 49).

In his book in which he analyzes "having" an "being", the two fundamental ways of human life, Erich Fromm alleges that the distinction between these two concepts in a healthy mind is similar to a normal function of human life. In his work presenting the opinions of certain philosophers, he states that:

> *"The Buddha teaches that in order to arrive at the highest stage of human development, we must not crave possessions... [whereas] Master Eckhart taught that to have nothing and make oneself open and "empty", not to let one's ego stand in one's way, is the condition for achieving spiritual wealth and strength. Marx taught that luxury is as much a vice as poverty and that our goal should be to be much, not to have much" (Fromm, 2003: 37–38).*

The changes in societal conditions brought about by the Industrial Revolution cause social and psychological problems for individuals while leaving them alone with their fate. The novel sense of freedom evoked by capitalism makes the individual lonelier and more isolated; it renders them a tool for greater external dominant powers (Fromm, 2011: 104–106). Unlike the fulfillment of basic needs, humanity has started manufacturing novel needs and items with the Industrial Revolution. What is meant here is that people's needs have always had variety. The important aspect it the existence of human desires and wants. However, nowadays these desires and wants are stimulated and nurtured from without. This shows that in today's economy, businesses rely on maximum production and maximum consumption for profit. "However, the economy in the 19th century was focused on maximizing savings. While people considered it as a flaw and shame when someone bought something that they could not afford back then, it is now considered an accomplishment. People without artificial needs who do not shop using credit cards and only spend real money are considered to be awkward. Self-esteem has become correlated with material possessions; this leads to a belief that if one wants to be the best, they have to own the most possessions. This perception is considered to be a part of the societal syndrome. At the same time, many people feel impoverished even if they own more than what they need since they cannot keep up with the consumption trend" (Fromm, 2004: 42–43).

Conclusion

The present study demonstrated the evolution of consumer society from the perspective of Zygmunt Bauman, Jean Baudrillard, Richard Sennett, and Erich Fromm. These philosophers emphasize the impact of changes brought about the Industrial Revolution on both society and individuals while underlining that consumption is not the solution for happiness and that individuals living in consumer societies, stimulated through various channels, feel increased pressure to consume due to globalization. At the same time, they point out the fact that products purchased by consumers within the context of the search for identity within contemporary society are used to express one's social identity and to differentiate oneself from the rest of the crowd.

Taking such developments into account, certain critics favor a model of "voluntary simplicity" regarding the attitudes towards and approaches to the world one lives in. At this point, carrying ambitions and desires related to consumption to a reasonable social context is considered essential (Ginsborg, 2010: 154). As for Fromm, he argues that the solution lies in the support of rational consumption as it is good and beneficial for humankind (Fromm, 2003: 212–218). In conclusion, consumption offers happiness sourcing from commodities and senses of ownership, equality, trendiness, power, image, and elevated status.

References

Baudrillard, J. (2015). *Şeytana Satılan Ruh*. 3rd Ed. (Trans. O. Adanır). Ankara: Doğu Batı Yayınları.

Baudrillard, J. (2018). *Tüketim Toplumu*. 11th Ed. (Trans. N. Tutal, & F. Keskin). İstanbul: Ayrıntı Yayınları.

Bauman, Z. (2015). *Akışkan Modern Toplumda Kültür.* 1st Ed. (Trans. İ. Çapcıoğlu, & F. Ömek). Ankara: Atıf Yayınları.

Bauman, Z. (2018). *Iskarta Hayatlar.* 1st Ed. (Trans. O. Yener). İstanbul: Can Yayınları.

Bauman, Z., & Lyon, D. (2013). *Akışkan Gözetim.* 1st Ed. (Trans. E. Yılmaz). İstanbul: Ayrıntı Yayınları.

Best, S., & Kellner, D. (2016). *Postmodern Teori.* 3rd Ed. (Trans. M. Küçük). İstanbul: Ayrıntı Yayınları.

Chaney, D. (1999). *Yaşam Tarzları.* 1st Ed. (Trans. İ. Kutluk). Ankara: Dost Kitabevi.

Çağlayan, S., & Bayrakcı, O. (2016). 'Emek süreçlerinde denetim'. *Süleyman Demirel Üniversitesi Fen-Edebiyat Fakültesi Sosyal Bilimler Dergisi,* 0 (39), pp. 257–274

Fromm, E. (2003). *Sahip Olmak Ya da Olmak.* (Trans. A. Arıtan). İstanbul: Arıtan Yayınevi.

Fromm, E. (2004). *Hayatı Sevmek.* (Trans. A. Köse). İstanbul: Arıtan Yayınevi.

Fromm, E. (2011). *Özgürlükten Kaçış.* 6th Ed. (Trans. Ş. Yeğin). İstanbul: Payel Yayınevi.

Giddens, A. (2008). *Sosyoloji.* 1st Ed. (Trans. Z. Mercan). İstanbul: Kırmızı Yayınları.

Ginsborg, P. (2010). *Gündelik Hayat Politikaları.* 1st Ed. (Trans. M. Ö. Mengüşoğlu). İstanbul: Açılım Kitap.

Hausel, H. G. (2007). Die Gesetze des Gehirns: Wie Kaufentscheidungen fallen. http://www.perspektive-blau.de/artikel/0701b/0701b.htm Accessed on: 15.03.2020.

McRobbie, A. (2013). *Postmodernizm ve Popüler Kültür.* 1st Ed. (Trans. A. Özdek). İstanbul: Parşömen Yayıncılık.

Meyer, E. (2008). Das Konsumverhalten von Jugendlichen. Welche Rolle spielt das Internet? München, Grin Verlag, https://www.grin.com/document/137560 Accessed on: 15.03.2020.

Odabaşı, Y., & Barış, G. (2010). *Tüketici Davranışı.* 10th Ed. İstanbul: Medicat Akademi.

Ritzer, G. (2016). *Büyüsü Bozulmuş Dünyayı Büyülemek.* 3rd Ed. (Trans. F. Payzın). İstanbul: Ayrıntı Yayınları.

Sarup, M. (2014). *Post-Yapısalcılık ve Postmodernizm.* 5th Ed. (Trans. A. Güçlü). Ankara: Pharmakon Yayınevi.

Sennett, R. (2010). *Kamusal İnsanın Çöküşü.* 3rd Ed. (Trans. S. Durak, & A. Yılmaz). İstanbul: Ayrıntı Yayınları.

Sennett, R. (2015). *Yeni Kapitalizm Kültürü.* 3rd Ed. (Trans. A. Onocak). İstanbul: Ayrıntı Yayınları.

Yanıklar, C. (2006). *Tüketimin Sosyolojisi.* İstanbul: Birey Yayınları.

Zum Kaufen verführt - Konsumpsychologie durchschauen. (28.06.2019), https://www.wissenschaft.de/gesellschaft-psychologie/zum-kaufen-verfuehrt-konsumpsychologie-durchschauen/ Accessed on: 15.03.2020.

Mutlu UYGUN and Ebru GÜNER

7 Spiritual Consumption as a Rising Trend in Consumer Psychology

Introduction

In today's world where life is full of uncertainties and the pace of life is unstoppable, people actively seek answers and meaning regarding their lives (Husemann & Eckhardt, 2019: 391), desiring more than ever to feel complete by attaining internal happiness. Upon realizing that this feeling cannot be achieved solely by materialistic means, it seems like people increasingly turn to spirituality (Marmor-Lavie & Stout, 2016: 169). In the present day, as traditional religions become more and more irrelevant particularly in Western societies, a more secular type of spirituality gradually becomes more significant and an understanding of spiritual consumption corresponding to this trend fills the gap left by organized religions (Shepherd & Kay, 2019: 467) in a fast-paced, high-tech, and commercialized world and consumer culture (Hemetsberger et al., 2019: 540). Ancient sites of pilgrimage, yoga, meditation, awareness workshops, seclusion in monasteries, and healing hotels become increasingly popular as sources of self-expression, getting rid of emotional distresses, and finding answers to spiritual questions about life (Hemetsberger et al., 2019: 540–541; Husemann & Eckhardt, 2019: 391) in modern societies shaped by the culture of pursuit stemming from a series of social and cultural transformations (Roof, 1999: 10). Consumers desiring to attain a more authentic and internally fulfilling life become more and more interested in their spirituality, acquire more knowledge about it, and actively seek spirituality in their lives. Therefore, spirituality has started to become a global phenomenon as a personalized and subjective form of contemplation and an internal immaterial pursuit (Hemetsberger et al., 2019: 541)

With the entanglement of the spiritual and the material, of the tangible and intangible, and of the sacred and the secular, consumers try to combine these elements in various aspects of their lives properly to achieve fulfillment (Marmor-Lavie & Stout, 2016: 169). As a result of the close interest among consumers in spirituality, the fact that marketing researchers pay more attention to the role of markets and consumption in the pursuit of meaning and that a new field of research emerges in the juncture of spirituality, religion, markets, and consumption is worthy of attention (Husemann & Eckhardt, 2019: 392). In this respect, the seminal study of Belk et al. (1989) focusing particularly on the role of consumption in one's experience of the sacred has laid the foundation of the examination of spirituality in consumer research. Previous research studies examine the way consumers sanctify earthly goods, services, and brands (Belk et al., 1989; Muniz & Schau, 2005); the immaterial needs of consumers and their spiritual motives for consumption (Dodds et al., 2018; Skousgaard, 2006); the way marketers use spirituality and religion to increase the value and appeal of their products and brands (Andreini et al., 2017; Askegaard & Eckhardt, 2012; Rinallo et al., 2013); the way religious and spiritual institutions, leaders, and movements adapt marketing techniques and practices for their applications (Kumar et al., 2014; Rinallo et al., 2016; Sardana et al., 2018); and the way businesses or brands make use of spiritual or religious symbols in their communication activities (Fischer, 2019; Kaur, 2016; Marmor-Lavie & Stout, 2016; Soldevilla et al., 2019).

In the consumer research literature, it can be seen that spiritual consumption is analyzed under two titles: spirituality as market supplies and spirituality as experiences from the consumer's perspective. The former handles the issue from the markets' perspective and focuses on the way spirituality is commodified and how the spiritual market is beneficial for consumers, whereas the latter focuses on personal and social experiences and the way consumers fill their lives with spiritual meanings (Hemetsberger et al., 2019: 541). These studies provide a theoretical and empirical basis for spiritual consumption, yet research studies on the way consumers experience spirituality, create spiritual value, develop spirituality, or embark on a transformative journey supported by non-consumption factors remain insufficient (Dodds et al., 2018: 288; Hemetsberger et al., 2019: 542). Therefore, this chapter examines the phenomenon of spiritual consumption within the framework of consumer psychology with a holistic approach along with its relational aspects; in this respect, it will deal with the concept of spirituality, its differences with religion, and its rising importance while elaborating on the concepts of consumer spirituality, spiritual consumption, and spiritual markets.

1 The Concept and Rise of Spirituality

Spirituality is a multifaceted concept discussed in many disciplines; the literature devoted to spirituality has expanded significantly throughout the years (Dodds et al., 2018: 291; Haq & Wong, 2010: 136). The word "spirituality" derives from the Latin root "spiritus" meaning "breath" or "breath of life" (Suri & Rao, 2014: 26). Signifying one's construction of the meaning of life (Ulvoas-Moal,

2010: 918), spirituality is a personal belief system denoting the constant pursuit of the meaning and purpose of life and gratitude towards the depth of life, the profundity of the universe, and natural powers (Basci, 2015: 446; Kale, 2006: 108). The individual is in a personal pursuit for answers to his/her questions regarding himself/herself, his/her place in the universe, the meaning of life, and God or a superior being considered to be sacred (Arslan & Konuk Şener, 2009: 54). Representing the meaning of each person's life (Kaur, 2016: 328), spirituality signifies the endeavor of the individual to connect their inner self to the known world and beyond in a deep and significant manner (Kale, 2006: 108). Therefore, whether aware of it or not, they strive to integrate themselves with something greater than them and being connected with other people, the environment, and the world (Kumar et al., 2014: 482). Spirituality is a perception of life beyond physical states, psychological emotions, and social roles; the assumption that one is more than they can perceive and comprehend completely; and looking beyond one's self considering integrity, inner harmony, the sense of peace, and the meaning of life (Kaur, 2016: 328).

It is possible to say that the definitions of spirituality are categorized under two different ideas. The first is the desire to find the meaning of one's life and his/her purpose of existence indicating an extremely individualized form of the belief system, whereas the other is the belief in the superiority of a God controlling the entire universe, emphasizing the standardized form of religion. This encompasses not only the structured and organized doctrine of religions but also imaginary and superstitious beliefs that are known to be unreal. In brief, spirituality in the modern world is considered to be an experiential and secular pursuit of the truth in nature against religious reactionism and hierarchy (Basci, 2015: 446).

Still controversial and vague in its current state, spirituality fundamentally represents a different kind of structure even though it is perceived to be synonymous with religion. Spirituality is an inherent human desire and transcends beyond the depths of religion (Marmor-Lavie & Stout, 2016: 171). It is a meaningful discovery of the reciprocal relationship between one's inner self and the wider truth (Kale, 2006: 109) and denotes the personalized and subjective aspect of the religious experience (Standifer et al., 2010: 134). As a social institution methodizing the belief in and worship of a God, supernatural forces, and various sacred beings, religion gathers and employs beliefs within the framework of rules, institutions, customs, and symbols. Being a cultural phenomenon, an organized belief system, and a set of worships and practices, religion envisages a lifestyle for its believers (Arslan & Konuk Şener, 2009: 54). The concept of religion denotes an organized societal system of beliefs, practices, and rituals officialized, institutionalized and designed to facilitate the affinity with God, whereas spirituality is different as it is less official, rigid, and institutionalized than religion (Rinallo et al., 2013: 3). Spiritual beliefs and values might or might not be with religion. Furthermore, one does not need to have strong religious beliefs in order to have a spiritual aspect to their personality. Spirituality is a wider concept than religious practices, yet it can also include such practices. Someone who is not affiliated with any religion might define themselves as someone with a strong spirituality.

One of the reasons underlying this difference between religion and spirituality is the rise of secularization with the modernization of society. With the advent of secularization, traditional religious institutions have started to lose their authority on society and personal life (Rinallo et al., 2013: 2–3; Shaw & Thomson, 2013: 559). After the Second World War, due to their inability to make satisfying explanations and provide emotional support, church attendance has started to decrease in many developed countries and Christianity has led to disappointment and lost its credibility among believers (Hosseini et al., 2017). In the West, this disappointment over religion and the loss of faith has become more evident with modernization and scientific inquiries providing alternative explanations for the existence of humankind (Sardana et al., 2018: 725). While there was a general pressure on individuals to adopt a religion, to have the same religious beliefs as their parents, and to follow the practices necessitated by their religion before the 1960s, the decade was the scene for a cultural revolution leading to a decrease in the importance of religious norms in many Western countries (Stolz & Usunier, 2019: 8). Profound changes in sexual behavior, the role of women in society, and migration in the 1960s brought about new religious movements, challenging Christian values (Shaw & Thomson, 2013: 559). The decay in the authority of organized religions as a result of such changes has led to the freedom of formulating belief systems based on various spiritual sources (Rinallo et al., 2013: 2). The search for wisdom, enlightenment, intuition, and one's true self has become popular, laying the foundations of a liberated context for different traditions, philosophies, and faiths described as "believing without belonging" to be practiced without complete attachment (Hosseini et al., 2017; Shaw & Thomson, 2013: 559). The rise of globalization and capitalism has also given impetus to the rise of spirituality. In addition to contributing significantly to the processes of capitalism and globalization, advancements in communication and transport technologies have given rise to individual mobility. Therefore, while people are presented with an opportunity to travel around the globe; they also had the chance to observe new religions, teachings, and beliefs, to obtain more knowledge about these, and combine these to obtain new systems (Husemann &

Eckhardt, 2019: 394; Stolz & Usunier, 2019: 9). Despite all these developments, late modernity did not transform into secularized societies in which the pursuits of spirituality, religion, and the supernatural have become insignificant and faith has declined (Husemann & Eckhardt, 2019: 392). Even though the significance of organized religions has relatively decreased, this decrease cannot be said to represent a loss of faith as people replace their new belief systems with the existing ones. Instead, individuals have gravitated towards the consumption of unsatisfying goods and services; therefore, the new age of spirituality has emerged as one's beliefs were integrated with the market (Hosseini et al., 2017).

Being values of modern society, individualism and the consumption trend seem to have created a new path as far as marketing is concerned. As the philosophy of marketing has gone through a profound transformation since brands and images have become more important than the functionality of products, spirituality has become a marketable commodity. More importantly, the ever-expanding market of spiritual goods, services, experiences, venues/places, and even people targeting individualized, secular, and socially competitive consumers is seen to be profitable and feasible in the new millennium. Whereas religion is considered to be a taboo, the use of spirituality was welcomed heartily by consumers (Basci, 2015: 447). Ultimately, "the realm of the spiritual is increasingly permeated by marketi[z]ation, which involves applying capitalist practices and principles to institutions and social fields that formerly were 'above' the logic of the market" (Laer & Izberk-Bilgin, 2019: 586). It has also become a significant subject within the scope of consumer behavior (in particular, consumer psychology) and consumer experience (Dodds et al., 2018: 291).

2 Consumer Spirituality and Spiritual Consumption

Today, many consumers want their preferred goods and services to not only satisfy their functional and emotional needs but also to be in touch with their spirituality (Dodds et al., 2018: 287; Kotler, et al., 2010: 4). Consumer spirituality can be defined as a set of interrelated practices and processes encountered while consuming market supplies (goods, services, places) providing a spiritual benefit (Kale, 2006: 109). In other words, within the scope of consumer spirituality, market supplies obtained are designed purposefully to satisfy consumer desires for significant encounters with one's inner self or a higher external power (Husemann & Eckhardt, 2019: 393). Spirituality is a pursuit of one's inner self and the exploration of the relationships between this self and the wider truth; self-exploration and self-integration are the two fundamental elements of spirituality. Designed and offered within the market to facilitate this exploration and integration of one's self, goods and services provide immaterial benefits for consumers (Kale, 2006: 109).

Today, with the rise of new-age spiritual discourses and practices, there is a significant increase in the number of consumers seeking spiritual experiences (Dodds et al., 2018: 291). Through spiritual consumption, consumers attempt to quench a thirst regarding their search for significance (Shaw & Thomson, 2013: 559). As a result, spirituality is marketed as a product of self-development, a social phenomenon, and a state of personal well-being (Suri & Rao, 2014: 27). As an art of persuasion, marketing often includes the formation of symbolic relationships between a product and certain cultural sources of resonance; therefore, religion and spirituality provide ample opportunities for symbolism. Businesses and brands aware of these opportunities seem to devote efforts to integrate qualities related to spirituality or religion into their market supplies; thus, market supplies with such spiritual qualities are generally considered by consumers to be superior to non-spiritual goods, services, and places (Shepherd & Kay, 2019: 467). These findings become evident each day.

Wanting to achieve spirituality through goods, services, and places, consumers might make use of three tools, namely materiality, embodiment, and technology (Husemann & Eckhardt, 2019: 393). Current studies on consumption and spirituality (Rauf et al., 2019; Santana & Botelho, 2019; Shepherd & Kay, 2019) indicate that there is a relationship between materiality and consumer spirituality and that consumers might attain and experience spirituality through material objects. In this respect, consumers have spiritual experiences by sanctifying and adding religious symbols to their material objects (Shepherd & Kay, 2019: 467), restraining their physical and corporal desires, decreasing and simplifying their consumption (Rauf et al., 2019: 500), and forming fluid and strong connections with material objects (Santana & Botelho, 2019: 514).

In today's societies that are digitalized gradually, technology has increasingly become a means of attaining spirituality. The metaphor of the Internet almost becoming a tool for reaching and communicating with God becomes significantly prevalent. Within this context, studies on pilgrimages show that online forums support and facilitate spiritual journeys through word-of-mouth communication in addition to helping with the practical search for information. Furthermore, talking about and evaluating one's pilgrimage on online platforms carry spirituality beyond a physical journey (Husemann & Eckhardt, 2019: 398–399).

3 Markets and Consumer Spirituality

In modern-day life becoming increasingly temporary, unstable, complex, and vague, people are more prone to search the meaning of life and go after a transformation to a better self (Kotler, 2019: 407). Many people seek spiritual solutions to the consumption behavior brought about by the current style of life (Haq & Wong, 2010: 136). Longing for relaxation, dreaming of a more romantic and fascinating lifestyle, and seeking ways to reconnect with nature (Hemetsberger et al., 2019: 540), people gravitate towards hopes, remedies, and foundations, leading to the gradual growth of the spiritual market (Kotler, 2019: 410). These advancements have culminated in the rise of a relatively novel market that might be able to respond to the transformation of one's inner world (Basci, 2015: 446).

A spiritual market consists of three basic components. First of all, a consumer wanting to change since they see a value in this transformation and willing to allocate money, time, attachment, and loyalty in exchange for this change is necessary for a spiritual market. Secondly, a seller of change as the exchanging party that might be a spiritual practitioner triggering the transformative process is required. Thirdly, the transformative market offer is supplied within the market in which the buyer and the seller come together for a change in the mind or body of the consumer. As far as transformative experiences are concerned, the place of transformation might be an ashram (a venue of seclusion in Hinduism), a seminar hall, or even someone's living room (Kotler, 2019: 407).

In terms of consumer spirituality, understanding the market first is a vital priority for businesses and marketers. In this respect, finding answers to questions such as the way spiritual markets are formed, expanded, and globalized; the actors present in these actors and the roles they play; or potential megatrends for the future (Husemann & Eckhardt, 2019: 394) might provide significant hints for businesses providing spiritual goods and services to survive in the market.

Conclusion

We live in a world order in which traditional religions coexist with new ones, the number of people placing great importance on spirituality yet not defining themselves as religious increases, and religion and spirituality intersecting politics, society, and culture affects and transforms the market and consumption (Rinallo & Oliver, 2019: 4). In such a context, there is a significant increase in the significance of spirituality and, therefore, spiritual goods and services for consumers. As a result, businesses becoming aware of the fact that they need to satisfy consumers with spiritual tendencies endeavor to transform themselves in this regard (Smith, 2003: 52) as demonstrated by their new practices. However, it must be acknowledged that marketing experts were quite late in examining spirituality within the context of marketing, consumer behavior, and, in particular, consumer psychology, and assessing its impact on the market (Kale, 2006: 108). Therefore, it can be said that any new research study, especially on spiritual consumption and consumer experiences, would contribute profoundly to both the existing academic literature and professional practice.

Businesses wanting to differentiate themselves from their competitors and to provide added value for their consumers need to be aware of the spiritual needs of consumers and to think about how to satisfy these needs. Evaluating consumers as a whole consisting of a mind, body, and soul seeking meaning and purpose in the products they consume has become an obligation for any kind of business (Dodds et al., 2018: 287). Therefore, in addition to providing functionally and emotionally-satisfying marketing supplies to consumers, businesses need to solidify them with spiritual benefits.

References

Andreini, D., Rinallo, D., Pedeliento, G., & Bergamaschi, M. (2017). Brands and religion in the secularized marketplace and workplace: Insights from the case of an Italian hospital renamed after a Roman Catholic Pope. *Journal of Business Ethics*, 141(3), pp. 529–550.

Arslan, H., & Konuk Şener, D. (2009). Stigma, spiritüalite ve konfor kavramlarının Meleis'in kavram geliştirme sürecine gore irdelenmesi. *Maltepe Üniversitesi Hemşirelik Bilim ve Sanatı Dergisi*, 2(1), pp. 51–58.

Askegaard, S., & Eckhardt, G. M. (2012). Glocal yoga: Re-appropriation in the Indian consumptionscape. *Marketing Theory*, 12(1), pp. 45–60.

Basci, E. (2015). 4P's and 1C of new age spirituality: A holistic marketing review. *International Journal of Social Science and Humanity*, 5(5), pp. 446–449.

Belk, R. W., Wallendorf, M., & Sherry Jr, J. F. (1989). The sacred and the profane in consumer behavior: Theodicy on the odyssey. *Journal of Consumer Research*, 16(1), pp. 1–38.

Dodds, S., Bulmer, S. L., & Murphy, A. J. (2018). Exploring consumers' experiences of spiritual value in healthcare services. *Social Responsibility Journal*, 14(2), pp. 287–301.

Fischer, J. (2019). Looking for religious logos in Singapore. *Journal of Management, Spirituality & Religion*, 16(1), pp. 132–153.

Haq, F., & Wong, H. Y. (2010). Is spiritual tourism a new strategy for marketing Islam? *Journal of Islamic Marketing*, 1(2), pp. 136–148.

Hemetsberger, A., Kreuzer, M., & Klien, M. (2019). From caterpillar to butterfly: experiencing spirituality via body transformation. *Journal of Marketing Management*, 35(5–6), pp. 540–564.

Hosseini, M. S., Akwei, C. A., McClelland, B., & Foster, S. (2017). Spirituality effects on consumption behaviour in the fashion market industry and its importance for the development of successful marketing strategies: A comparative study of female consumers in the UK and Iran. In *BAM 2017 Conference Proceedings*, BAM, September. https://www.bam.ac.uk/home Accessed Date: 15.04.2020

Husemann, K. C., & Eckhardt, G. M. (2019). Consumer spirituality. *Journal of Marketing Management*, 35(5–6), pp. 391–406.

Kale, S. (2006). Consumer spirituality and marketing. *ACR Asia-Pacific Advances*, 7, pp. 108–110.

Kaur, G. (2016). Customer interface in spiritual tourism via "synaptic CRM gap": An integrative technology-based conceptual model for relationship marketing. *Journal of Relationship Marketing*, 15(4), pp. 326–343.

Kotler, P. (2019). The market for transformation. *Journal of Marketing Management*, 35(5–6), pp. 407–409.

Kotler, P., Kartajaya, H., & Setiawan, I. (2010). *Marketing 3.0: From products to customers to the human spirit*. New Jersey: John Wiley & Sons.

Kumar, V., Jain, A., Rahman, Z., & Jain, A. (2014). Marketing through spirituality: A case of PatanjaliYogpeeth. *Procedia-Social and Behavioral Sciences*, 133, pp. 481–490.

Laer T. V., & Izberk-Bilgin, E. (2019). A discourse analysis of pilgrimage reviews. *Journal of Marketing Management*, 35(5–6), pp. 586–604.

Marmor-Lavie, G., & Stout, P. A. (2016). Consumers' insights about spirituality in advertising. *Journal of Media and Religion*, 15(4), pp. 169–185.

Muniz Jr, A. M., & Schau, H. J. (2005). Religiosity in the abandoned Apple Newton brand community. *Journal of Consumer Research*, 31(4), pp. 737–747.

Rauf, A. A., Prasad, A., & Ahmed, A. (2019). How does religion discipline the consumer subject? Negotiating the paradoxical tension between consumer desire and the social order. *Journal of Marketing Management*, 35(5–6), pp. 491–513.

Rinallo, D., & Oliver, M. A. (2019). The marketing and consumption of spirituality and religion. *Journal of Management, Spirituality & Religion*, 16(1), pp. 1–5.

Rinallo, D., Maclaran, P., & Stevens, L. (2016). A mixed blessing: Market-mediated religious authority in Neopaganism. *Journal of Macromarketing*, 36(4), pp. 425–442.

Rinallo, D., Borghini, S., Bamossy, G., & Kozinets, R. T. V. (2013). *When Sacred Objects Go B®a(n)d: Fashion Rosaries and the Contemporary Linkage of Religion and Commerciality*. In Consumption and spirituality (Eds. D. Rinallo, L. Scott, P. Maclaran), New York: Taylor & Francis, pp. 29–40.

Roof, W. C. (1999). *Spiritual Marketplace: Baby Boomers and the Remaking of American Religion*. New Jersey: Princeton University Press.

Santana, J., & Botelho, D. (2019). 'If it comes from Juazeiro, it's blessed'! Liquid and solid attachment in systems of object itineraries of pilgrimages. *Journal of Marketing Management*, 35(5–6), pp. 514–539.

Sardana, D., Gupta, N., & Sharma, P. (2018). Spirituality and religiosity at the junction of consumerism: Exploring consumer preference for spiritual brands. *International Journal of Consumer Studies*, 42(6), pp. 724–735.

Shaw, D., & Thomson, J. (2013). Consuming spirituality: The pleasure of uncertainty. *European Journal of Marketing*, 47(3–4), pp. 557–573.

Shepherd, S., & Kay, A. C. (2019). 'Jesus, take the wheel': The appeal of spiritual products in satiating concerns about randomness. *Journal of Marketing Management*, 35(5–6), pp. 467–490.

Skousgaard, H. (2006). *A Taxonomy of Spiritual Motivations for Consumption*. In NA – Advances in Consumer Research, Vol. 33, Eds. C. Pechmann and L. Price, Duluth, MN: Association for Consumer Research, pp. 294–296.

Smith, J. W. (2003). Marketing that's good for the soul. *Marketing Management*, January/February, 12, 52.

Soldevilla, S., Palao Errando, J. A., & Marzal-Felici, J. (2019). Advertising communication and spirituality: A critical approach of academics and professionals. *Communication & Society*, 32(3), pp. 139–153.

Standifer, R. L., Evans, K. R., & Dong, B. (2010). The influence of spirituality on buyer perception within business-to-business marketing relationships: A cross-cultural exploration and comparison. *Journal of Relationship Marketing*, 9(3), pp. 132–160.

Stolz, J., & Usunier, J. C. (2019). Religions as brands? Religion and spirituality in consumer society. *Journal of Management, Spirituality & Religion*, 16(1), pp. 6–31.

Suri, R., & Rao, J. (2014). Impact of spiritual marketing on different segments of tourists and their evaluation of the site. *Journal of Business & Economic Policy*, 1(1), pp. 26–34.

Ulvoas-Moal, G. (2010). *Exploring the Influence of Spirituality: A New Perspective on Senior Consumers' Behavior*. in NA-Advances in Consumer Research Vol. 37, Eds. M. C. Campbell, J. Inman, and R. Pieters, Duluth, MN: Association for Consumer Research, pp. 917–919.

Özlem AKBULUT DURSUN

8 Thorstein Veblen and Conspicuous Consumption

Introduction

There are many elements behind the purchasing decisions of consumers. Individuals express their social statuses and economic powers based on the prices and quantities of the commodities they use. However, consuming products is not sufficient on its own since individuals also need to display the products they consume to society. In this context, one approaches consumption regarding its dimension of vanity. "Conspicuous consumption" is a phenomenon of long standing. It is defined as shopping activities with the objective of demonstrating one's social status and prestige. With conspicuous consumption, individuals of higher social classes endeavor to demonstrate their wealth through consumption to differentiate themselves from lower social classes. The concept was analyzed for the first time by Thorstein Veblen. In his book titled "The Theory of the Leisure Class" published in 1899, Veblen discussed the concept openly within the cultural context of the United States during the 1800s. Today's world of consumption has significantly changed and conspicuous consumption has become increasingly prevalent in alignment with cultural, economic, and technological developments when compared with the context in which Veblen lived and made his observations.

The present study initially makes a brief introduction to the distinguished book titled "The Theory of the Leisure" by Thorstein Bundy Veblen, the first researcher to deal with the concept of conspicuous consumption. Then, it delineates the concept along with its precursors and stimulants. Ultimately, it elaborates on the concept of status consumption, occasionally used interchangeably with conspicuous consumption despite certain structural differences.

1 Thorstein Veblen and the Theory of the Leisure Class

Considered to be the founder of institutional economics, Thorstein Bundy Veblen indicated that the leisure class emerged with the rise of private property and that leisure is the consumer and not the maker of time. However, what must be underlined here is that how a group of people making a living without working was created by society. In his famous work titled "The Theory of the

Leisure Class", he discussed the development of the perceptions regarding consumption. In this context, he explained the evolutionary pattern of the consumption relationship between women and men from primitive societies to modern ones (Genç & Yardımcı, 2016: 108). He defined the leisure class as "the social class following the nobility and the clergy, along with much of their retinue" (Veblen, 2005: 19). He handles leisure as the lifestyle reserved to the upper classes in society, delineating it as the aimless waste of time. Within the context of leisure, purposeful labor like errands one does in order to earn a livelihood or fulfill their needs is scorned, whereas having free time or spending this free time in an unproductive way is glorified (Babür Tosun & Karşu Cesur, 2018).

Veblen discusses the three stages of society, namely the peaceful savages, barbarians, and the pecuniary culture. The cultural features of underdeveloped societies without a leisure class show that this class emerges during the transition from the primitive savages to warlike barbarians (Heilbroner, 2008: 200). Stating that the textbook examples of the leisure class were in feudal Germany and Japan that display the strongest features of the barbarian culture, Veblen indicates that the class distinction in the said societies was rigid. In this class discrimination, the upper classes are exempted from industrial work and have jobs with "honor/dignity" reserved for them while lower classes deal with the industrial work. This exemption is an economic indicator of the superiority of the upper class. The jobs considered to be dignified in all feudal societies are within the sectors of government, religious and military services, and sports (Veblen, 2005: 20).

Veblen states that the leisure class flourishes as the society in question transitions from peaceable savages to warrior barbarians and relates it to the rise of private property as a result of this cultural evolution. According to him, the advancement of the industry brought about an increased significance of having material wealth as the foundation of fame and reputation. Instead of enjoying remarkable success, the ownership of material wealth and property through either personal achievement or inheritance brought about increased reputation and was considered as a condition of obtaining a reputable place within society. In fact, inheriting material wealth was deemed more honorific than acquiring wealth through one's own endeavors (Veblen, 2005: 35).

He claimed that the increase in wealth has led to the functional and structural development of the leisure class, resulting in differences within the same social class. He expressed that there was a delicate system of social ranking and levels and that differences in the hierarchy and social levels were deepened as a result of the inheritance of wealth and, consequently, of nobility. According to Veblen, leisure is inherited along with nobility (Veblen, 2005: 62).

2 The Concept of Conspicuous Consumption

Consumption is an inevitable action in one's life from the moment they were born. Therefore, people are innately consumers. Consumption bears a significance transcending merely fundamental needs such as nutrition and clothing and goods and services consumed are assessed based on their symbolic meanings. Raymond Williams defines consumption as "erasure, usage, and waste" (Featherstone, 2007: 21). According to Douglas and Isherwood (1996: viii), consumption is considered to be "an integral part of the same social system that accounts for the drive to work, itself part of the social need to relate to other people, and to have mediating materials for relating to them". Generally speaking, consumption is examined in two ways, as an economic activity and a cultural practice. When considered as an economic activity, consumption ends when a product is purchased. However, the product in question might be used multiple times and brings about instances of consumption that cannot be explained through economic terms. In other words, the purchase is merely the beginning of consumption. However, one can consume a product without necessarily buying it, i.e. by borrowing it. All these moments outside the time of the actual purchase are when consumption becomes cultural. The products that the individual consumes and the way the consumption takes place might be an expression of their actual or desired identity, an indicator of the lifestyle they want to attain or maintain, and a symbol of an achievement or level of income they want to extol or demonstrate (Storey, 2017: xii).

The type of consumption aiming to obtain or maintain a certain social status or prestige as an indicator of one's wealth is called "conspicuous consumption". The concept was coined by the American economist Thorstein Veblen. In his work titled "The Theory of the Leisure Class" published in 1899 based completely on his observations, Veblen argued that wealthy individuals consume eye-catching goods and services to parade their wealth and, therefore, to obtain social status. Based on this argument, he referred to the unnecessary and inefficient spending in this respect as "conspicuous consumption" (Bagwell & Bernheim, 1996).

Veblen stated that consumption is truly a process of socialization and that goods function as indicators of one's social class (Memushi, 2013: 250). Furthermore, he claimed that the aim of consumption not only satisfying biological needs but also to display their superiority, basing the relationship between the society and economy on a class distinction. Veblen alleges that money is "extravagantly spent on materialistic excesses, and purchasing as an act meant purely for display" (Chaudhuri & Majumdar, 2006: 3). Within this framework, Veblen argues that conspicuous consumption denotes the case in which upper classes and those who want to look like upper classes shop for the purpose of display (Güllülü, Ünal & Bilsen, 2010: 107). Therefore, goods and services act as a bridge between one's actual social class and the social class they want to be a part of, distinguishing them from lower classes. Even though Veblen portrays the concept of conspicuous consumption clearly through many examples in his work mentioned above, it must not be forgotten that he formulated his observations based on the American lifestyle and culture in the 1800s.

Conspicuous consumption aiming to display one's social status and reputation to their social environment has certain features that can be listed as follows:

- Conspicuous consumption is the pecuniary measure of reputation and it is relatively expensive.
- Conspicuous consumption is considered to be a means of prestige.
- Within the scope of conspicuous consumption, the wealth obtained is displayed in a way making others envious.
- Conspicuous consumption occurs only through extravagance.
- Instead of providing a functional benefit, conspicuous consumption is a status symbol indicating an aesthetic value, beauty, and prestige.
- Goods of conspicuous consumption are hard to obtain, rare, personal, expensive, hand-made, and exclusive.

3 Precursors and Stimulants of Conspicuous Consumption

Conspicuous consumption is observed among middle and upper classes in developing countries because they continuously strive to display their social ranking to others, opting for expensive and socially visible products of luxury brands. In developed countries, individuals from the middle class opt for extravagant products to be associated with wealthier and upper classes. The middle class in developed countries and the upper class of developing countries show similarities in terms of conspicuous consumption patterns: they buy expensive products to display their wealth and impress others (Ryu, 2015). In both developing and developed countries, there are various reasons behind conspicuous consumption. Conspicuous consumption is thought to be influenced by certain factors such as power, social class, culture, economic development, age, social exclusion, psychological needs, and materialism.

Power signifies the capacity to govern others and having authority and influence over other individuals (Johnson & Lennon, 1999). People lacking power attempt to display power to increase their perceived influence through other means and, therefore, opt for goods associated with conspicuous consumption.

This is because such goods are visible, offering them an easy way for powerless individuals to display their power to others. For instance, Rucker and Galinsky (2009) indicated in their study that powerless individuals are more likely to opt for clothes clearly showing the brand logo when compared with powerful people.

Social class denotes a hierarchy within which individuals of the same class generally have similar statuses. Individuals of other classes have varying levels of social standings, either higher or lower (Schiffman & Wisenblit, 2015: 60). As ostentatious products grant the user additional social status, individuals coming from lower social classes focusing on their social positions tend to choose these products over less conspicuous ones. Therefore, they attempt to resemble individuals of higher social standing. Ordabayeva and Chandon (2011) revealed that in lower social classes, an increase in equality gives rise to conspicuous consumption. Han, Nunes, and Drèze (2010) stated that individuals from lower and middle classes perceive conspicuous and luxury products to be more expensive than non-conspicuous luxury products.

Culture consists of beliefs, attitudes, and values held among many people within a society as well as rules, traditions, and norms adhered to by the majority (Peter & Olson, 2010: 279). Societies with individualistic or collective cultures differ in terms of their conspicuous consumption tendencies. Collective societies attaching significant importance to external values are more prone to conspicuous consumption as stratification and the acquiring of status symbols is more acceptable when compared with other cultures (Güllülü, Ünal, & Bilsen, 2010). In collective cultures, people might even opt for less convenient products to impress others (Ratner & Kahn, 2002). In individualistic societies in which people have higher self-orientation and the concept of private property has more significance on a personal level, individuals are less prone to conspicuous consumption (Güllülü, Ünal, & Bilsen, 2010; Wong & Ahuvia, 1998).

Conspicuous consumption varies depending on the economic development level of each country. In under-developed countries, social status denotes inherited income and wealth rather than acquired fortune. Even though wealth and material properties are allowed on a personal level in such countries, conspicuous consumption is not observed as they are not indicative of one's social standing. However, characteristics of conspicuous consumption can manifest themselves in the number of spouses and children (Chaudhuri & Majumdar, 2006).

Age is an important factor affecting the consumption of conspicuous products. In a research study, Belk et al. (1982) revealed that young children make random decisions that the inferences made by older children are more consistent with adults and, consequently, they are able to make more assumptions about consumption as they grow older. Adolescents prefer conspicuous products to reduce social pressure coming from their peers and to display their self-identities (Piacentini & Mailer, 2004; Wooten, 2006).

Social exclusion has an impact on conspicuous consumption. Socially excluded individuals experience negative emotions like anxiety, depression, and loneliness and their basic needs like a sense of belonging, control, meaningful existence, and respect are therefore in danger (Williams, 2001). These individuals react differently, seeking alternative ways to connect with their societies. Since they believe that they will become more significant and valuable as a person by drawing attention from others, they opt for conspicuous products (Rucker & Galinsky, 2008; Rucker & Galinsky, 2009).

One's quality of life depends on the fulfillment of physiological and psychological needs. Particularly, individuals feeling that their needs for security, esteem, and efficacy are denied tend to opt for conspicuous products. When one feels insecure as a person (in terms of wealth, personal capabilities, or other sources of security), they engage in conspicuous consumption as they think doing so would enable them to conceal their weaknesses. Someone who has yet to gain experience in their profession preferring branded products to render themselves worthy of praise in the eyes of others is an example of this phenomenon (Braun & Wicklund, 1989). Furthermore, individuals with low self-efficacy attempt to increase their self-worth through conspicuous products (Sivanathan & Pettit, 2010). An example of this would be someone with low income and self-esteem buying a luxurious handbag from an esteemed brand to feel more worthy. Finally, individuals whose needs of self-sufficiency are neglected opt for conspicuous products to draw the attention of others and make their presence felt more strongly (Lee & Shrum, 2012).

Defined as a value steering consumption decisions and individuals in certain conditions (Richins & Dawson, 1992: 307), materialism signifies one's strong attachment to material possessions and, as a result, their central position in one's life (Belk, 1984). Individuals with greater materialistic tendencies place a high value on products visible for others in public. They usually want to display these products to others rather than actually using them, feeling great satisfaction from this act of boasting (Podoshen & Andrzejewski, 2012).

In the present day, developments in consumption have led to an increase in the number of stimulants of conspicuous consumption including technological advancements, mass communication tools, advertising, fashion, and shopping venues (Güner Koçak, 2017: 88).

4 The Concept of Status Consumption

Status consumption is one of the important concepts regarding conspicuous consumption. The concept of status is an indicator of presence stemming from the consumption of conspicuous products that individuals consider important, evoking envy in others (Eastman & Liu, 2012: 94). As for status consumption, it denotes a process of motivation in which individuals aim to improve their social standing through the consumption of conspicuous products (Eastman & Thomas, 2013: 58). In status consumption, the product in question does not need to be expensive. The precursors of status consumption include supporting one's self, the desire to climb the social ladder, and culture. As for its outcomes, they can be listed as the preference of status-related products and brands, using different sources of media and communication for status-related products, associating reputable brands with positive attributes, and benefiting lower prices (Aslay, Ünal, & Akbulut, 2013: 45).

The concepts of conspicuous consumption and status consumption are sometimes used interchangeably by researchers. In fact, Kilsheimer (1993: 341) defines status consumption as they type of consumption aiming to display one's status and prestige to others around them. However, these two concepts are structurally different even though they are related to one another (O'Cass & Frost, 2002; O'Cass & McEwen, 2004). The fundamental difference between status consumption and conspicuous consumption is that the desire to buy a product indicating one's social status to oneself and others is the motivation behind status consumption whereas the desire to boost one's ego and buy an expensive product underlies conspicuous consumption. At the same time, owning a product deemed to be a status symbol helps one in terms of self-respect and social acceptability (Eastman, Goldsmith, & Flynn, 1999: 43). Another significant difference is that in status consumption, consumers obtain esteemed products and brands to gain prestige, whereas in conspicuous consumption focuses on the visual display and open use of the product in question while others are present. A consumer opting for Calvin Klein underwear might be regarded as an example. In the context of status consumption, one proves the status of a product they own to oneself and not to others around them (O'Cass & McEwen, 2004: 27).

Conclusion

Conspicuous consumption has a distant past. In his work titled "The Theory of the Leisure Class" in which the assesses the concept scientifically, Veblen coined the term to indicate unnecessary and inefficient spending made by wealthy individuals to parade their wealth and, therefore, improve their social standing and argued that they consume conspicuous goods and services (Bagwell & Bernheim, 1996). He defined the leisure class as "the social class following the nobility and the clergy, along with much of their retinue" (Veblen, 2005: 19).

Indicating that consumption is truly a process of socialization and products are the indicators of social class (Memushi, 2013: 250), Veblen also alleged that the aim of consumption is not only satisfying biological needs but also displaying one's assets. It predicates the relationship between society and the economy on class distinctions.

Generally speaking; having precursors such as power, social class, culture, age, social exclusion, economic development, psychological needs, and materialism, conspicuous consumption is based on the perception of products one purchases by others around them as indicators of status and prestige. Occasionally used synonymously with conspicuous consumption despite structural differences, the concept of status consumption is the motivational process of one's endeavors to manifest their social standing by purchasing products symbolizing status for oneself and others (Heaney, Goldsmith, & Jusoh, 2005: 85).

References

Aslay, F., Ünal, S., & Akbulut, Ö. (2013). Materyalizmin statü tüketimi üzerindeki etkisini belirlemeye yönelik bir araştırma. *Atatürk Üniversitesi İktisadi ve İdari Bilimler Dergisi, 27*(2), pp. 43–62.

Babür Tosun, N., & Karşu Cesur, D. (2018). Tüketimin paranormali: Gösterişçi tüketim ve paranormal inanç ilişkisi. *Marmara Üniversitesi Öneri Dergisi, 13*(49), pp. 167–186.

Bagwell, L. S., & Bernheim, B. D. (1996). Veblen effects in a theory of conspicuous consumption. *The American Economic Review, 86*(3), pp. 349–373.

Belk, R. W. (1984). Three scales to measure constructs related to materialism: Reliability, validity, and relationships to measures of happiness. *Advances in Consumer Research, 11*(1), pp. 291–297.

Belk, R., Mayer, R., & Bahn, K. (1982). The eye of the beholder: Individual differences in perceptions of consumption symbolism. *Advances in Consumer Research, 9*, pp. 523–530.

Braun, O. L., & Wicklund, R. A. (1989). Psychological antecedents of conspicuous consumption. *Journal of Economic Psychology, 10*(2), pp. 161–187.

Chaudhuri, H. R., & Majumdar, S. (2006). Of diamonds and desires: Understanding conspicuous consumption from a contemporary marketing perspective. *Academy of Marketing Science Review, 11*, pp. 1–18.

Douglas, M., & Isherwood, B. (1996). *The World of Goods: Towards an Anthropology of Consumption*. London. UK: Routledge.

Eastman, J. K., & Liu, J. (2012). The impact of generational cohorts on status consumption: An exploratory look at generational cohort and demographics on status consumption. *Journal of Consumer Marketing, 29*(2), pp. 93–102.

Eastman, J. K., & Thomas, S. P. (2013). The impact of status consumption on shopping styles: An exploratory look at the millennial generation. *Marketing Management Journal, 23*(1), pp. 57–73.

Eastman, J. K., Goldsmith, R. E., & Flynn, L. R. (1999). Status consumption in consumer behavior: Scale development and validation. *Journal of Marketing Theory and Practice, 7*(3), pp. 41–52.

Featherstone, M. (2007). *Consumer Culture and Postmodernism*. London: Sage Publications.

Genç, S. Y., & Yardımcı, M. E. (2016). Neoklasik iktisadi düşünceye eleştirel bir bakış: Thorstein bunde veblen. *Balka Sosyal Bilimler Dergisi, 5*(9), pp. 106–114.

Güllülü, U., Ünal, S., & Bilsen, B. (2010). Kendini gösterim ve kişilerarası etkileşimin gösterişçi tüketim üzerindeki etkilerini belirlemeye yönelik bir araştırma. *Hacettepe Üniversitesi İktisadi ve İdari Bilimler Fakültesi Dergisi, 28*(1), pp. 105–139.

Güner Koçak, P. (2017). Gösterişçi tüketim üzerine teorik ve uygulamalı bir çalışma: Pamukkale üniversitesi örneği. *Erciyes Üniversitesi Sosyal Bilimler Enstitüsü Dergisi, 43*, pp. 79–112.

Han, Y. J., Nunes, J. C., & Drèze, X. (2010). Signaling status with luxury goods: The role of brand prominence. *Journal of Marketing, 74*(4), pp. 15–30.

Heaney, J.-G., Goldsmith, R. E., & Jusoh, W. J. (2005). Status consumption among Malaysian consumers. *Journal of International Consumer Marketing, 17*(4), pp. 83–98.

Heilbroner, R. L. (2008). *İktisat Düşünürleri: Büyük İktisat Düşünürlerinin Yaşamları ve Fikirleri*. (Trans.: A. Tartanoğlu) Ankara: Dost Kitapevi.

Johnson, K. K., & Lennon, S. J. (1999). *Appearance and Power*. Oxford, United Kingdom: Berg.

Kilsheimer, J. C. (1993). *Status consumption: The development and implications of a scale measuring the motivation to consume for status*. The Florida State University, PhD. Dissertation, UMI.

Lee, J., & Shrum, L. J. (2012). Conspicuous consumption versus charitable behavior in response to social exclusion: A differential needs explanation. *Journal of Consumer Research, 39*(3), pp. 530–544.

Memushi, A. (2013). Conspicuous consumption of luxury goods: Literature review of theoretical and empirical evidences. *International Journal of Scientific & Engineering Research, 4*(12), pp. 250–255.

O'Cass, A., & Frost, H. (2002). Status brands: Examining the effects of non-product-related brand associations on status and conspicuous consumption. *Journal of Product & Brand Management, 11*(2), pp. 67–88.

O'Cass, A., & McEwen, H. (2004). Exploring consumer status and conspicuous consumption. *Journal of Consumer Behaviour, 4*(1), pp. 25–39.

Ordabayeva, N., & Chandon, P. (2011). Getting ahead of the joneses: When equality increases conspicuous consumption among bottom-tier consumers. *Journal of Consumer Research, 38*(1), pp. 27–41.

Peter, J. P., & Olson, J. C. (2010). *Consumer Behavior and Marketing Strategy* (9th Edition b.). New York: McGraw-Hill.

Piacentini, M., & Mailer, G. (2004). Symbolic consumption in teenagers' clothing choices. *Journal of Consumer Behaviour, 3*(3), pp. 251–262.

Podoshen, J. S., & Andrzejewski, S. A. (2012). An examination of the relationships between materialism, conspicuous consumption, impulse buying, and brand loyalty. *Journal of Marketing Theory and Practice, 20*(3), pp. 319–334.

Ratner, R. K., & Kahn, B. E. (2002). The impact of private versus public consumption on variety-seeking behavior. *Journal of Consumer Research, 29*(2), pp. 246–257.

Richins, M. L., & Dawson, S. (1992). A consumer values orientation for materialism and its measurement: Scale development and validation. *Journal of Consumer Research, 19*(3), pp. 303–316.

Rucker, D. D., & Galinsky, A. D. (2008). Desire to acquire: Powerlessness and compensatory consumption. *Journal of Consumer Research, 35*(2), pp. 257–267.

Rucker, D. D., & Galinsky, A. D. (2009). Conspicuous consumption versus utilitarian ideals: How different levels of power shape consumer behavior. *Journal of Experimental Social Psychology, 45*(3), pp. 549–555.

Ryu, J. S. (2015). The emergence of new conspicuous consumption. *Journal of Distribution Science, 13*(6), pp. 5–10.

Schiffman, L. G., & Wisenblit, J. (2015). *Consumer Behavior.* USA: Pearson.

Sivanathan, N., & Pettit, N. C. (2010). Protecting the self through consumption: Status goods as affirmational commodities. *Journal of Experimental Social Psychology, 46*(3), pp. 564–570.

Storey, J. (2017). *Theories of Consumption.* New York: Routledge.

Veblen, T. (2005). *Aylak Sınıfın Teorisi.* (Trans.: Z. Gültekin, & C. Atay) İstanbul: Babil.

Williams, K. D. (2001). *Ostracism: The Power of Silence.* New York: Guilford Publications.

Wong, N. Y., & Ahuvia, A. C. (1998). Personal taste and family face: Luxury consumption in Confucian and Western societies. *Psychology and Marketing.* (15).

Wooten, D. B. (2006). From labeling possessions to possessing labels: Ridicule and socialization among adolescents. *Journal of Consumer Research, 33*(2), pp. 188–198.

Mehmet Said KÖSE

9 Minimalism in Consumption

Introduction

Being as old as human existence, the phenomenon of consumption will not cease until the end of life itself. A wide range of meanings has been attributed to the concept of consumption, in alignment with contemporary circumstances throughout history. Consuming for survival in times of scarcity and poverty, individuals also consume for the sake of vanity, socialization, and an elevated social status in times of abundance and prosperity. Essentially a vital necessity for survival in this regard, consumption has become, in time, an end in itself rather than a means to an end. Consumers have started to perceive the accumulation of possessions and increased consumption as a way of making their existence significant, going beyond the mere aim of staying alive. The complementation of functional benefits with hedonistic ones has culminated in the belief in the statement "I consume, therefore I am".

Beyond individuals, companies, societies, and even states have adapted their systems to a "consumption-driven economic system". This system is based on increased consumption and has become a cycle in which interest groups reap more benefits as the individual consumes more. To maintain their existence, these elements of the capitalist system encourage consumers to buy and consume more by exposing them to a plethora of stimuli. Strengthened by globalization and technological advancements, these stimuli urging consumption have turned consumers into dissatisfied communities always wanting more and believing that consuming more will make them happier.

The gradual increase of the global population has led to the unconscious consumption of finite resources. Companies and states incessantly focusing on the necessity of increased consumption among individuals might think that we are the only ones entitled to use these finite resources. Yet the resources belong not only to the people currently living on this planet but also to future generations. In the present day, where the concepts of needs and wants are used interchangeably, we are trying to satisfy our limited needs with unlimited wants. Consumers consuming more than they need try to feel happy by dissipating resources that could have been used by those who cannot consume enough due to economic constraints and by future generations. Consumers questioning this mindset hold the opinion that the concept of happiness is not only related to pleasure and that consuming more does not bring about increased happiness. Therefore, minimalist thought has found a place in marketing and consumption activities. Consumers arguing increased consumption leads to increased happiness have adopted a minimalistic lifestyle.

Upon analyzing literature on the relationship between marketing and minimalism, two different ways in which minimalism influences marketing are observed. The first way is that companies engaging in marketing activities can be more effective and efficient by using fewer resources while developing and implementing marketing strategies. This can be named as business-oriented minimalism. The second way in which minimalism affects marketing is the impact of minimalist consumer activities on consumption and consumer behavior, examined under the title of consumer psychology. This can be named as consumer-oriented minimalism. This study will deal with the effect of a minimalistic lifestyle on marketing and consumption. Furthermore, it will also examine the concept of minimalism through the concepts of anti-consumption and boycotting, voluntary simplicity, and the sharing economy.

1 How Minimalism and Marketing Are Related

The concept of minimalism first emerged as a school of thought based on the philosophy of "less is more" proposed by the architect Ludwig Mies van der Rohe. Minimalism can be defined as the elimination of all unnecessary elements and the focus on the essentials and necessities. It has been included in many different fields such as architecture, art, programming, and data processing design. In time, the minimalist though has become a subject of particular interest among researchers in the fields of marketing, advertising, and consumption (Kumar, Joshi, & Avinash, 2018; Margariti, Boutsouki, Hatzithomas, & Zotos, 2017; Tanase, 2019). Described as a movement against excessive consumption, minimalistic consumption today is considered to be an understanding affecting the lifestyles and consumption patterns of consumers. Based on the idea of seeing consumption as a means to an end rather than an end in itself, minimalistic consumption adopts a perspective according to which consumption is an intermediary to attain the truly important values in life (Köksalan, 2019: 638).

When people want to simplify their lives, they get rid of unnecessary elements. This signifies the increased and more creative use of fewer elements. In other words, it denotes liberation and making fewer decisions (Tanase, 2019). The number of consumers adopting a minimalistic outlook in their thinking increases each day, creating more pressure on businesses. Thus, businesses apply minimalist thought into their marketing activities. Minimalist marketing is an approach in which redundant marketing applications are eliminated and marketers focus on the crucial and essential elements of marketing. This approach highlights the ultimate goal of marketing necessary for the goods and services in question. Although it seems to be simple; more thinking, application, and time contribute to the generation and development of a minimalistic idea. Minimalist marketing (1) is more systematic while employing fewer people, (2) prioritizes quality over quantity, (3) acts with a strategy, (4) consists of successive processes, and (5) focuses fundamentally on important, successful, and precise tasks (Kumar et al., 2018: 313).

The case in which the individual, bothered by excessive consumption due to both personal and societal/environmental factors, reduces their purchasing and consumption activities forms the basis of minimalism in consumption. Excessive consumption will potentially put human health, future, and welfare in danger as a result of the attenuation and deterioration of resources, considering the increase in the global population. For this reason, consumers believe they can minimize these threats by reducing and controlling their consumption (Dursun, Kabadayı, & Tuğer, 2016: 14). Consumers adopting minimalism would, therefore, support the efforts to eliminate societal and environmental damages caused by unconscious consumption while increasing their awareness with reduced consumption and attaining a level of understanding brought about by living with fewer but more functional possessions. Both outcomes would contribute to the search of consumers for happiness and satisfaction. Çevik (2019: 183) lists the features of a minimalist consumer as follows:

The minimalist consumer likes simplicity in their daily life: The most significant characteristic of minimalist consumers is that they prefer simplicity in their daily lives. By consuming less, consumers create simple and spacious environments to live in. Consumers first get rid of certain objects in their lives; then, they eliminate items they do not miss permanently after a certain time.

The minimalist consumer knows what they want: Minimalism allows consumers to know beforehand what they will consume. Knowing what they really need, consumers are able to make accurate and swift decisions accordingly. As a result, consumers list their needs and the items they need to buy, therefore making more conscious purchases.

The minimalist consumer knows how to use their time properly: As minimalist consumers tend to shop only if necessary, they spend less time in the pre- and post-purchase processes.

The minimalist consumer knows consumption does not bring happiness: Nowadays, consumers assign different meanings to consumption apart from satisfying needs. One of these meanings is the goal of attaining happiness and pleasure through consumption. In other words, they believe that the more an individual consumes, the more they feel happy and vice versa. However, minimalist consumers have experienced that the road to happiness goes through reduced consumption rather than increased consumption.

The minimalist consumer believes liberation comes from not consuming: The idea of "I consume, therefore I am" has led consumption to become an end rather than a means. This caused the contemporary consumer to feel drained as they consume, to never be satisfied with what they already own, and become addicted to their material possessions. The minimalist consumer sees consumption merely as a means and is aware of the fact that they are not liberated through consumption.

2 Minimalism in Consumption

Consumers might reduce their consumption due to various reasons. This chapter will attempt to explain minimalistic consumption under the titles of anti-consumption, voluntary simplicity, and the sharing economy.

2.1 Anti-Consumption

Anti-consumption means "being against consumption". Research studies on anti-consumption focus on the reasons why consumers avoid a certain product or brand (Lee, Fernandez, & Hyman, 2009: 145). Anti-consumption signifies avoiding the use of a good or service harmful for others and one's own health, not consuming more than fundamentally necessary, and refraining from products that might damage the environment. Consumers refuse to buy the products of organizations harmful to the environment (Moisander, 2007; Moisander & Pesonen, 2002), disregarding social responsibility from an ethical perspective (Ozcaglar-Toulouse, Shiu, & Shaw, 2006), not in alignment with their ideological beliefs (Cherrier & Murray, 2007; Micheletti, Follesdal, & Stolle, 2008; Sandıkcı & Ekici, 2009), and negatively affecting the society (Klein, Smith, & John, 2004). In fact, even though anti-consumption seems to mean not consuming, it is not an economic threat. In order for an action to be evaluated within the scope of anti-consumption, it needs to fulfill the following criteria (Basci, 2014):

(1) The reduction of consumption or selective consumption is a prerequisite for anti-consumption,
(2) The anti-consumption act needs to be linked to a societal problem on the local and/or national level (e.g. environmental problems, economic injustice, social problems, unethical marketing...),

(3) The consumer in question should be aware of why they act this way,
(4) Non-purchase of a product due to dissatisfaction with its functional attributes should not be confused with anti-consumption,
(5) Non-consumption due to reasons related to an insufficient budget or the inaccessibility of the product should not be confused with anti-consumption.

Anti-consumption emerges in the form of ethical concerns, environmental concerns, consumer resistance, and symbolic concerns. Boycotts within ethical concerns, green activism within environmental concerns, backlash within consumer resistance, and avoidance behavior within symbolic concerns are the outcomes of anti-consumption (Uz, 2016: 15). Boycotting means protesting products, businesses, and activities that harm or might harm nature, society or the economy. Boycotts act as an impetus for anti-consumption action and product avoidance (Kozinets & Handelman, 1998: 475). They might aim to avoid the use of a certain good or service; they can also target a certain country of origin (Chatzidakis & Lee, 2012: 190).

2.2 Voluntary Simplicity

The concept of voluntary simplicity was coined by Richard Gregg in 1936; it was defined as "avoiding accumulating possessions in a way incompatible with the primary objective of life and wasting energy". The concept has gained gradual importance with the increase in the number of consumers wanting to simplify their daily lives and minimize their possessions in the 1970s and 80s (Özgül, 2010: 126).

Voluntary simplicity aims purity in the external sense and enrichment in the internal sense. Such a lifestyle encompasses a strong sense of environmental sensitivity, the desire to go back to more human-oriented living and working environments, and the intention to realize one's potential in both psychological and moral senses by having higher human values. Voluntary simplicity denotes a self-sufficient lifestyle having certain responsibilities towards the environment and aiming for minimized consumption (Elgin & Mitchell, 1977: 5). The concept has come to the forefront with an increase in the number of consumers reacting against consumption. It can be defined as "the avoidance of ownership of material goods to an extent contradicting with the meaning of life as well as energy waste" (Özgül, 2010: 126). In other words, voluntary simplicity signifies a limitation of material consumption, which has been centralized in one's life in order to get pleasure. These individuals limit material consumption and look for satisfaction in the immaterial aspects of life (Özgül, 2011: 28).

The current economic system encourages the individual to consume constantly and unconsciously, making consumption as a goal of existence while voluntary simplicity implies the awareness of values besides consumption and the renouncement of selfish consumption. What should be underlined here is that voluntary simplicity does not mean complete avoidance of consumption but an increased focus on immaterial values and personal development by getting rid of redundancies (Babaoğul & Buğday, 2012: 85).

Shama (1985: 57) indicates that voluntary simplicity has six basic dimensions. These can be listed as follows:

Material Simplicity: It signifies the simplification of daily life and the elimination of complexity as both an individual and a consumer. Buying only what is necessary and consuming less is better than excessive consumption. In order to achieve material simplicity, one needs to opt for higher quality products that are generally hand-crafted. These products have higher prices and might provide an elevated profit margin. Therefore, the principle of "less is more" can be rewarding for both marketers and voluntary simplifiers.

Human Scale: It signifies the aim of small-scale organization and technology as well as the minimization of the living and working space. Taking the principle of "small is beautiful" as their basis, one can opt for smaller, more personalized shops instead of giant stores and malls.

Appropriate Technology: It denotes the functional, efficient, and energy-conserving use of technology. Therefore, products and services using technology appropriately provide novel marketing opportunities. More efficient cars, energy-saving products, and some solar energy systems can be given as examples to appropriate technology.

Self-determination: It signifies the need to have increased control over one's life as well as less dependency on other organizations such as businesses or marketing channels. It represents the marketing opportunities within the "do-it-yourself (DIY)" market that have been expanding recently.

Ecological Awareness: It denotes the realization that humans and environmental factors are interdependent, resources are limited, and pollution reduction is imperative. Products and practices that help consumers conserve are examples of new marketing opportunities.

Personal Growth: It signifies the desire to explore oneself, free oneself and develop one's inner life both psychologically and spiritually. Personal growth denotes the preference for personalized products and services.

It should be kept in mind that voluntary simplifiers do not have explicitly similar demographic characteristics and that their income level must be sufficient to obtain many things they want. The most significant common feature of voluntary simplifiers is that they have the potential for earning a high income. Furthermore, they are usually well-educated families without children (Cengiz, 2014: 35). In addition to eliminating excessive and redundant consumption in their daily lives, voluntary simplifiers also do the following in the same order: avoiding impulse purchases, recycling products, getting rid of chaos, doing elating jobs, buying local produce, avoiding exposure to advertisements, purchasing environmentally-friendly products, limiting the use of vehicles like cars, and purchasing the products of socially-responsible producers (Huneke, 2005: 538).

Voluntary simplicity and a lifestyle adhering to this principle might occasionally create certain misunderstandings. Having become a popular concept in recent years, minimalism, one of its reflections being voluntary simplicity, may be misinterpreted by various media outlets and related circles. Cengiz (2014: 42) lists the misconceptions about voluntary simplicity as follows: (1) *Voluntary simplicity is synonymous with poverty.* Voluntary simplifiers have either a high income or a potential to earn a high income. (2) *Voluntary simplicity requires one to live in rural regions.* There is no obligation to live in rural areas among the fundamental values of a lifestyle adhering to the principle of voluntary simplicity. Voluntary simplicity concerns the way of life of an individual rather than the place in which they live. (3) *Voluntary simplicity brings about economic stagnation.* As it is the case in anti-consumption, voluntary simplicity is argued to decrease the demand for goods and services, leading to an increase in unemployment. Even though such an assumption might be considered to be true in the short term, these elements of minimalist consumption are crucial for achieving sustainability in the economy in the long term.

2.3 The Sharing Economy

Advancements in information and communication technologies have brought about the development of the concept of "the sharing economy". The sharing economy might be defined as the sum of the activities taking place between parties regarding the provision of access to goods and services coordinated through online services. It is expected to reduce economic costs while alleviating societal problems such as excessive consumption, pollution, and poverty. Diverted from ethical consumption due to economic and institutional reasons, individuals resolve these unethical problems and reach solutions by developing new ways of consumption such as the common consumption economy (Hamari, Sjöklint, & Ukkonen, 2016: 2047).

The act of sharing, mostly occurring between individuals who know and trust each other, has become a common practice among people who do not know one another with the development and proliferation of the Internet. Owing to these developments in online networks, consumers have started to offer their idle assets for the use of unfamiliar consumers. In other words, various platforms allowing consumers wanting to capitalize on their underused assets to meet other consumers wanting to use these assets without owning them have emerged (Ayazlar, 2018: 1186).

The sharing economy has found ample opportunities to thrive in many markets ranging from traveling to accommodation, from food to the sharing of goods and services. Some prominent sectors and companies within the sharing economy can be listed as follows (Gül, Dinçer, & Çetin, 2018: 9):

- Transport: Uber, Bla Car, Lyft, Scoot, Zipcar
- Accommodation: Airbnb, HomeExchange, Couchsurfing, HomeAway, Pivotdesk
- Finance: Bitcoin, LendingClub, Kickstarter
- Food: EatWith, BlueApron, Mealsharing
- Services: TaskRabbit, Freelancer, Elance, CrowdSpring
- Goods: eBay, Quirky, Etsy

Conclusion

Technological advancements, the proliferation of the Internet and online networks, and the consequent globalization have influenced individuals and societies in many domains, ranging from culture to lifestyle, from thoughts and emotions to beliefs and attitudes, from needs to consumption. This change has inevitably affected our consumption behavior we display to satisfy our needs. Apart from functionality, symbolic and hedonistic values of goods and services have gradually become more significant. One of the smallest but most significant components of the consumption system, individuals encounter countless stimuli indoctrinating them into the necessity of consuming more to obtain happiness and pleasure. Successful and effective marketing strategies developed by companies lead consumers to consume more and unconsciously. Increasing consumer demands cause finite resources to be used insensibly and distributed unjustly while leading to environmental damages and unethical practices.

Consumers believing that the current consumption system is not sustainable and that more consumption will not bring more happiness have associated other meanings to happiness by changing their lifestyles and consumption habits.

This group of consumers has adopted a minimalist lifestyle by consuming less and more consciously. Within the context of consumer psychology, the minimalist lifestyle manifests itself in the following ways: boycotts against companies harming the environment, wasting resources, and disregarding ethical values and the avoidance of purchases from such companies; less consumption; the preference of a simpler lifestyle; offering possessions for use by others.

The popularity of minimalism and the minimalist lifestyle increases each day. At this point, one should ask if consumers opt for a minimalist lifestyle due to their increased awareness or the trendiness of minimalism. Businesses finding an answer to this question are probably producing products tailored for the minimalist lifestyle, including minimalist consumers in their targeted market segments.

References

Ayazlar, R. A. (2018). Paylaşım ekonomisi ve turizm endüstrisine yansımaları. *Gaziantep University Journal of Social Sciences, 17*(3), pp. 1185–1202.

Babaoğul, M., & Buğday, A. G. U. E. B. (2012). Gösteriş tüketimine karşı gönüllü sadelik. *Tüketici Yazıları (III)*, 76.

Basci, E. (2014). A revisited concept of anti-consumption for marketing. *International Journal of Business and Social Science, 5*(7), p. 1.

Cengiz, H. (2014). *Gönüllü sade yaşam davranışının ölüm tüketimi davranışına yönelik tutumlar üzerine etkisi: Türk ve Amerikan kültürleri arasında bir karşılaştırma.* PhD Thesis, Eskişehir Osmangazi University.

Chatzidakis, A., & Lee, M. S. (2012). Anti-consumption as the study of reasons against. *Journal of Macromarketing, 33*(3), pp. 190–203.

Cherrier, H., & Murray, J. B. (2007). Reflexive dispossession and the self: constructing a processual theory of identity. *Consumption Markets & Culture, 10*(1), pp. 1–29.

Çevik, D. (2019). Çoğu Zarar, Azı Karar! Tüketim Karşıtı Akımlar - Gönüllü Sade Yaşam ve Paylaşım Ekonomisi. In R. Altunışık (Ed.), *Tüketimin 1001 Hâli*. pp. 179–196: Beta.

Dursun, İ., Kabadayı, E. T., & Tuğer, A. T. (2016). Sorumlu tüketim: Neden? Nasıl? In M. Babaoğul, A. Şener & E. B. Buğday (Eds.), *Tüketici Yazıları (V)*. pp. 9–39.

Elgin, D., & Mitchell, A. (1977). Voluntary simplicity. *The Co-Evolution Quarterly, 3*(1), pp. 4–19.

Gül, İ., Dinçer, M. Z., & Çetin, G. (2018). Paylaşım ekonomisi ve turizme etkileri üzerine bir değerlendirme. *Güncel Turizm Araştırmaları Dergisi, 2*(1), pp. 7–16.

Hamari, J., Sjöklint, M., & Ukkonen, A. (2016). The sharing economy: Why people participate in collaborative consumption. *Journal of the Association for Information Science and Technology, 67*(9), pp. 2047–2059.

Huneke, M. E. (2005). The face of the un-consumer: An empirical examination of the practice of voluntary simplicity in the United States. *Psychology & Marketing, 22*(7), pp. 527–550.

Klein, J. G., Smith, N. C., & John, A. (2004). Why we boycott: Consumer motivations for boycott participation. *Journal of Marketing, 68*(3), pp. 92–109.

Kozinets, R. V., & Handelman, J. (1998). Ensouling consumption: A netnographic exploration of the meaning of boycotting behavior. *ACR North American Advances,* 25(1), 475–480.

Köksalan, N. (2019). *Minimalist Tüketim.* Paper presented at the XI. International Balkan and Near Eastern Social Sciences Congress Series, Tekirdağ/Turkey.

Kumar, S., Joshi, S., & Avinash, S. (2018). Minimalistic marketing: The perfect blend of creativity and simplicity. *International Research Journal of Management Science & Technology, 9*(2), pp. 312–322.

Lee, M. S., Fernandez, K. V., & Hyman, M. R. (2009). Anti-Consumption: An Overview and Research Agenda. *Journal of Business Research*, 62(2), pp. 145–147.

Margariti, K., Boutsouki, C., Hatzithomas, L., & Zotos, Y. (2017). A typology of minimalism in advertising. *Advances in Advertising Research VIII*, pp. 1–15. Wiesbaden: Springer.

Micheletti, M., Follesdal, A., & Stolle, D. (2008). Politics, products, and markets: Exploring political consumerism past and present. *Economic Geography, 84*(1), pp. 123–125.

Moisander, J. (2007). Motivational complexity of green consumerism. *International Journal of Consumer Studies, 31*(4), pp. 404–409.

Moisander, J., & Pesonen, S. (2002). Narratives of sustainable ways of living: constructing the self and the other as a green consumer. *Management Decision, 40*(4), pp. 329–342.

Ozcaglar-Toulouse, N., Shiu, E., & Shaw, D. (2006). In search of fair trade: ethical consumer decision making in France. *International Journal of Consumer Studies, 30*(5), pp. 502–514.

Özgül, E. (2010). Tüketicilerin değer yapıları, gönüllü sade yaşam tarzı ve sürdürülebilir tüketim üzerindeki etkileri. *Hacettepe Üniversitesi İktisadi ve İdari Bilimler Fakültesi Dergisi, 28*(2), pp. 117–150.

Özgül, E. (2011). Tüketicilerin sosyo-demografik özelliklerinin hedonik tüketim ve gönüllü sade yaşam tarzları açısından değerlendirilmesi. *Ege Academic Review, 11*(1), pp. 25–38.

Sandıkcı, Ö., & Ekici, A. (2009). Politically motivated brand rejection. *Journal of Business Research, 62*(2), pp. 208–217.

Shama, A. (1985). The voluntary simplicity consumer. *Journal of Consumer Marketing, 2*(4), pp. 57–63.

Tanase, C. (2019). Minimalism: A Marketing Approach of Creativity and Simplicity. *Romanian Distribution Committee Magazine, 10*(2), 31–35.

Uz, N. N. (2016). Tüketim karşıtlığı. *İktisat ve Toplum, 73*, pp. 14–17.

Selçuk Yasin YILDIZ and Sezen GÜLEÇ

10 Consumer Regret

Introduction

With the impact of globalization, businesses aiming to adapt to the increasingly competitive environment place consumer and customer satisfaction at the center of their marketing activities. Consumer behavior is a complex issue since human behavior cannot be measured clearly and is influenced by a plethora of factors (İslamoğlu & Altunışık, 2013). Psychological, cultural, social, and personal factors affect individuals, who are social beings, in their communicative processes with others. These factors might lead one to behave differently or make different decisions when compared with other individuals. Consumer behavior involves the examination of many domains, including the selection, purchase, use, and disposal of goods, services, ideas, and experiences by individuals or groups to satisfy their desires and needs (Solomon, Bamossy, Askegaard, & Hogg, 2006). Owing to the complexity of consumer behavior, individuals might regret their purchasing decisions from time to time. Consumer regret may arise in different stages such as pre-purchase, purchase and post-purchase. Factors affecting consumer regret include certain variables such as uncertainties in the consumer's mind, various pricing policies, and time-related issues. An initial analysis of decision-making processes is considered crucial to understanding the phenomenon of regret within the context of consumer psychology. Consumers aim to select the most suitable option from the alternatives within the sector of which they solicit the services. The consumer believing that they made the best decision is not expected to feel regretful. Taking the significance of this feeling into account, this chapter deals with the issue of consumer regret. Furthermore, it also treats the issue and theories of decision-making based on the assumption that consumer regret is a result of the consumer's way of reaching decisions.

1 Decision-Making

Instead of displaying reactive behavior, individuals intellectualize their surroundings and adapt to life. In this respect, they encounter many daily situations in which they have to make a decision. These situations are pervasive in life and a natural part of one's living experience.

When they encounter a situation in which they have to make a decision, individuals try to reach the best decision possible for their gratification. They need to evaluate their alternatives in order to be able to do so. With the advancements in social life, the increase in the number of alternatives is evident. This increase urges people to make more comprehensive assessments, rendering it more difficult to arrive at decisions.

In the most general sense, decision-making is defined as the process of selecting the best option among others by minimizing uncertainty and doubt (Doğan, 2014: 102). According to Kuzgun (2006), decision-making is acting to alleviate distress in case there are multiple ways of attaining an object, person, or situation or if one is going towards an unknown target. The process of decision-making is a complex one. As the number of criteria and alternatives regarding the situation in question increases, arriving at a decision becomes increasingly difficult. Mentally listing different alternatives in order of suitability with the criteria facilitates decision-making. The purpose of reaching a decision is to actualize the best option rather than creating new alternatives. Therefore, an option that had been previously deemed to be the best solution might also be put into practice (Doğan, 2014).

Decision-making has been an important research topic in many areas including business, economics, career consultancy, and the military. For this reason, different theories examining the process of decision-making and the components affecting the process have been put forward. Some of these theories are explained further in the subsequent section.

1.1 Theories of Decision-Making

Theories of decision-making can be categorized under three headings. Rational decision-making theories indicate that the decision-maker acts based on calculations, evidence, and analytical methods and not on emotions and past experience. Intuitive decision-making theories claim that the decision-maker makes the most satisfactory decision through their emotions and past experiences without any rational evidence or criterion. As for multi-criteria decision-making theories, they combine the strengths of rational and intuitive theories and, consequently, allow the individual to make a selection through effective methods such as prioritizing certain options over other contradictory alternatives. In recent years, multi-criteria theories are the most well-accepted ones.

1.1.1 Rational Decision-Making Theories

A rational individual is expected to opt for the most gratifying and pleasurable alternative among others. As far as consumers are concerned, it is considered that they tend to buy products and services appealing to their taste the most and providing the most benefits in alignment with their income levels (Camerer, 1999). In this respect, rational approaches to decision-making encompass certain principles.

a. *The principle of expected utility* assumes that people are rational beings. A rational person is emancipated from sentimentality and, therefore, will select the alternative that will benefit them the most in a very objective manner. When making decisions during risky and uncertain circumstances, individuals compare the potential benefits of the alternatives before them (Kahneman & Tversky, 1979). The principle of expected utility relies on certain assumptions. These assumptions can be listed as follows (Bailey, 2005):
   - In cases of uncertainty, individuals determine the objective probability,
   - "More" is better than "less",
   - If there are more than one beneficial alternatives with varying levels of utility, the individual selects the most beneficial one,
   - The decision-maker examines the possibilities brought about by each alternative and ranks them in order of utility. They opt for the most suitable alternative for their objective.
b. *The principle of exponential discounting* states that people need to make utility and cost analysis in the future to be able to make a decision in the economic sense. According to this principle, the time difference is taken into consideration while assessing benefits. People opt for an instant benefit over more benefits in one week. Yet when this time frame is extended, the opposite occurs. Therefore, the principle of exponential discounting does not always allow pleasure by postponing positive outcomes and people are always favor increased benefits (Loewenstein & Prelec, 1992).
c. A majority of economic theories allege that individuals only consider their welfare instead of making sacrifices to help or harm others. According to *the principle of social utility*, individuals do not like situations in which they benefit differently from others and they enjoy reciprocating (Camerer, 1999).

1.1.2 Intuitive Decision-Making Theories

Intuitions are known to affect frequently the evaluation of potential alternatives during the decision-making process (Tversky & Kahneman, 1982). For instance, intuitions might manifest themselves in the case when people believe they have control over the results of lotteries. Alternatively, they might lead to misinterpretations regarding the frequency of a negative event when the individual or someone close to them experiences the said event (Byrnes, 2013). The intuitive approach to decision-making, unlike others, makes a holistic perception and faster processing possible without analytical assessments (Lauri et al., 2001).

From the consumer's perspective, for example, if one has someone close to them experiencing distress caused by a product they purchased due to misuse might develop negative attitudes towards the product in question and might not prefer buying it through intuitive decision-making.

Intuitive decision-making theories denote reaching decisions based on experiences, through the fastest assessment of significant aspects, similarities, and differences of the situation along with necessary clues (Lauri et al., 2001). Furthermore, rather than a systematic analysis and data processing, individuals tend to take details into consideration and rely on emotions and intuitions. Decision-makers opting for intuitive methods focus more on imagery, perception, and sensation (Scott & Bruce, 1995).

1.1.3 Multi-Criteria Decision-Making Theories

The multi-criteria decision-making theory was first proposed by Kenneth R. MacCrimmon (1968) and signifies cases in which one needs to make a decision based on two or more criteria. It is considered to be one of the best approaches to be used in cases in which the number of criteria affecting the alternatives is high. Encompassing objective and subjective criteria of assessment, the theory allows one to make comparisons regarding the consistency of evaluations and facilitates the prioritization of alternatives (Higgins, Hajkowicz, & Bui, 2008).

Thomas L. Saaty (2000) put forward the model of analytic hierarchy based on the multi-criteria theory, facilitating decision-making in complex circumstances. The analytic hierarchy process is one of the multi-purpose decision-making processes including objective and subjective assessments, the testing of the validity of these assessments, and determining the priorities of different alternatives based on multiple criteria. It consists of the following sequential stages:

- Structuring the problem within the context of a system or hierarchy,
- Making evaluations reflecting opinions and emotions,
- Enumerating these evaluations in order of priority,
- Determining the priority of alternatives based on these numbers,
- Making a general assessment of the alternatives,
- Analyzing the changes in the assessments.

Situations entailing purchasing and economic decision-making seem to include multiple criteria (Ballı, Karasulu, & Korukoğlu, 2007). Based on the assumption that the increasing number of criteria makes decision-making more difficult, multi-criteria decision-making approaches were put forward. This is important for understanding the prevalence of multi-criteria approaches to decision-making.

In reference to the theories of decision-making, the consumer making the most suitable decision for their circumstances is expected to feel less regret. However, there are also some factors impacting the purchasing decision of the consumer. In this respect, the following section elaborates on the factors influencing consumers while making decisions regarding the purchase of the best good or service for their needs. There are academic studies in the relevant literature that mention the role of regret in consumer behavior (Anderson, 2003) and the impact of regret on the factors influencing the purchasing decision (Bui, Krishen, & Bates, 2011; Lynch Jr & Zauberman, 2007; Tsiros & Mittal, 2000).

2 Factors Affecting the Purchasing Decision

Consumer behavior includes the examination of a plethora of domains like the selection, purchase, usage, or disposal of goods, services, ideas, or experiences to satisfy their needs and desires (Solomon et al., 2006). Purchasing decisions of consumers are profoundly affected by cultural, social, personal, and psychological factors (Kotler & Armstrong, 2012).

Cultural factors: The possibility and desire of consumers to buy goods and services provided by the modern world are evaluated within a wide social and cultural context (Bocock, 2009). As cultural characteristics change, so should the way of developing, marketing, and selling many goods and services to serve the changing customers better (Anderson, Hair, & Bush, 1999). It is possible to list cultural factors affecting the purchasing behavior of consumers as culture, sub-culture, and social class. Cultural factors play a key role in the purchasing behavior of consumers (Kotler, 2000).

Social factors: In addition to cultural factors, consumer behavior is influenced by social factors such as small groups to which consumers belong, families, social roles, and social status. Since these social factors might impact consumer reactions, businesses are ought to take them into account while formulating their marketing strategies (Kotler & Armstrong, 2012).

Personal factors: The aging and life cycle, economic situation, character, and lifestyle of an individual are the personal factors influencing their purchasing decisions. As many of these factors have a direct impact on consumer behavior, marketers need to follow these factors closely (Kotler, 1991).

Psychological factors: These factors influence purchasing preferences as much as cultural, social, and personal factors. Psychological factors discussed here consist of four components: motivation, perception, learning, and beliefs and attitudes (Kotler, 2000; Loken, 2006).

The social class, culture, family structure, personality, way of perception and learning, attitudes, and beliefs of consumers might affect regret as well. Among the factors mentioned above, psychological factors are particularly considered to trigger regret.

3 Consumer Regret

When they make a bad decision while opting for purchasing alternatives, consumers blame themselves and feel regret as they consider the negative consequences of their decision (Zeelenberg et al., 2002).

In consumer psychology, regret denotes "a negative emotion that occurs when a forgone option is (or is thought to be) better than the selected alternative" (Patrick, Lancellotti, & Demello, 2009: 464). While making a choice, consumers attempt to maximize their satisfaction or benefits to avoid such negative emotions (Inman & Zeelenberg, 2002).

Regret emotions experienced by consumers might differ in the temporal. In their studies, Abendroth and Diehl (2006) state that the regret arising from purchasing a product is more effective than the regret stemming from inaction for the consumer. While not acting in any way is generally considered to be normal behavior, the purchasing behavior of consumers entails more responsibilities and risks. These risks and responsibilities result in greater regrets. However, research shows that regret sourcing from purchasing decreases in time, whereas regret due to inaction exacerbates as time passes (Gilovich & Medvec, 1995).

Consumers might change their preferences of products among different alternatives or the time of purchase in order to relieve or avoid regret (Tsiros, 2009) because consumer regret depends on the wrong choice of brand, quantity, purchasing price, or the time of purchase. If the consumer starts blaming themselves after comparing the foregone alternative and the product they purchased, regret occurs. Such regret following the purchase takes its toll on customer satisfaction (Abendroth & Diehl, 2006).

The factors of dissatisfaction leading to consumer regret can be categorized as pre-purchase, during-purchase, and after-purchase stages (Jarrar, Ruben, & Meersman, 2003). There are several theories explaining regret.

4 Theories of Regret

Various studies in the academic literature (George & Edward, 2009; Hunt, 1970; Kaish, 1967; Korgaonkar & Moschis, 1982; Sweeney, Hausknecht, & Soutar, 2000; Tanford & Montgomery, 2015; Veer & Shankar, 2011) consider the theory of cognitive dissonance as one of the significant frameworks to assess purchasing processes.

The theory was developed by Leon Festinger (1957). It suggests that cognitive dissonance is a psychologically uncomfortable condition that the individual is motivated to reduce. The theory of cognitive dissonance is sometimes referred to as consumer regret.

Individuals obliged to make a choice out of many appealing alternatives encounter a psychologically bothersome situation. This is called cognitive dissonance or disharmony (Sweeney, Soutar, & Johnson, 1996). Consumers frequently experience cognitive dissonance. This might occur before, during, and after the purchasing decision. Cognitive dissonance is particularly prevalent in cases where the purchasing decision and its consequences are deemed important and the decision is irreversible; it depends on whether the decision is made voluntarily (Hausknecht et al., 1998; Sweeney, Soutar, & Johnson, 1996). In other words, it arises when consumer uncertainty is more evident (Koller & Salzberger, 2007). In marketing, the theory of cognitive dissonance might be considered in many studies on various topics ranging from purchasing behavior to consequent disharmonies, from the changes in attitudes and perceptions to brand loyalty and service quality (Telci, 2014).

Another framework in this respect is the regret theory proposed by Loomes and Sugden (1982). The theory is studied in many disciplines such as consumer psychology, consumer behavior, business administration, psychology, finance, and economics. It suggests that when people make decisions in uncertain circumstances, regret might affect their decision-making processes. It alleges that individuals might diverge from their ideal behavior at the moment they reach a decision due to the fear of regret in the future.

Marketing professionals study the regret felt after a purchase in detail to understand the decision-making processes of individuals (Bui, Krishen, & Bates, 2011). The concept of regret is considered to be a powerful incentive for motivation and to influence consumer behavior significantly (Zeelenberg & Pieters, 2007). The regret theory does not only assume that people might feel regret after a negative purchasing experience but also suggests that they might experience the feeling before making the purchase (Sugden, 1985).

Conclusion

In the ever-developing world, the number of alternatives seems to increase as far as the purchase of goods and services is concerned, as it is the case in every sector. Particularly, digital and mobile marketing made many alternatives regarding the good or service the consumer intends to buy available to the consumer. Each alternative has many different features. While the increase in the number of options and features offers the advantage of receiving top-quality services, it also brings about certain disadvantages such as the difficulty of making a decision and regret. A high number of alternatives and criteria render decision-making challenging; individuals might believe that they did not choose the best option after making a purchase. This may lead to consumer regret.

It is plausible to indicate that the anxiety of not being able to make a decision and regretting a decision causes cognitive dissonance. Within this context, regret is better explained with the theory of cognitive dissonance. According to Odabaşı and Barış (2014), negative characteristics of the selected alternative and the positive aspects of the foregone alternatives also give rise to cognitive dissonance. This is also related to the regret arising from a purchasing decision.

While making a purchasing decision, the consumer has certain desires and expectations regarding the product in question. These expectations persist during the entire decision-making process, from the initial consideration to consumption. In other words, expectations are visible throughout the decision-making and purchasing process.

However, desires and expectations are related more to post-purchase behavior. In order for the individual to feel a high level of satisfaction, the product needs to live up to the wants and expectations of the consumer after the purchase (Kotler & Armstrong, 2012). If this is not the case, the customer feels dissatisfied; dissatisfaction is thought to lead to regret.

In this context, consumer regret, explained with various theories, might arise as a result of the processes in which the consumer aims to make the right decisions and, therefore, tries to make the best decisions regarding their purchases.

References

Abendroth, L. J., & Diehl, K. (2006). Now or never: Effects of limited purchase opportunities on patterns of regret over time. *Journal of Consumer Research*, *33*(3), pp. 342–351.

Anderson, C. J. (2003). The psychology of doing nothing: forms of decision avoidance result from reason and emotion. *Psychological Bulletin*, *129*(1), p. 139.

Anderson, R. E., Hair, J. F., & Bush, A. J. (1999). *Professional Sales Management*. Huston: Dame Publications, Inc.

Bailey, R. E. (2005). *The Economics of Finansal Market.* 1st Ed. UK: Cambridge University Press.

Ballı, S., Karasulu, B., & Korukoğlu, S. (2007). En uygun otomobil seçimi problemi için bir bulanık PROMETHEE yöntemi uygulaması. *Dokuz Eylül Üniversitesi İktisadi İdari Bilimler Fakültesi Dergisi, 22*(1), pp. 139–147.

Bocock, R. (2009). *Tüketim*. Ankara: Dost.

Bui, M., Krishen, A. S., & Bates, K. (2011). Modeling regret effects on consumer post-purchase decisions. *European Journal of Marketing, 4*(7/8), pp. 1068–1090.

Byrnes, J. P. (2013). *The Nature and Development of Decision-Making: A Self-Regulation Model.* New York: Psychology Press.

Camerer, C. (1999). Behavioral economics: Reunifying psychology and economics, *Proceedings of the National Academy of Sciences of the USA*, 96, pp. 10575–10576.

Doğan, H. (2014). Çağdaş kariyer karar verme yaklaşım ve modellerinin incelenmesi. *OPUS Uluslararası Toplum Araştırmaları Dergisi, 4*(6), pp. 100–130.

Festinger, L. (1957). *A Theory of Cognitive Dissonance.* Stanford, CA: Stanford University Press.

George, B. P., & Edward, M. (2009). Cognitive dissonance and purchase involvement in the consumer behavior context. *IUP Journal of Marketing Management, 8.*

Gilovich, T., & Medvec, V. H. (1995). The experience of regret: what, when, and why. *Psychological Review, 102*(2), p. 379.

Hausknecht, D., Sweeney, J., Soutar, G., & Johnson, L. (1998). "After I had made the decision, I...:" Toward a scale to measure cognitive dissonance. *Journal of Consumer Satisfaction, Dissatisfaction and Complaining Behavior, 11.*

Higgins, A. J., Hajkowicz, S., & Bui, E. (2008). A multi-objective model for environmental investment decision making. *Computers & Operations Research, 35*(1), pp. 253–266.

Hunt, S. D. (1970). Post-transaction communications and dissonance reduction. *Journal of Marketing, 34*(3), pp. 46–51.

Inman, J. J., & Zeelenberg, M. (2002). Regret in repeat purchase versus switching decisions: The attenuating role of decision justifiability. *Journal of Consumer Research, 29*(1), pp. 116–128.

İslamoğlu, A. H., & Altunışık, R. (2013). *Tüketici Davranışları*. İstanbul: Beta.

Jarrar, M., Ruben, V., & Meersman, R. (2003). Ontology-based customer complaint management. *In OTM Confederated International Conferences "On the Move to Meaningful Internet Systems"*, pp. 594–606. Lecture Notes in Computer Science, vol 2889, Berlin: Springer.

Kaish, S. (1967). Cognitive dissonance and the classification of consumer goods. *Journal of Marketing, 31*(4), pp. 28–31.

Kahneman, D., & Tversky, A. (1979). Prospecteory: An analysis of decision under risk. *Econometrica: Journal of the Econometric Society, 47*(2), pp. 263–264.

Koller, M., & Salzberger, T. (2007). Cognitive dissonance as a relevant construct throughout the decision-making and consumption process-an empirical investigation related to a package tour. *Journal of Customer Behaviour, 6*(3), pp. 217–227.

Korgaonkar, P. K., & Moschis, G. P. (1982). An experimental study of cognitive dissonance, product involvement, expectations, performance and consumer judgement of product performance. *Journal of Advertising, 11*(3), pp. 32–44.

Kotler, P. (1991). *Marketing Management: Analysis, Planning, Implementation, and Control.* New Jersey: Prentice-Hall, Inc.

Kotler, P. (2000). *Marketing Management.* Millenium ed. New Jersey: Prentice-Hall, Inc.

Kotler, P., & Armstrong, G. (2012). *Principles of Marketing.* New Jersey: Pearson Education, Inc.

Kuzgun, Y. (2006). İlköğretimde Rehberlik. *Hacettepe Üniversitesi Eğitim Fakültesi Dergisi, 8*(8).

Lauri, S., Salanterä, S., Chalmers, K., Ekman, S. L., Kim, H. S., Käppeli, S., & Macleod, M. (2001). An exploratory study of clinical decision-making in five countries. *Journal of Nursing Scholarship, 33*(1), pp. 83–90.

Loewenstein, G., & Prelec, D. (1992). Anomalies in ıntertemporal choice: Evidence and an ınterpretation. *The Quarterly Journal of Economics, 107*(2), pp. 573–597.

Loken, B. (2006). Consumer psychology: Categorization, inferences, affect, and persuasion. *Annual Review of Psychology, 57*, pp. 453–485.

Loomes, G., & Sugden, R. (1982). Regret theory: An alternative theory of rational choice under uncertainty. *The Economic Journal, 92*(368), pp. 805–824.

Lynch Jr, J. G., & Zauberman, G. (2007). Construing consumer decision making. *Journal of Consumer Psychology, 17*(2), pp. 107–112.

MacCrimmon, K. R. (1968). *Decision Making among Multiple-Attribute Alternatives: A Survey and Consolidated Approach*. Santa Monica, CA: Rand Corp Santa Monica Ca. https://www.rand.org/pubs/research_memoranda/RM4823.html Accessed on: 15.04.2020

Odabaşı, Y., & Barış, G. (2014). *Tüketici Davranışı*. İstanbul: MediaCat Akademi.

Patrick, V. M., Lancellotti, M. P., & Demello, G. (2009). Coping with non-purchase: Managing the stress of inaction regret. *Journal of Consumer Psychology, 19*(3), pp. 463–472.

Saaty, T. L. (2000). *Fundamentals of Decision Making and Priority Theory with the Analytic Hierarchy Process*. Pittsburgh, PA: RWS Publications.

Scott, S. G., & Bruce, R. A. (1995). Decision-making style: The development and assessment of a new measure. *Educational and Psychological Measurement, 55*(5), pp. 818–831.

Solomon, M., Bamossy, G., Askegaard, S., & Hogg, M. K. (2006). *Consumer Behavior: A European Perspective*. Essex: Pearson Education Limited.

Sugden, R. (1985). Regret, recrimination and rationality. *Theory and Decision, 19*(1), pp. 77–99.

Sweeney, J. C., Soutar, G. N., & Johnson, L. W. (1996). Are satisfaction and dissonance the same construct? *Journal of Consumer Satisfaction, Dissatisfaction and Complaining Behavior, 9*, pp. 138–143.

Sweeney, J. C., Hausknecht, D., & Soutar, G. N. (2000). Cognitive dissonance after purchase: A multidimensional scale. *Psychology & Marketing, 17*(5), pp. 369–385.

Tanford, S., & Montgomery, R. (2015). The effects of social influence and cognitive dissonance on travel purchase decisions. *Journal of Travel Research, 54*(5), pp. 596–610.

Telci, E. E. (2014). Bilişsel uyumsuzluk teorisi. Yağcı, M. İ. & Çabuk, S. (Eds.) *Pazarlama Teorileri* (211–223). MediaCat Yayınları.

Tsiros, M. (2009). Releasing the regret lock: Consumer response to new alternatives after a sale. *Journal of Consumer Research, 35*(6), pp. 1039–1059.

Tsiros, M., & Mittal, V. (2000). Regret: A model of its antecedents and consequences in consumer decision making. *Journal of Consumer Research, 26*(4), pp. 401–417.

Tversky, A., & Kahneman, D. (1982). *Judgment under uncertainty. Heuristics and biases*. Cambridge: Cambridge University Press.

Veer, E., & Shankar, A. (2011). Forgive me, Father, for I did not give full justification for my sins: How religious consumers justify the acquisition of material wealth. *Journal of Marketing Management, 27*(5–6), pp. 547–560.

Zeelenberg, M., & Pieters, R. (2007). A theory of regret regulation 1.0. *Journal of Consumer Psychology, 17*(1), pp. 3–18.

Zeelenberg, M., Van den Bos, K., Van Dijk, E., & Pieters, R. (2002). The inaction effect in the psychology of regret. *Journal of Personality and Social Psychology, 82*(3), pp. 314.

İlknur TÜFEKÇİ

11 The Relationship between Consumer Guilt and Shame and Impulse Buying

Introduction

An integral part of human personality, emotions have been a common research subject in the field of marketing. With emotions being revealed primarily by psychological research studies to affect all aspects of life, marketing scholars have developed an interest in the issue in question. In particular, consumer research studies revealed that emotions affect consumer decisions and actions (de Hooge et al., 2007).

The emotional experiences of consumers during their purchases are of vital importance because consumers would consider their next purchase based on their emotional experiences. Therefore, emotions are used to define consumer experiences and to create an impact among consumers. It is necessary to detect the emotions influential throughout the process of consumption for marketing strategies to be successful (Cacioppo & Gardner, 1999). Emotions are generally divided into two categories: positive and negative. Marketing studies focus primarily on positive emotions (King & Meiselman, 2010). Although consumption is generally considered to be fun, it can also lead to negative emotions such as shame, guilt, and sadness. Consumers might feel such emotions especially when they think that they bought unnecessary, expensive and meaningless products and this might affect future purchases (Lamb, 1983). Negative emotions were found to be much more influential on future purchases when compared with positive emotions as consumers remember negative emotions more clearly than positive ones (Inman et al., 1997).

Tronvoll (2010) indicated that negative emotions are evoked when the consumer encounters unwanted situations or experiences and that this triggers complaints by the consumer. Such emotions can be observed while the consumer spends time in the store for shopping, talks to the salesperson, uses the product or watches advertisements. The positive or negative nature of these emotions might lead the consumer to purchase or not to purchase the product in question (Kabadayı & Alan, 2013). Furthermore, emotions also influence attitudes towards the retailer and satisfaction. Understanding negative emotions and preventing customer complaints are crucial (Inman et al., 1997). Owing to the significance of the issue, this chapter evaluates consumer guilt and shame, the difference between these concepts and their relationship with impulse buying.

1 Guilt and Consumer Guilt

According to the definition made in the dictionary of the Turkish Language Association, guilt is *an emotion evoked either consciously or unconsciously as a result of their realization that someone violated moral or religious codes, unsettling the value judgments a person has of themselves* (TDK, 15.04.2020). Izard (1977) suggested that guilt emerges with the development of the senses of self and responsibility. Guilt can be defined as the unpleasant emotional state related to the individual's actions, conditions, or intentions as a function of the social relationships they establish (Baumeister et al., 1994: 261).

Huhmann and Brotherton (1997) explained three main types of guilt: reactive, existential, and anticipatory. Reactive guilt occurs after an individual act in a way that contradicts their internal behavior standards. Existential guilt arises when the individual feels more privileged or luckier than others. Anticipatory guilt signifies the emotion that an individual might experience when they think of contradicting their personal standards in the future or imagine doing so (Hanks, 2012). Guilt encompasses feelings of anxiety, sadness, and regret as a result of a negative evaluation of individual behavior, such as the realization of a mistake. When people feel guilty, they are concerned with the impacts of their behaviors on others (Tangney & Dearing, 2003). Unlike shame, guilt focuses on the individual's actions rather than the individual themselves. Research studies show that although an unpleasant emotion, guilt produces functional reactions. Apart from harmonious and reparative behaviors like apologizing and helping someone with something, guilt also makes the individual get perspectives and display constructive reactions (Tangney et al., 2007).

Yet certain studies provided evidence for the influence of guilt on behavior or behavioral intentions. Studies show that guilt is an important emotion as far as ethical decision-making is concerned (Steenhaut & van Kenhove, 2006). Other studies report that individuals with high scores on guilt-proneness are less likely to act unethically and tend to distance themselves from wrong behaviors and illegal actions (Cohen et al., 2011).

The concept of guilt was studied in the marketing literature starting from the 1980s (Elgaaied, 2012). It was defined to be a key emotion in the context of purchases. Consumer guilt particularly concerns consumption decisions and is defined as an effect triggered by the anxiety stemming from the thought of having violated a moral, societal, or ethical principle (Lascu, 1991: 290). Burnett and

Lunsford (1994) explained four variety of guilt in consumer decision-making processes: financial guilt, health guilt, moral guilt, and social responsibility guilt. Financial guilt arises in cases of unnecessary or extravagant spending. For example, impulse purchases can lead to financial guilt. Health guilt emerges if an individual believes that they are not paying attention to their physical well-being. It includes purchasing decisions that are not good for one's health, such as eating high-fat foods or smoking. Moral guilt surfaces when the purchasing decision in question is in contradiction with the individual's moral values. The feeling originating from the purchase of a product prohibited by one's religious beliefs can be given as an example of this type of guilt. Social responsibility guilt occurs in the case in which the individual shirks their perceived social responsibilities as a result of their purchasing decision. This type of guilt can stem from the decision to or not to buy a product, including donations, environmental issues, familial responsibilities, and gift purchases. Consumer guilt might occur before or after the purchasing decision. The majority of the studies concerning guilt tend to focus on the type of guilt conveyed by a marketing message or an advertisement. Guilt is one of the strategies used by marketers to influence consumers (Haynes & Podobsky, 2016). Particularly as a persuasive method, guilt was observed frequently in advertisements. As a result, consumers were motivated to purchase the product to avoid this emotion (Steenhaut & van Kenhove, 2006).

2 Shame and Consumer Shame

The Turkish Language Association defines shame as *a sense of abashment or embarrassment*. Being ashamed signifies *the sadness and distress due to the fear of finding oneself in a situation considered to be dishonorable or laughable* (TDK, 15.04.2020). It is defined as the sense of self-evaluation causing anxiety about how the individual is judged by others (Velleman, 2001). It arises when the individual violates a moral standard in their society. The individual criticizes themselves in a painful manner as they experience a moral self-defect (Gausel & Leach, 2011).

Shame encompasses the self-evaluations of an individual. Its focus is a defective self and it is related to an undesirable personality. Shame is described as a painful emotion related to the individual's identity, originating from a discreditable, inappropriate act causing them to feel insufficiency within themselves. The individual might feel themselves to be imperfect, worthless, unsuccessful, and inadequate (Lewis, 1971). Experiencing shame causes the individual to withdraw and cower (Greenberg & Watson, 2006). Shame also gives rise to an unwillingness within the individual to make up for their actions when they act negatively (Barrett, 1995).

Research studies are conducted to observe how emotions affect the science of marketing. Even though the field of psychology is a basis particularly for comprehending consumer mentality, marketers also undertake research studies in this regard. However, the impact of emotions cannot be explained in a systematic manner in the present day. This creates the gap in the discipline of marketing. Understanding emotions, the key determinants of social behavior, is vital for the literature of consumer behavior and marketing (Aydın, 2015).

Various studies in the literature revealed that there is a correlation between purchasing behavior and emotional reactions. Consumer shame was analyzed by only a few cases. In a study by Zielke (2014), it was revealed that negative emotions like shame influence purchasing intentions. The studies to this day examine the relationship between consumer shame and compulsive buying (Johnson & Attman, 2009), impulse buying (Aydın, 2015; Yi & Baumgartner, 2011), consumer ethics (Arli et al., 2016; Eisenberg, 2000; Tangney et al., 2007), guilt and empathy (Tangney 1991).

3 Differentiating Guilt and Shame

Tangney (1995) indicates that although guilt and shame have different characteristics, they also share many similar characteristics. Some of their common features can be listed as follows: Both emotions generally emerge in interpersonal relationships and contexts, are moral, include internal judgments, are negative, concern the sense of self and have similar influencing factors (Baumeister et al., 1994).

Shame and guilt arise when the individual makes an assessment of the situation they are in and finds it to be disharmonious with their sense of self (Tangney & Dearing, 2003). Thus, shame and guilt are considered to be self-conscious emotions. Although shame and guilt can be experienced simultaneously, they are different emotions with different aspects (Lewis, 1971). While guilt is about the actions of the individual, shame generally concerns the sense of self. Guilt emerges when the individual focuses on their behavior. Considering the statement "I did something bad", if the individual focuses on "something bad", that might lead to guilt while if the focus is on "I", this might evoke shame. In other words, while guilt is about doing something wrong, shame is about the negative way in which the individual is perceived by others as a result of the wrong action. Shame is generally more painful and destructive. In this sense, it is easier to cope with guilt (Tangney, 1995). The person feeling guilty can get rid of this emotion by means of reparation, confession or apology. Guilty individuals have a higher chance of acting generously and in a co-operative manner (Ketelaar & Au, 2003). On the other hand, shame goes beyond actions and focuses on the faulty and worthless perception of the self. In addition to the sense of abasement, this negative assessment of self is also related to the wish of being invisible or disappearing (Hoffman, 1982).

Another point in which guilt and shame differ from one another is that while guilt is more private and personal, shame is a social emotion (Deonna & Teroni, 2011). Shame lasts longer than guilt. While shame produces more intense emotional reactions, those evoked by guilt are less intense. Individuals feeling guilty are empathetic but those feeling shame tend to display less empathy (Lindsay-Hartz et al., 1995). Within the interpersonal context, guilt and shame also differ in the sense that they create dissimilar impulses for the behavior following the emotions (Ferguson et al., 1991).

4 How Impulse Purchases Are Related to Guilt and Shame

A common behavior among people, impulse buying can be seen within the context of any type of goods and services (Kacen & Lee, 2002). The fact that many purchases made by modern-day consumers are related to impulse buying underlines the importance of impulse purchases (Dawson & Kim, 2010).

Comprehensive research studies on impulse buying date back to the early 1950s. Initially, impulse buying was defined as an "unplanned" purchase. In later studies, it was revealed that impulse purchases and unplanned purchases are different (Stern, 1962). Impulse buying can be defined as "purchases made with an irresistible instinct as a result of being stuck between self-control and desires" (Baumeister, 2002: 670).

Although perceived as a problematic behavior from the consumers' point of view, impulse buying is an imperative method for marketers in order to increase sales volumes (Akram et al., 2018). However, a rapid decision-making process might lead to negative emotions (Youn & Faber, 2000). Consumers might make impulse purchases to get rid of negative emotional states or to change negative emotions (Rook & Gardner, 1993). Some consumers might resort to impulse buying upon encountering emotional distress, in order to alleviate negative emotions such as disappointment, loneliness or sadness (Silvera et al., 2008) or to unbend and cheer up (Verplanken & Herabadi, 2001).

Consumers may make impulse purchases to free themselves of negative moods, yet they can also experience negative emotions after the impulse purchase. Research studies have shown that impulse buying is linked to emotions such as post-purchase financial problems, product disappointment, and social disapproval (Rook 1987; Rook & Fisher, 1995), guilt (Miao, 2011) and anxiety (Roberts & Roberts, 2012). Among these negative emotions, guilt plays an important role in shaping behavior (Dahl et al., 2003). Although these emotions are complex and many factors contribute to their emergence, impulsive shopping is one of the important factors (Aydın & Ünal, 2017).

In a strong competition environment, the consumer is stimulated to buy a good or service right away (King, Dennis, & Wright, 2008). Consumers might experience these emotions when the good or service in question is defected or incomplete. Furthermore, the consumer blames themselves when they do not do enough research or realize later on that the alternative they thought to be better is not the right choice (Engin, 2011). Guilt can interrupt the purchasing behaviors of the consumer (Dahl et al., 2003). The limitation of such purchases by consumers due to their negative impacts might produce adverse effects for marketers and retailers (Zhang & Fengjuan, 2010).

Research studies within the academic literature reveal that a negative mood affects impulse buying (Bahrainizad & Rajabi, 2018; Youn & Faber, 2000) and leads to negative emotions such as guilt and regret (Dahl et al., 2003; King et al., 2008). A study by Aydın and Ünal (2017) examines the impact of impulse buying on shame and guilt. It was revealed that these emotions are negative self-conscious emotions arising after impulse purchases and that they affect the repurchasing behavior of the consumer. In their study, Yi and Baumgartner (2010) found that consumers with a tendency towards impulse buying experience guilt and shame more intensely.

Conclusion and Suggestions

Today, businesses are aware that consumers decide and buy products based on their emotions. As competition has increased, the gap between the qualities of different goods and services has narrowed, the product range has increased and consumer demands have changed accordingly in the present day, consumer experience is interpreted through emotions. Therefore, consumer emotions are of vital importance for brands or businesses. Despite this level of significance, upon reviewing the literature on consumer psychology or consumer behavior, it can be seen that only a few studies examine the emotions of guilt and shame when compared with other negative emotions. Shame, in particular, is one of the rarely studied subjects. This might restrain the ability of businesses and scholars to understand consumers and to foresee their future behavior. For this reason, it seems to be necessary to increase the number of qualitative and quantitative studies to explain the consumer decision-making process.

In addition to its contribution to the existing literature, the present study provides certain suggestions to businesses. For instance, businesses can utilize these negative emotions for their promotional activities. Using these negative emotions specifically in advertisements might help businesses create a positive image. For example, companies producing healthy food and insurance companies may increase their market shares with these emotions.

Businesses must make an effort for consumers not to feel guilt and shame after their purchases. In particular, post-purchase dissatisfaction negatively affects businesses and decrease their market shares. Considering that most present-day consumers make impulse purchases, developing post-sales services and implementing easy return policies should be used to attract customers in order to reduce the feelings of guilt and shame after a purchase.

References

Akram, U., Hui, P., Khan, M. K., Tanveer, Y., Mehmood, K., & Ahmad, W. (2018). How website quality affects online impulse buying. *Asia Pacific Journal of Marketing and Logistics*, 30(1), pp. 235–256.

Arli, D., Leo, C., & Tjiptono, F. (2016). Investigating the impact of guilt and shame proneness on consumer ethics: a cross national study. *International Journal of Consumer Studies*, 40, pp. 2–13. doi:10.1111/ijcs.12183 Accessed on: 15.03.2020.

Aydın, H. (2015). *İçgüdüsel alımlarda tüketici suçluluğu ve utancı ile başa çıkma stratejilerinin değerlendirilmesi: Üniversite öğrencileri üzerine bir araştırma*. Unpublished PhD Thesis, Atatürk Üniversitesi Sosyal Bilimler Enstitüsü, Erzurum.

Aydın, H., & Ünal, S. (2017). İçgüdüsel alımlardan sonra meydana gelen negatif özbilinç duyguları. *Atatürk Üniversitesi İktisadi ve İdari Bilimler Dergisi*, 31(1).

Baumeister, R. F. (2002). Yielting totemptation: Self-control failure, impulsive purchasing and consumer behavior. *Journal of Consumer Research*, 28(4), pp. 670–676.

Bahrainizad, M., & Rajabi, A. (2018). Consumer' perception of usability of product packaging and impulse buying: Considering consumers' mood and time pressure as moderating variables. *Journal of Islamic Marketing*, 9(2), pp. 262–282.

Barrett, K. C. (1995). A functionalist approach to shame and guilt. In Tangney & Fischer (Eds.), *Self-Conscious Emotions* (pp. 25–63). New York: Guilford Press.

Baumeister, R. F., Stillwell, A. M., & Heatherton, T. F. (1994). Guilt: An interpersonal approach. *Psychological Review*, 115, pp. 243–267.

Burnett, M. S., & Lunsford, D. A. (1994). Conceptualizing guilt in the consumer decision-making process. *Journal Consumer Market*, 11(3), pp. 33–43.

Cacioppo, J. T., & Gardner, W. L. (1999). Emotion. *Annual Review of Psychology*, 50, pp. 191–214.

Cohen, T. R., Wolf, S. T., Panter, A. T., & Insko, C. A. (2011). Introducing the gasp scale: A new measure of guilt and shame proneness. *Journal of Personality and Social Psychology*, 100(5), pp. 947–966.

Dahl, D. W., Honea, H., & Manchanda, R. V. (2003). The nature of self-reported guilt in consumption context. *Marketing Letters*, 14(3), pp. 159–171.

Dawson, S., & Kim, M. (2010). Cues on apparel web sites that trigger impulse purchases. *Journal of Fashion Marketing and Management*, 14(2), pp. 230–246.

De Hooge, I. E., Zeelenberg, M., & Breugelmans, S. M. (2007). Moral sentiments and cooperation: Differential influences of shame and guilt. *Cognition & Emotion*, 21, pp. 1025–1042. doi:10.1080/ 02699930600980874 Accessed on: 15.03.2020.

Deonna, J., & Teroni, F. (2011). Is shame a social emotion? In *Self-Evaluation* (pp. 193–212). Netherlands: Springer.

Eisenberg, N. (2000). Emotion, regulation, and moral development. *Annual Review Psychology,* 51, pp. 665–697.

Elgaaied, L. (2012). Exploring the role of anticipated guilt on pro-environmental behavior: A suggested typology of residents in France based on their recycling patterns, *Journal of Consumer Marketing*, 29(5), pp. 369–377.

Engin, M. B. (2011). *Tüketici karar alma sürecinde pişmanlık ve Türkiye' de esnek iade politikalarının uygulanabilirliği: Hazır giyim sektörü üzerine bir inceleme.* Unpublished PhD Thesis, İstanbul Üniversitesi Sosyal Bilimler Enstitüsü. İstanbul.

Ferguson, T. J., Stegge, H., & Damhuis, I. (1991). Children's understanding of guilt and shame. *Child Development,* 62(4), pp. 827–839.

Gausel, N., & Leach, C. W. (2011). Concern for self-image and social-image in the management of moral failure: Rethinking shame. *European Journal of Social Psychology*, 41, pp. 468–478. doi: 10.1002/ejsp.803 Accessed on: 15.03.2020.

Greenberg, L. S., & Watson, J. C. (2006). *Emotion-Focused Therapy for Depression*. Washington, DC: American Psychological Association.

Hanks, L. (2012). *The impact of purchase type, pre-purchase mood, and gender on levels of consumer guilt in an impulse purchase context*. Doctoral Thesis, The Pennsylvania State University. USA.

Haynes, P., & Podobsky, S. (2016). Guilt-free food consumption: One of your five ideologies a day. *Journal of Consumer Marketing*, 33(3), pp. 202–212.

Hoffman, M. L. (1982). *Development of Prosocial Motivation: Empathy and Guilt*. In N. Eisenberg-Berg (Ed.), Development of prosocial behavior (pp. 281–312). San Diego, CA: Academic Press.

Huhmann, B. A., & Brotherton, T. P. (1997). A content analysis of guilt appeals in popular magazine advertisements. *Journal of Advertising*, 26, 35.

Inman, J. J., Dyer, J. S., & Jia, J. (1997). A generalized utility model of disappoinment and regret effects on post-choice valuation. *Marketing Science*, 16, pp. 97–111.

Izard, C. E. (1977). *Human Emotions*. New York: Plenum Press.

Johnson, T., & Attmann, J. (2009). Compulsive buying in a product specific context: Clothing. *Journal of Fashion Marketing and Management: An International Journal*, 13(3), pp. 394–405.

Kabadayı, E. T., & Alan, A. K. (2013). Duygu tipolojilerinin tüketici davranışları üzerindeki etkisi ve pazarlamadaki önemi. *İşletme Araştırmaları Dergisi*, 5(1), pp. 93–115.

Kacen, J. J., & Lee, J. A. (2002). The influence of culture on consumer impulsive buying behavior. *Journal of Consumer Psychology*, 12(2), pp. 163–176.

Ketelaar, T., & Au, W. T. (2003). The effects of feelings of guilt on the behaviour of uncooperative individuals in repeated social bargaining games: An affect-as-information interpretation of the role of emotion in social interaction. *Cognition and Emotion*, 17, pp. 429–453.

King, S. C., & Meiselman, H. L. (2010). Development of a method to measure consumer emotions associated with foods. *Food Quality and Preference*, 21(2), pp. 168–177.

King, T., Dennis, C., & Wright, L. T. (2008). Myopia, customer returns and the theory of planned behaviour. *Journal of Marketing Management*, 24(1–2), pp. 185–203.

Lamb, R. E. (1983). Guilt, shame and morality. *Philosophy and Phenomenological Research*, 43(3), pp. 329–346.

Lascu, D. N. (1991). Consumer guilt: Examining the potential of a new marketing construct. *Advances in Consumer Research*, 18, p. 290.

Lewis, H. B. (1971). *Shame and Guilt in Neurosis*. New York: International Universities Press.

Lindsay-Hartz, J., De Rivera, J., & Mascolo, M. F. (1995). Differentiating guilt and shame and their effects on motivation. In J. P. Tangney & K. W. Fischer (Eds.), *Self-Conscious Emotions: The Psychology of Shame, Guilt, Embarrassment, and Pride* (pp. 274–300). New York: Guilford Press.

Miao, L. (2011). Guilty pleasure or pleasurable guilt? Affective experience of impulse buying in hedonic-driven consumption. *Journal of Hospitality & Tourism Research*, 35(1), pp. 79–101.

Roberts, J. A., & Roberts, C. (2012). Stress, gender and compulsive buying among early adolescents. *Young Consumers: Insight and Ideas for Responsible Marketers*, 13(2), pp. 113–123.

Rook, D. W. (1987). The buying impulse. *Journal of Consumer Research*, 14(2), pp. 189–199.

Rook, D. W., & Fisher, R. J. (1995). Normative influences on impulsive buying behavior. *Journal of Consumer Research*, 22(3), pp. 305–313.

Rook, D. W., & Gardner, M. (1993). In the mood: Impulse buying's affective antecedents. *Research in Consumer Behavior*, 6(1), pp. 1–28.

Silvera, D. H., Lavack, A. M., & Kropp, F. (2008). Impulse buying: The role of affect, social influence, and subjective wellbeing. *Journal of Consumer Marketing*, 25(1), pp. 23–33.

Steenhaut, S., & Van Kenhove, P. (2006). The mediating role of anticipated guilt in consumers' ethical decision making. *Journal of Business Ethics*, 69(3), pp. 269–288.

Stern, H. (1962). The significance of impulse buying today. *Journal of Marketing*, 26(2), pp. 59–62.

Tangney, J. P. (1991). Moral affect: The good, the bad, the ugly. *Journal of Personality and Social Psychology*, 61(4), pp. 598–607.

Tangney, J. P. (1995). Shame and guilt in interpersonal relationships. In J. P. Tangney, K. W. Fischer (Eds.), *Self Conscious Emotions*. New York: Guildford Press, pp. 114–139.

Tangney, J. P., & Dearing, R. L. (2003). *Shame and Guilt*. New York: Guilford Press.

Tangney, J. P., Stuewig, J., & Mashek, D. J. (2007). Moral emotions and moral behavior. *Annual Review of Psychology*, 58, pp. 345–372.

Tronvoll, B. (2010). Negative emotions and their effect on customer complaint behavior. *Journal of Service Management*, 22, pp. 111–134.

TDK, The Turkish Language Association, 'Guilt', https://sozluk.gov.tr/?kelime=su%C3%A7luluk Accessed on: 15.04.2020.

TDK, The Turkish Language Association, 'Shame', https://sozluk.gov.tr/?kelime=utan%C3%A7 Accessed on: 15.04.2020.

Velleman, J. D. (2001). The genesis of shame. *Philosophy and Public Affairs*, 30(1), pp. 27–52.

Verplanken, B., & Herabadi, A. (2001). Individual differences in impulse buying tendency: Feeling and no thinking. *European Journal of Personality*, 15(1), pp. S71–S83.

Yi, S., & Baumgartner, H. (2011). *Coping* with guilt and shame in the impulse buying context. *Journal of Economic Psychology*, 32(3), pp. 458–467.

Youn, S., & Faber, R. J. (2000). Impulse buying: İts relation to personality traits and cues. *ACR North American Advances*, 27, pp. 179–185.

Zhang, Y., & Fengjuan, W. (2010). *The Relationship between Impulse Buying, Negative Evaluations and Customer Loyalty*. Orient Academic Forum. http://www.seidatacollection.com/upload/product/201004/2010glhy03a6.pdf. Accessed on 15.04.2020

Zielke, S. (2014). Shopping in discount stores: The role of price-related attributions, emotions and value perception. *Journal of Retailing and Consumer Services*, 21(3), pp. 327–338.

Melih BAŞKOL

12 The Relationship between Subjective Well-Being and Consumer Well-Being

Introduction

Consumer well-being (CWB) has drawn significant attention from managers and public policy experts, as well as scholars and practitioners (Pancer & Handelman, 2012). Analyzing factors affecting subjective consumer well-being is crucial for consumer behavior research, lawmakers, and marketers. Examining the question of whether subjective well-being has the potential of influencing consumer trust and spending at the macro level is also vital (Petrescu & Kara, 2018).

Research on CWB is usually dated back to the late 1970s to the macro marketing school of thought, but the CWB understanding of the CWB has existed with the development of marketing as a discipline. CWB started to be deemed important by scholars and organizations in the early 19th century. Towards the late 1940s, the convergence of the production efficiency obtained from the wartime economy and the appearance of the suburban class consumer solidified the place of the operational marketing understanding. The rise of production efficiency brought about a need for new factories, an increased variety of consumer goods and, most importantly, new markets. The transition from satisfying basic needs to wanting to purchase hedonic products made producers and consumers shift their focus from finding exclusively pragmatic products. In this new era, the concept of CWB has started to carry the same meaning with consumer choices and producers have made the significance of the concept even more apparent by competing with other companies to provide a wide range of products for competitive prices (Pancer & Handelman, 2012).

The primary objective of this study is to make a conceptual analysis of consumer well-being and other related elements. The study will examine the concepts of well-being, SWB, and CWB with regards to consumption.

1 Literature Review

There is a plethora of research studies on subjective well-being (SWB) and consumer well-being (CWB). Diener (1984) developed single and multi-item psychometric well-being scales and evaluated the correlation between demographic factors and SWB. Another macro-scale study is based on the idea that the satisfaction from purchase, ownership, consumption, conservation, and organization of costumer products and services defines CWB (Lee, Sirgy, Larsen, & Wright, 2002).

Relationship measurements between psychological, objective and economic well-being based on life cycle income, relative income and resource deficit theories; income is observed to be the most crucial factor (Macdonald & Douthitt, 1992). Psychology has been particularly used to explain the concept of well-being (Seegebarth, Peyer, Balderjahn, & Wiedmann, 2016). Yet personality is not the sole determining or explanatory factor for SWB; factors like culture, relationships, and social activities might also affect the perception of SWB (Holm, Lugosi, Croes, & Torres, 2017).

Various research studies were conducted regarding the relationship between materialism and well-being within the context of the value system of the individual throughout the years. The analysis of the relationship between material values and life values showed that an excessive focus on material objects and the sense of possession harm well-being levels (Burroughs & Rindfleisch, 2002). Notably, the examination of the impacts of consumer expenses for hedonic products on SWB revealed that satisfied consumers primarily choose making expenditure on less costly recreation events to develop long-term personal resources such as physical health and social connectedness (Zhong & Mitchell, 2012). However, some studies reported that hedonic purchases trigger varying levels of increase in well-being depending on the type of purchase, i.e. material elements (in other words, tangible assets) or life experiences (in other words, events experienced by the individual making the purchase). This produces three fundamental outcomes: (a) life experiences have a stronger impact on well-being than material elements, (b) experiential products have a more significant effect on well-being than material products, and (c) experiential products and life experiences generate similar levels of increase in well-being (Guevarra & Howell, 2015). In their study Oral and Thurner (2019) confirmed that there was a positive connection between anti-consumption and CWB which means that low-level materialistic desires have a positive effect of on CWB. This conclusion is compatible with preceding research studies explaining how disproportionate consumption negatively influences the well-being of the individual.

A wide range of research studies in the literature confirms the positive correlation between marketing activities and well-being (Peterson & Ekici, 2007). For instance; a research study revealed that a marketing variable (per capita advertising expenditure) has a strong correlation with SWB while another variable (per capita retail sales) does not display such a strong correlation with SWB (Yue, Zinkhan, & Shibin, 2007).

Another study demonstrated that consumption has a positive effect on well-being only if it serves to improve the quality of the related living spaces. The study revealed that the subjective cognitions of consumers (e.g. being satisfied with what one has) play a vital role and that the frequent consumption of low-cost hedonic products instead of expensive products is related to the subjective satisfaction of consumers within their living spaces (Zhong & Mitchell, 2010). In this regard, a discussion of attitudes of the individual towards consumption at both individual (micro) and social (macro) levels as well as their SWB in terms of cognitive and emotional well-being shows that micro attitudes, positive or negative, has a positive correlation with the SWB of the consumer while macro attitudes are negatively correlated with SWB, a statement supported by certain studies in the literature (Iyer & Muncy, 2016).

2 Well-Being and Subjective Well-Being

There is a wide range of comprehensive concepts used for well-being (WB). The concept of WB is described on one hand as 'individual well-being' with physical and biological terms and, in other words, as 'an affirm of happiness'. Happiness can be regarded as an outcome of a prudent life or, within the scientific context, it can be examined from the perspective of hedonic philosophy (Suranyi-Unger, 1981: 132). Well-being is not only about financial growth or the absence of disease; it is a broad concept encompassing the basis of life satisfactions such as happiness, vitality, and patience. Generally, well-being consists of both objective and subjective parameters (Taneja, 2017).

Diener (1984) divides the definitions of WB into three categories. In definitions made on the basis of normative evaluations, happiness is considered to be the state of having the desired quality rather than a subjective state. Such definitions are normative as they describe what is desired. In the second set of definitions, social scientists focus on what causes people to describe their lives using positive terms. For instance, individuals can create evaluation criteria for their lives (life satisfaction) and certain aspects of their lives (e.g. career or marriage satisfaction) (Diener, 1996). This definition of WB is called life satisfaction and it relies on the individual's personal standards while defining what a good life is. The third meaning of happiness can be described as the superiority of positive effects over negative effects; it is the most frequently used definition in daily life. Therefore, this definition of WB mostly underlines pleasant and positive emotional experiences (Diener, 1984). According to Guillen-Royo (2019), WB is evaluated under two main categories. The first category is used in social psychology, within the scope of which researchers distinguish between hedonia or SWB and eudaimonia or psychological WB. Employed in the economics of happiness and traditional welfare economics, the second category makes a distinction between subjective and objective perspectives. Hedonic approaches account for feelings, moods, and emotions, yet they are usually considered as constituting SWB, occurring as a result of the cognitive evaluation of life and satisfaction generally felt without the sense of ownership (Guillen-Royo, 2019).

3 Elements of Subjective Well-Being

An analysis of the related literature reveals that SWB is the most common subject of research studies on WB. SWB consists of a vast array of concepts ranging from momentary moods to global judgments of life satisfaction, and from depression to euphoria (Diener, Scollon, & Lucas, 2003). Taneja (2017) states that the concept of SWB signifies the psychological and emotional valuations of individuals concerning their lives, enabling them to measure their level of life satisfaction. SWB is a key concept particularly for research studies on social indicators to analyze the quality of life. More importantly, SWB, which is a way of appraising people's own lives, is an essential component of the comprehensive positive WB (Bearden & Wilder, 2007). Being relatively more stable and lasting unlike momentary or daily happiness, SWB is a more significant goal for people (Zhong & Mitchell, 2010). In this respect, subjective well-being is a relatively stable cognitive orientation towards life (Maggioni, Sands, Kachouie, & Tsarenko, 2019). According to Holm et al. (2017), SWB consists of not only cognitive components like happiness but also of experiences that have the potential of affecting the stability of the concept. The relative significance of cognitive and emotional components in determining general SWB partly depends on the national culture (Ahuvia & Friedman, 1998).

As social scientists were not satisfied with the evaluation of human well-being solely based on macro-economic indicators (e.g. GDP, employment rates, etc.), the scientific evaluation of subjective well-being gained significance in the 1960s (Burroughs & Rindfleisch, 2002). In the existing academic literature, there are three different sources of SWB researched by sociologists and psychologists: (a) demographic factors and personality; (b) unemployment, inflation, and socio-economic conditions such as the income level of the place one lives in; (c) institutional and cultural conditions within the economy and society (Yue et al., 2007). Market-centric arguments provide both macro and micro-level explanations on the question of why SWB is a function of economic activities. At the macro level, the organization of production and distribution to maximize material wealth is the central problem of society. In modern market economies, this issue is addressed by the activities of both economic and political organizations (Oropesa, 1995). Subjective well-being consists of emotional experiences and life satisfaction. According to Luhmann (2017), SWB focuses on the definition, evaluation, and correlations of happiness. Based on the principle arguing that each individual knows if they are happy or not, SWB is considered to be an inherently subjective experience. In particular, the consumption experience of hedonic products leads to the characterization of emotional and life experiences (Zhong & Mitchell, 2012).

There is a hierarchical structure among the components of SWB according to their specific level of originality. This structure is shown in Figure 12.1. The concept of SWB is at the top of this hierarchical model. At this stage, SWB denotes a general assessment of one's life. Right below this level, four components give an additional definite insight of one's SWB. These elements (i.e. pleasurable emotions, unpleasant emotions, opinions on life, and satisfaction of all areas of life) are moderately linked with others, and they are all conceptually correlated (Diener et al., 2003).

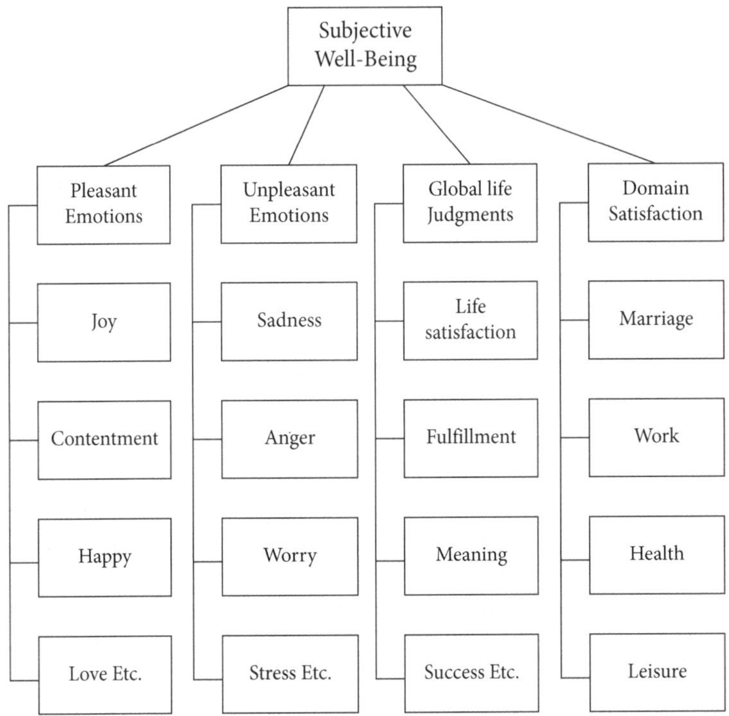

Fig. 12.1: The Components of Subjective Well-Being. **Source:** Diener et al., 2003

4 Consumer Well-Being

The consumer society is a complex system of technologies, cultures, institutions, markets, and business models steered by neoliberalism and the ideology of endless growth (Brown & Vergragt, 2016). The concept of CWB represents a state of development with health and happiness (Fitzgerald, Bias, & Gurley-Calvez, 2017). At the micro-level, individuals increase their levels of well-being by accumulating economic rewards, with income or products being the most valuable economic rewards. CWB depends on the consumption of goods offered in the market as products provide satisfaction (Oropesa, 1995). Consumer well-being can be defined as the assessment of consumers' lives with a cognitive component such as life satisfaction and an emotional component such as happiness (Oral & Thurner, 2019: 278). The difference between SWB and CWB reveals certain differences between the two concepts. These differences can be listed as follows: a) While SWB is in question in the general life of the individual, CWB is valid in personal consumption life; b) While SWB is valid for a wide variety of information and events produced from different sources; CWB applies to consumption-related stimuli and consumer behavior. Despite these differences, the relationship between them is that CWB is an important part of SWB (Zhao & Wei, 2019).

Suranyi-Unger (1981) argues that in economics, individual well-being constitutes one of the cornerstones of the discipline and is concerned primarily with the results of consumptive activity. Therefore, individual WB and CWB are synonymous. In the present day, many scales and indices are used to explain CWB. Although these models measure CWB in different ways, they basically agree on making measurements of CWB on economic bases. According to this orientation, as consumers spend, the level of satisfaction in meeting their needs increases, and the economy develops more and this process causes the increase of the overall CWB (Pancer & Handelman, 2012).

In research studies on psychology and consumer behavior, CWB and happiness have lately regained their central positions due to the rise of the transformative research movement. An important stream of research in this area concentrates on the motivational enhancement of the CWB level. It suggests that successfully attaining individual objectives devotes to the improvement of SWB. Another approach to SWB research focuses on the psychological structure of self-control. It argues that consumers need to control momentary impulses to obtain long-term benefits (Tang, Guo, & Gopinath, 2016).

CWB concerns the points of consideration and self-esteem of consumers as much as their attitudes and behavior. Both individual characteristics and societal forces make consumers focus on their identities and be affected by SWB (Petrescu & Kara, 2018). CWB signifies the assessment of experiences of consumers with products and services (related to the purchase, preparation, utilization, ownership, maintenance, and removal of specific categories of products and services in their regional environment) (Sirgy & Lee, 2006). The purchasing model alleges that CWB is defined by the satisfaction with the purchase of consumer products and services. Product purchasement satisfaction denotes consumer satisfaction due to realization of the purchasing of consumer products and services from retailer. On the other hand, satisfaction stemming from product ownership focuses on subjective experiences regarding material possessions and the contentment arising from these possessions. Purchasing satisfaction can be defined as consumer satisfaction resulting from other activities within the scope of shopping and the acquisition of consumer goods and services. Ownership satisfaction can be described as the contentment originating from the ownership of big-ticket consumer goods such as housing or other properties, consumer electronics, or private transports. Consumption satisfaction stems from the use of goods and services. Maintenance satisfaction arises when the consumer wants to have a product repaired or sent to the technical service. It has two sub-dimensions: a) satisfaction with the maintenance and repair services offered by service providers as well as with the prices of elements like replacement parts (owned goods service), and b) satisfaction with the services making it easier for the consumer to maintain and repair the product on their own (DIY support services) (Lee & Sirgy, 2004). In this regard, CWB can be explained as a process-based, need-based, and community-based concept (Taneja, 2017).

Various issues concerning the correlations between consumer products, attitudes regarding consumption, and SWB are frequently studied. The first issue is the question of whether the accumulation of different consumer goods and the expectations related to this foster SWB. The second issue concerns the question of whether the current and future accumulation can explain the well-established relationship between the income level and SWB. These issues are examined through two alternative methods of assessment consisting of different assumptions regarding the significance of ownership and innovation levels of products. The third issue deals with the question of whether passions for innovation have a positive or negative correlation with subjective well-being (Oropesa, 1995). Similarly, Burroughs and Rindfleisch (2002) underlined that one of the vital subjects of consumer research is the nature of the relationship between consumers and the objects they consume and its impact on CWB levels.

Marketing has the potential to contribute significantly to the improvement of CWB by allowing the production of various goods and services. This potential of marketing not only helps with the improvement of overall quality of life but also contributes to the consumer, society, and environment by enabling the safe production of goods and services (Sirgy & Lee, 2008). Marketing activities might affect well-being positively or negatively. For instance, investment in advanced distribution networks has the potential to create time and space services; therefore it can help with generating wealth and increasing the perceived quality of life. Within the marketing system, it is improbable to provide a high standard of living without a major retail component. Advertising may have a positive impact owing to the increase in the volume of information within the market. However, it might also create the opposite effect due to its annoying and repetitive nature. Furthermore, marketing communication efforts may contradict the goal of reaching SWB standards when institutions use deceptive tools to reinvigorate demand, reinforce certain negative stereotypes, and create inappropriate cultural values (Yue et al., 2007). Through goods and services, consumers can satisfy their physical, material, social, and emotional needs and, consequently, experience happiness. Many definitions of CWB support this argument (Zhao & Wei, 2019).

Conclusion

The present study aimed to present the relationship between CWB and other related concepts. The contemporary consumer has become a factor of pressure for businesses owing to both the abundance of choices of goods/services and the surge in income levels. This has also increased the intent among consumers to maximize their well-being through the goods and services they purchase. Marketing has a substantial influence on CWB as it directly affects satisfaction in the consumer life domain (experiences regarding the marketplace) and indirectly in other aspects of life like health and safety, work, family, leisure, and finance (Sirgy, Lee, & Rahtz, 2007). Consumer well-being might be affected by personal values, social and cultural factors, brand factors, good and service factors, and behavioral factors. Furthermore, it also has an impact on physical and psychological health, consumer loyalty, and word-of-mouth communication (Zhao & Wei, 2019). Businesses ought to provide values for their customers by preserving and improving the well-being of the consumer and society. In this respect, they need to formulate a CWB-oriented marketing philosophy aimed to increase CWB in each stage of consumption.

References

Ahuvia, A. C., & Friedman, D. C. (1998). Income, consumption, and subjective well-being: Toward a composite macromarketing model. *Journal of Macromarketing, 18*(2), pp. 153–168. https://doi.org/10.1177/027614679801800207 Accessed on: 15.03.2020.

Bearden, W. O., & Wilder, R. P. (2007). Household life-cycle effects on consumer wealth and well-being for the recently retired. *Journal of Macromarketing, 27*(4), pp. 389–403. https://doi.org/10.1177/0276146707307142 Accessed on: 15.03.2020.

Brown, H. S., & Vergragt, P. J. (2016). From consumerism to wellbeing: Toward a cultural transition? *Journal of Cleaner Production, 132*, pp. 308–317. https://doi.org/10.1016/j.jclepro.2015.04.107 Accessed on: 15.03.2020.

Burroughs, J. E., & Rindfleisch, A. (2002). Materialism and well-being: A conflicting values perspective. *Journal of Consumer Research, 29*(3), pp. 348–370. https://doi.org/10.1086/344429 Accessed on: 15.03.2020.

Diener, E. (1984). Subjective well-being. *Psychological Bulletin, 95*(3), pp. 542–575.

Diener, E. (1996). Traits can be powerful but are not enough: Lessons from subjective well-being. *Journal of Research in Personality, 30*(0027), pp. 389–399.

Diener, E., Scollon, C. N., & Lucas, R. E. (2003). The evolving concept of subjective well-being: The multifaceted nature of happiness. *Advances in Cell Aging and Gerontology, 15*(03), pp. 41–88. https://doi.org/10.1016/S1566-3124(03)15003-1 Accessed on: 15.03.2020.

Fitzgerald, M. P., Bias, T. K., & Gurley-Calvez, T. (2017). The affordable care act and consumer well-being: Knowns and unknowns. *Journal of Consumer Affairs, 51*(1), pp. 27–53. https://doi.org/10.1111/joca.12059 Accessed on: 15.03.2020.

Guevarra, D. A., & Howell, R. T. (2015). To have in order to do: Exploring the effects of consuming experiential products on well-being. *Journal of Consumer Psychology, 25*(1), pp. 28–41. https://doi.org/10.1016/j.jcps.2014.06.006 Accessed on: 15.03.2020.

Guillen-Royo, M. (2019). Sustainable consumption and wellbeing: Does on-line shopping matter? *Journal of Cleaner Production, 229*, pp. 1112–1124. https://doi.org/10.1016/j.jclepro.2019.05.061 Accessed on: 15.03.2020.

Holm, M. R., Lugosi, P., Croes, R. R., & Torres, E. N. (2017). Risk-tourism, risk-taking and subjective well-being: A review and synthesis. *Tourism Management, 63*, pp. 115–122. https://doi.org/10.1016/j.tourman.2017.06.004 Accessed on: 15.03.2020.

Iyer, R., & Muncy, J. A. (2016). Attitude toward consumption and subjective well-being. *Journal of Consumer Affairs, 50*(1), pp. 48–67. https://doi.org/10.1111/joca.12079 Accessed on: 15.03.2020.

Lee, D. J., & Sirgy, M. J. (2004). Quality-of-life (QOL) marketing: Proposed antecedents and consequences. *Journal of Macromarketing, 24* (1), pp. 44–58. https://doi.org/10.1177/0276146704263922 Accessed on: 15.03.2020.

Lee, D. J., Sirgy, M. J., Larsen, V., & Wright, N. D. (2002). Developing a subjective measure of consumer well-being. *Journal of Macromarketing, 22*(2), pp. 158–169. https://doi.org/10.1177/0276146702238219 Accessed on 15.04.2020.

Luhmann, M. (2017). Using big data to study subjective well-being. *Current Opinion in Behavioral Sciences, 18*, pp. 28–33. https://doi.org/10.1016/j.cobeha.2017.07.006 Accessed on: 15.03.2020.

Macdonald, M., & Douthitt, R. A. (1992). Consumption theories and consumers' assessments of subjective well-being. *Journal of Consumer Affairs, 26*(2), pp. 243–261. https://doi.org/10.1111/j.1745-6606.1992.tb00026.x Accessed on: 15.03.2020.

Maggioni, I., Sands, S., Kachouie, R., & Tsarenko, Y. (2019). Shopping for well-being: The role of consumer decision-making styles. *Journal of Business Research, 105*(August), pp. 21–32. https://doi.org/10.1016/j.jbusres.2019.07.040 Accessed on: 15.03.2020.

Oral, C., & Thurner, J. Y. (2019). The impact of anti-consumption on consumer well-being. *International Journal of Consumer Studies, 43*(3), pp. 277–288. https://doi.org/10.1111/ijcs.12508 Accessed on: 15.03.2020.

Oropesa, R. S. (1995). Consumer possessions, consumer passions, and subjective well-being. *Sociological Forum, 10*(2), pp. 215–244. https://doi.org/10.1007/BF02095959 Accessed on 15.04.2020.

Pancer, E., & Handelman, J. (2012). The evolution of consumer well-being. *Journal of Historical Research in Marketing, 4*(1), pp. 177–189. https://doi.org/10.1108/17557501211195118 Accessed on: 15.03.2020.

Peterson, M., & Ekici, A. (2007). Consumer attitude toward marketing and subjective quality of life in the context of a developing country. *Journal of Macromarketing, 27*(4), pp. 350–359. https://doi.org/10.1177/0276146707307125 Accessed on: 15.03.2020.

Petrescu, M., & Kara, A. (2018). Consumer aspirations and subjective well-being. *Journal of International Consumer Marketing, 30*(5), pp. 304–316. https://doi.org/10.1080/08961530.2018.1459219 Accessed on: 15.03.2020.

Seegebarth, B., Peyer, M., Balderjahn, I., & Wiedmann, K. P. (2016). The sustainability roots of anticonsumption lifestyles and initial ınsights regarding their effects on consumers' well-Being. *Journal of Consumer Affairs*, *50*(1), pp. 68–99. https://doi.org/10.1111/joca.12077 Accessed on: 15.03.2020.

Sirgy, M. J., & Lee, D. J. (2006). Macro measures of consumer well-being (CWB): A critical analysis and a research agenda. *Journal of Macromarketing*, *26*(1), pp. 27–44. https://doi.org/10.1177/0276146705285669 Accessed on: 15.03.2020.

Sirgy, M. J., & Lee, D. J. (2008). Well-being marketing: An ethical business philosophy for consumer goods firms. *Journal of Business Ethics*, *77*(4), pp. 377–403. https://doi.org/10.1007/s10551-007-9363-y Accessed on: 15.03.2020.

Sirgy, M. J., Lee, D. J., & Rahtz, D. (2007). Research on consumer well-being (CWB): Overview of the field and introduction to the special issue. *Journal of Macromarketing*, *27*(4), pp. 341–349. https://doi.org/10.1177/0276146707307212 Accessed on: 15.03.2020.

Suranyi-Unger, Jr., T. (1981). Consumer behavior and consumer well-being: An economist's digest. *Journal of Consumer Research*, *8*(2), pp. 132. https://doi.org/10.1086/208849 Accessed on: 15.03.2020.

Taneja, R. (2017). Consumer well-being – Contemporary conceptualization. *Indian Journal of Economics and Development*, *5*(1), pp. 1–4.

Tang, C., Guo, L., & Gopinath, M. (2016). A social-cognitive model of consumer well-being: A longitudinal exploration of the role of the service organization. *Journal of Service Research*, *19*(3), pp. 307–321. https://doi.org/10.1177/1094670516637675 Accessed on: 15.03.2020.

Yue, P., Zinkhan, G. M., & Shibin, S. (2007). The subjective well-being of nations: A role for marketing? *Journal of Macromarketing*, *27*(4), pp. 360–369. https://doi.org/10.1177/0276146707307211 Accessed on: 15.03.2020.

Zhao, C., & Wei, H. (2019). The highest hierarchy of consumption: A Literature review of consumer well-being. *Open Journal of Social Sciences*, *07*(04), pp. 135–149. https://doi.org/10.4236/jss.2019.74012 Accessed on: 15.03.2020.

Zhong, J. Y., & Mitchell, V. W. (2010). A mechanism model of the effect of hedonic product consumption on well-being. *Journal of Consumer Psychology*, *20*(2), pp. 152–162. https://doi.org/10.1016/j.jcps.2010.01.001 Accessed on: 15.03.2020.

Zhong, J. Y., & Mitchell, V. W. (2012). Does consumer well-being affect hedonic consumption? *Psychology & Marketing*, *8*, pp. 583–594. https://doi.org/10.1002/mar Accessed on: 15.03.2020.

Elif KARA

13 Consumer Wisdom

Introduction

Consumption has become the most significant concept used for defining present-day societies and as a means of one's self-expression. It is no longer exclusively about the fulfillment of needs. In modern societies shaped by consumer culture, the main purpose of individuals in life is consumption as they express themselves and maintain their existence through it. This results in the rapid and uncontrolled depletion of resources. Today, consumption is not only an economic concept. As it occurs, concepts like time, knowledge, and culture are used up at a fast pace and eviscerated. In modern societies, consumption is being transformed into a craze as it is an expression of one's personality and social status. The changing perception of consumption leads people to consume unconsciously, which is costly in the social sense.

Currently, we are faced with the COVID-19 pandemic threatening the whole world. Everyone around the globe is confined in their homes, world economies have come to a screeching halt, and everyone tries to adapt to the confinement. Daily activities like working, meetings, gatherings, classes take place between four walls. Our slogan is: "Life fits inside your home". This pandemic is one of the catastrophes experienced by humankind in the past couple of years. Lately, the world struggles with major earthquakes, droughts, forest fires, tsunamis, and landslides. Do these natural disasters take place by themselves or do they stem from the imbalances by human activities? Unfortunately, most of such geo-climatic events show similarities with the worst scenarios indicated by climate change activists. In this regard, what must humankind do to achieve a sustainable economic model without harming the environment and ecological balance?

That is to say, many present-day problems like natural disasters or health conditions arise from irresponsible consumption and the wastage of resources. The present outlook proves that the current mindset cannot acknowledge the facts and cope with these problems. The idea that older civilizations could have had economic systems and practices based on a life in harmony with nature gradually becomes more prevalent. Therefore, making use of the wisdom of older generations, integrating their ideas and practices into the present day, or, in other words, "learning from the philosophies that have stood the test of time" (Kakoty, 2017: 3215) has become increasingly important. Ancient wisdom and philosophy are considered to play a guiding role in achieving sustainability and using resources. The failure to use resources properly and efficiently, a world order based on consumption, the disregard of the environment, ecology and the finiteness of resources, the perception of the human merely as a material belief, and the neglection of spirituality have culminated in the current state of the world. At this juncture, the concept of wisdom comes into play. So, what is wisdom? What are the aspects of wisdom signifying the increasing awareness of the consumer? How is this wise consumer expected to behave?

This chapter will examine the concept of wisdom from the point of various scientific disciplines and philosophy while discussing the components of consumer wisdom. It will also clarify the common characteristics of and differences between consumer wisdom and other similar concepts.

1 The Concept of Wisdom

Wisdom is the capacity of internalizing important matters and putting them into practice through common sense, good manners, comprehension, knowledge acquisition, and intuitive understanding. It is related to other personal characteristics such as ethics and kindness, going beyond oneself, self-knowledge based on experience, mercy, impartial judgment, and non-attachment. A wise person is considered to be an individual having these traits. The Oxford Dictionary defines wisdom as the capacity of making accurate evaluations about issues related to life and behavior; the soundness of judgment in the choice of means and ends; or enlightenment, learning, and honesty (Oxford English Dictionary, 2019).

Wisdom denotes the use of knowledge to pursue an honest and good life. In Ancient Greek philosophy, wisdom is defined as rational behavior; Socrates identified it as knowing oneself while Epicurus describes it as a serene and indifferent state of mind attained through virtue. The philosophy underlying wisdom is that wise people know they know little, therefore they embark on a long and arduous journey of further self-development. This journey is a life-long one that does not end at a certain point (Eflatun, 1999: 86; Epikuros, 1949: 65).

From a mythological and philosophical perspective, the Ancient Greek associated wisdom with a virtue represented by goddesses Athena and Metis. For Plato and Socrates, the word "philosophy" denotes the love of wisdom. As for Aristotle, he defined wisdom as the act of understanding why things are the way they are through rationality. In Plato's Apology of Socrates, Socrates sought for people that might be wiser than him and saw that they did not have the right knowledge. On top of that, they were not aware of this and they did not know that they did not know. In response, saying that wisdom is one's humility and awareness of their ignorance, he uttered these immortal words: "Well, although I do not suppose that either of us knows anything really beautiful and good, I am better off than he is - for he knows nothing, and thinks that he knows. I neither know nor think that I know". Indicating he knows that he knows nothing, he goes down in history (Fine, 2008: 52; Ryan, 2018: 234).

From a pedagogical perspective on wisdom, Nicholas Maxwell believes that the purpose of academia is the search for, not the impartation of, knowledge. He states that one's experience and knowledge make one stronger but without the search and love of wisdom, this knowledge can harm one as much as it can help (Maxwell, 2007: 56).

From a psychological point of view, wisdom is perceived to be the ability to adapting to difficult living circumstances and coping with problems even though it is similar to intelligence, perceptiveness, and shrewdness. There are different opinions on the psychological definitions of wisdom. Yet what is important is that wisdom encompasses metacognitive processes with deep thoughts on life and serious matters. There is a general consensus regarding these processes. The processes of wisdom include one's awareness of their limits, the focus on contexts and the whole picture, acceptance of change and uncertainty, the capacity to look at an event from different perspectives, and the ability to merge these perspectives. Experimental research studies show that wisdom is different from one's IQ level (Grossmann et al., 2010: 7247).

The concept of consciousness is often defined as "awareness" (Tulving, 1985: 2). As for wisdom, it denotes the use of inferences from knowledge and experience for a virtuous and honest life. As seen in these definitions, consciousness and wisdom are different concepts. While the former signifies the awareness of events, the latter denotes the act of taking a stance towards these events and making this a philosophy of life. Based on this, a conscious consumer is an individual with a sense of social responsibility considering the factor and groups that might be affected by their purchases and does shopping with this awareness; this way of consuming goods and services is called conscious consumption (Karaca, 2019: 149). A conscious consumer engages in consumption to satisfy their needs without waste, with an awareness of their responsibilities towards the natural environment and other people, within the framework of universal rights (Özbölük, 2010: 53).

2 Consumer Wisdom

Human beings have lived by consuming the resources around them and altering their environment since the first day they came into existence. Consumer behavior brought about by the modern world has led to an increase in overall consumption. The concept of consumer wisdom has emerged with the objectives of controlling this increase in consumption, saving resources for future generations, and eliminating the risks for them arising from unconscious consumption. Environmental pollution and the emergence of overwhelming evidence for the danger to natural life due to the surge in consumption has led to the discussions regarding concepts such as conscious consumerism/consumption and voluntary simplicity.

Similar to consumer wisdom, the concept of voluntary simplicity was defined by Richard Gregg in 1936 as a philosophy of life according to which the individual gets rid of insignificant masses of material possessions while leading an honest, simple, and sincere life (Argan et al., 2012: 205). Voluntary simplicity also includes the lessened use of material goods and self-sufficiency (Iwata, 1997: 223). Voluntary simplifiers adopt an environmentally-conscious and simple lifestyle without any external pressure (Özgül, 2010: 119). The concept signifies knowing how to consume for a simple life and achieving happiness with this understanding of simplicity (Alexander, 2011: 113). Despite their material wealth, voluntary simplifiers feel spiritual peace brought about by a simple life instead of consuming resources unconsciously (Walther et al., 2016: 38).

Recently, a concept pushing beyond the limits of voluntary simplicity has emerged. Research inquiries study a significant social concept that dates back a long time, underlies the philosophy of many religions. These studies indicate that consumers have developed a novel kind of purchasing behavior. This is called "consumer wisdom" or "mindful shopping". Studies conducted by Djelassi et al. (2009: 38) demonstrate that consumers become gradually more mindful, cautious, and controlled while shopping. This movement has three strategies. Buying less, buying for lower prices, and not falling for material temptations. Consumer wisdom is similar to the movement of voluntary simplicity, but they are fundamentally different concepts. The aim of voluntary simplicity is to reduce consumption, to overcome the addiction to consumption, and to lead a self-sufficient life that relies less on material objects by taking control of one's life. In consumer consumption, however, this kind of conscious behavior is translated into a philosophy of life with a deeper meaning.

There are only a few studies on consumer wisdom. Other studies on this subject were compiled by Luchs and Mick (2018), defining five dimensions of consumer wisdom. These dimensions are intentionality, contemplation, emotional mastery, openness, and transcendence.

2.1 Intentionality

It signifies the intent in consumption. With an awareness of the significant and systematic role consumer behavior plays in the construction and maintenance of one's lifestyle, the individual accepts their responsibility for the management of a lifestyle within the scope of one's existing resources (Kakoty, 2017: 3215). One's intent is the most important step for accomplishing something. A positive intent makes it more likely for a thought to be translated into action. All behavior goes through a cognitive process occurs within the framework of an intention in a rational manner (Buğday & Babaoğlu, 2016: 201). In other words, intentionality signifies the case in which the individual intends to adopt and maintain a wise style of consumption.

Underlying the theory of planned behavior, rational consumption denotes the argument alleging that individuals think rationally while making a decision, make rational decisions by collecting and using information and act according to a certain plan. The behavior displayed by individuals is a result of a rational process in which factors affecting personal behavior go through a cognitive process (Ajzen & Fishbein, 1975: 304). According to this theory, the most important determinant of behavior is intention. A positive intent increases the chances of a behavior occurring. If the means and resources are not sufficient for an action or behavior, the possibility of intent formation is also reduced. Here, it is important to underline the difference between the intention for a purpose and the intention for a behavior. For instance, "the intention to buy environmentally-friendly products" signifies the intention for a behavior whereas "helping with the preservation of natural resources" denotes an intention for a purpose. What is important here is not the type of intention but the existence of a behavioral intention for the protection of natural resources (Buğday & Babaoğlu, 2016: 201).

2.2 Contemplation

Intentionality and contemplation are related to one another in consumer decisions. This relationship in which wise consumer decisions are governed by sincere intentions denotes the contemplation on the lessons learned from the outcomes of past choices and behavior. What makes intentionality and contemplation different is that while intentionality signifies a model of collective choices and behavior in time, it also denotes a series of superordinate consumption intentions.

Having intentions means that the consumer intends to adopt wise consumption. It signifies a model of collective choices and behavior of consumers in time. As for contemplation, it denotes the process in which one thinks about and evaluates one's consumption choices within a certain time. This occurs in three ways: through retrospection, prospection, and prudent reasoning (Luchs & Mick, 2018: 376).

Retrospection: It signifies the lessons learned from the past consumption behavior of the consumer in question. It also means the influence of these outcomes and lessons on future purchases and consumer behavior. For instance, clothes bought with the thought of wearing after losing some weight yet left in the closet with its tags on or tools bought thinking that they would be useful but never used are clues for one's consumer behavior. In their study, Luchs and Mick (2018) saw that the items participants purchased impulsively without any consideration (e.g. a small trinket) only served to occupy space on the shelves. They indicated that particular attention must be paid to fast decisions and unrestrained hopes or expectations in certain contexts. This insight does not come with old age; it completely depends on one's awareness of mindful consumption. Some individuals make use of the experiences and mistakes of others to achieve wisdom in consumption. For example, one participant observed the purchases of their grandfather buying a new car even though he already has multiple vehicles in his garage and saw that he was not happy at all. This guided them to form their consumption habits.

Prospection: The first method uses past experiences, whereas the method of prospection denotes the use of experiences related to the future. It is about the visualization of future purchasing behavior and simulating it to the maximum extent possible. In the aforementioned study by Luchs and Mick (2018: 377), one of the participants tests whether the house they think of buying will meet their expectations before and after the purchase and, therefore, be worth buying. For instance, they once went to work from the location of the house as if they were living there to see if the house is convenient for them. The participant imagines how such big-ticket purchases will change their life and makes their purchases accordingly.

Prudent Reasoning: Prudent reasoning is not limited to important decisions such as whether to buy an automobile. Even if the item considered for purchasing it a small object like a pair of sunglasses, prudent reasoning plays a role. For instance, why would one buy a pair of sunglasses for $130 when they can get two pairs for $15? In the case of mindful shopping, one needs to opt for the purchase of $15 based on the price difference. But if one thinks that they spend too much time under the sun and good health has no price, they must buy a single pair for 130$. Besides, instead of buying ten pairs of low-quality sunglasses is almost the same as the price of one good-quality pair. Prudent reasoning calls for such a way of thinking.

Contemplation is a novel concept within the scope of consumer psychology. It means that the consumer is satisfied with what they have, does not purchase more than they need, and questions their consumption behavior. This questioning includes the assessment and research of the need for the good or service concerned and the functionality of these products in fulfilling the need(s) in question if there is a need. As far as this feature of contemplation is concerned, they guide individuals while giving up the patterns of automatic thinking and harmful behavior. It is possible to say that "mindful consumption is an inquiry-based process that endows consumers with awareness and insight to choose their responses rather than react blindly or habitually" (Bahl et al., 2016: 200).

2.3 Emotional Mastery

It denotes one's capacity to manage their present and future emotions. Emotional maturity transcends the mere regulation of purchasing behavior (Kidwell et al., 2008: 156). At the same time, it also helps one avoid situations leading to unwanted emotional states like regret, guilt, and anxiety. In other words, the consumer is able to prevent regrettable and unpleasant situations by questioning their purchase and, therefore, protect themselves from negative emotional states. Emotional mastery also induces positive emotions like joy, peace, and flow (Luchs & Mick, 2018: 378).

Socially responsible individuals look at consumption from a critical standpoint. Fundamentally, these individuals do not perceive consumption negatively and believe that it might contribute to the development of societies. However, they need to get rid of the destructive and devastating effects of consumption while doing so. One needs to be aware of the fact that the meaning of life is not hidden within commodities and objects but within emotions (Gomez & Toulouse, 2008: 493). In this respect, emotional mastery allows one to be aware of the emotions related to consumption and use them strategically. Mastery prevents us from experiencing negative emotions while inducing positive ones (Luchs & Mick, 2018: 378).

2.4 Openness

In consumer wisdom, openness means that the consumer is willing to try new consumption habits. Studies show that individuals are open to consuming more or to try new products, similarly, they are also open to experiences that would allow them to attain wisdom in their consumption habits (Luchs & Mick, 2018: 380).

2.5 Transcendence

It denotes the impact of one's consumption on others. The entire world faces the consequences of one's consumption. Intrinsically, we are all connected with invisible bonds. In the study of Luchs and Mick (2018: 380), participants talked about consumption behavior including kindness and empathy with compassion as their starting point. Thinking of and empathizing with others starts from one's closest circle and spreads around in waves. This compassion consists of a multifaceted caring not only for other people but also for the natural environment.

Socially-responsible consumption and environmentally-friendly consumption is often used synonymously (Roberts, 1995: 110). Roberts (1995) indicated that socially-responsible consumption has two dimensions: societal and environmental. The purpose of the environmental dimension is the avoidance to buy products that might harm the environment, whereas the objective of the societal dimension is to avoid using the products of companies disregarding societal welfare. Individuals with a sense of social responsibility are aware of the problems that might arise from their consumption as much as they are aware of the functional benefits of the products concerned. To this end, they utilize their consumer behavior to draw attention to social events (Webster & Frederich: 1975: 188).

One must assume responsibility to protect the natural environment and to support its improvement. This is necessary for our society, culture, and the world to be left for future generations. There is no second world and we need to take good care of it.

Wise consumption is attained through the compilation of various resources including the observation of others, knowledge acquisition, and religion. Wise consumption is a lifestyle embraced by many individuals ranging from animal rights activists to local farmers not using non-recyclable packaging and people adopting philosophies like anti-consumption or pro-consumption. Research studies on the concept of wise consumers revealed that individuals with environmental and social concerns are driven by a sense of *compassion* (Luchs & Mick, 2018: 382). Environmentally-conscious individuals are aware of their responsibilities entailed by their purchasing and consumption decisions. These individuals have a sense of responsibility for the use of resources and towards the heritage to be left for future generations. For this reason, they buy products based on their packaging, content, production conditions, usage, and their decomposition in nature. Therefore, they make producers consider the ways their products are produced, influencing various product types. They provide an incentive for companies to produce recyclable products the packaging of which does not harm the environment, using less energy (Buğday, 2015: 74). The compassion towards the environment, future generations, and other people encourages the adoption of such a consumption style and translates this attitude into action.

Conclusion and Suggestions

Research studies manifest that consumer research on wisdom is not sufficient. More than half of the results of studies and articles on wisdom indicate the prevalence of the five factors discussed above. The explanations and inferences indicated in this chapter lead to a definition of consumer wisdom as follows: "Consumer wisdom is the pursuit of well-being for oneself and for others through mindful management of consumption-related choices and behaviors, as realized through the integrated application of Intentionality, Contemplation, Emotional Mastery, Openness, and Transcendence" (Luchs & Mick, 2018: 384).

We are not the only ones affected by the outcomes of our consumption behavior. They affect the environment and the entire world. It is necessary to develop a style of action based on environmental consciousness and social responsibility. Consumer wisdom is a philosophy of life essential for environmental protection and to leave a beautiful world with preserved natural resources. This is therapeutic for both the world and for our existence.

Future studies might deal with certain aspects and dimensions of wisdom in a more in-depth manner.

References

Ajzen, I. & Fishbein, M. (1975). *Belief, Attitude, Intention and Behavior: An Introduction to Theory and Research*. Reading: Addison-Wesley. https://trove.nla.gov.au/work/14275432?q&versionId=26117886 Accessed on: 25.04.2020.

Alexander, S. (2011). The voluntary simplicity movement: Reimagining the good life beyond consumer culture. University of Melbourne. *International Journal of Environmental, Cultural, Economic, and Social Sustainability*, 7(3), pp. 133–150.

Argan, M., Argan Tokay, M. & Sevim, N. (2012). Tükenmeden tükettiren yaşam tarzı: gönüllü sadelik, *17. Ulusal Pazarlama Kongresi Bildiri Kitabı*, Balıkesir, Üniversitesi Yayın No 39, Burhaniye Uygulamalı Bilimler Yüksekokulu, Yayın No:1, pp. 201–220.

Bahl, S., Milne, G. R., Ross, S. M., Mick, D. G., Grier, S. A., Chugani, S. K. & Boesen-Mariani, S. (2016). Mindfulness: Its transformative potential for consumer, societal, and environmental well-being. *Journal of Public Policy & Marketing*, 35, pp. 198–210.

Buğday, E. B. (2015). *Bilinçli Tüketici Ölçeği Geliştirme Çalışması*, PhD Thesis, Hacettepe Üniversitesi Sosyal Bilimler Enstitüsü, Ankara.

Buğday, E. B. & Babaoğlu, M. (2016). Bilinçli tüketici kavramının boyutları: Bilinçli tüketim davranışının yeniden tanımlanması. *SosyoEkonomi*, 24(30), pp. 187–206.

Djelassi, S., Collin-Lachaud, I. & Odou, P. (2009). Crise des pouvoirs d'achat: Les Fosse-Gomez, M. H., Ozcarlar-Toulouse, N. (2008). Towards an Understanding of Consumption Objectors. *European Advances in Consumer Research*, 8, pp. 493–497.

Eflatun (1999). Sokrates'in Savunması. (Trans. Numan Özcan). Şule Yay., İstanbul.

Epikuros (1949). Herotodos'a Mektup. (Büyük Filozoflar Antolojisi). (Trans. Mehmet Karasan). Meb Yay. İstanbul.

Fine, G. (2008). Does Socrates Claim to Know that He Knows Nothing? *Oxford Studies in Ancient Philosophy*, 35, pp. 49–88.

Gomez, M. H. & Toulouse, N. (2008). Towards an understanding of consumption objectors. *European Advances in Consumer Research*, 8, pp. 493–497.

Grossmann, I., Na, J., Varnum, M. E., Park, D. C., Kitayama, S. & Nisbett, R. E. (2010). Reasoning about social conflicts improves into old age. *Proceedings of the National Academy of Sciences*, 107(16), pp. 7246–50.

Iwata, O. (1997). Attitudinal and behavioral correlates of voluntary simplicity lifestyles. *Social Behavior and Personality*, 25(3), pp. 223–240.

Kakoty, S. (2017). Ecology, sustainability and traditional wisdom. *Journal of Cleaner Production*, 172, pp. 3215–3224.

Karaca, Ş. (2019). Bireysel sosyal sorumluluğun bilinçli tüketim davranışı üzerindeki etkisini incelemeye yönelik bir çalışma. *Dokuz Eylül Üniversitesi Sosyal Bilimler Enstitüsü Dergisi*, 21(1), pp. 147–172.

Kidwell, B., Hardesty, D. M. & Childers, T. L. (2008). Consumer emotional intelligence: Conceptualization, measurement, and the prediction of consumer decision making. *Journal of Consumer Research*, 35, pp. 154–166.

Luchs, M. G. & Mick, D. G. (2018). Consumer wisdom: A theoretical framework of five integrated facets. *Journal of Consumer Psychology*, 28(3), pp. 365–392.

Maxwell, N. (2007). From knowledge to wisdom: The need for an academic revolution. *London Review of Education*, 5(2), pp. 97–115(19).

Oxford English Dictionary (2019). "Wisdom". https://www.oed.com/view/Entry/229491 Accessed on: 26.05.2020.

Özbölük, T. (2010). *Pazarlamada Bilinçli Tüketim ve Tüketicilerin Bilinçli Tüketime İlişkin Tutumlarının Belirlenmesine Yönelik Bir Araştırma*. Master Thesis. Cumhuriyet Üniversitesi, Sosyal Bilimler Enstitüsü, Sivas.

Özgül, E. (2010). Tüketicilerin değer yapıları, gönüllü sade yaşam tarzı ve sürdürebilir tüketim üzerindeki etkisi. *H.Ü. İktisadi ve İdari Bilimler Dergisi*, 28(2), pp. 117–150.

Roberts, J. A. (1995). Profiling levels of socially responsible consumer behavior: A cluster analytic approach and its implications for marketing. *Journal of Marketing Theory and Practice*, 3(4), pp. 97–117.

Ryan, S. (2018). Zalta, E. N. (Ed.), The Stanford Encyclopedia of Philosophy (Fall 2018 edition), Metaphysics Research Lab, Stanford University, https://plato.stanford.edu/contents.html Accessed on: 12.04.2020.

Tulving, E. (1985). Memory and consciousness. *Canadian Psychology*, 26(19), pp. 1–12.

Walther, C. S., Sandlin, J. A. & Wuensch, K. (2016). Voluntary simplifiers, spirituality and happiness. *Humanity & Society*, 40(1), pp. 22–42.

Webster, Jr. & Frederich, E. (1975). Determining the characteristics of the socially conscious consumer. *The Journal of Consumer Research*, 2(3), pp. 188–196.

Section 2 Theories of Consumer Psychology

Hayrettin ZENGİN and Eda KUTLU

14 Customer Evangelism and Its Theoretical Bases

Introduction

In the present chapter of this book dealing with many dimensions of the psychology of consumption, theoretical dimensions of evangelism, a concept borrowed from the phenomenon of religion, with which consumption is related in a reciprocal and dialectic way, will be examined. Consumption can be defined simply as the fulfillment of human needs by goods and services. As for religion, it can be explained as a phenomenon playing a crucial role in meeting the individual and societal needs of people in social life (Demirezen, 2015). Taking the simplest definitions of the two concepts into account, the relationship between consumption and religion has a dialectic aspect as far as the common point of satisfying human needs and wants is concerned. The reciprocity and dialectic nature of the relationship between these two phenomena bring about the transitivity of the concepts related to them. A good example of the transitivity between concepts is the concept of "evangelism".

Evangelism can be defined as the zealous act of disseminating the gospels in the holy scripture among those who have yet to hear of them and converting them (into Christianity). Evangelism, a religious term, has been used in marketing literature following the second half of the 2000s. Initially coined by the CEO of Apple in the literature on marketing, the concept of evangelism has started to be used by other global companies like Google, Microsoft, and Adobe regarding their clients.

Introduced to marketing literature with the book titled *Selling The Dream* by Guy Kawasaki, the concept of evangelism was defined as the devotion to a brand like being devoted to a religion and, as it is the case with religious missionaries, as the considerable effort to convince others to become clients of the brand in question through word-of-mouth communication (Kawasaki, 1992). Explained as customer evangelism by Kawasaki, the concept signifies a group of clients conveying their positive emotions and thoughts about a specific brand to other clients with a desire to influence their consumption behaviors. The way of communication conducted by this group can be likened to a preaching aimed to convince others to become clients of the brand in question (Doss, 2014). The source of this strong motivation to convince other consumers to become customers of the said brand is the so-called "holy" bond with the brand.

Evangelist customers are passionately devoted to the brand and considered themselves as a part of the organization/brand in question.

Furthermore, this group of customers also states that nothing would be the same in their lives should they abandon the brand (McConnell & Huba, 2007; Collins et al., 2015). Reflecting this strong bond with the brand to their behavior as well, evangelist customers provide significant advantages to businesses in the present-day market conditions, in which finding new clients has become increasingly difficult, by trying to convince other consumers to become customers of the brand in question with no thought of personal gain. The competitive advantage of having evangelist customers has resulted in an increase in the interest in customer evangelism among researchers.

This chapter begins with a description of the concept of customer evangelism. In addition, it also examines the reasons behind customer evangelism or, in other words, the strong bond between the client and the brand, using theories from psychology/social psychology. The chapter also includes a review of marketing literature regarding the concept.

1 Customer Evangelism

Signifying a "bringer of good news", the word *"evangelist"* derives from the Greek root *euangelos* (Meiners et al., 2010: 89). As for the term "evangelism", it means preaching the holy scripture, delivering it to people who have never heard of it, and trying to convert them into Christianity while defending this faith at an advanced level (Green, 1984: 34). Known as brand evangelism or customer evangelism in marketing literature, the concept was first used in the book titled *Selling the Dream* penned by Guy Kawasaki, an Apple employee, within the context of marketing. Kawasaki (1992: 4) defines customer evangelists as clients with an inner drive to spread positive word-of-mouth, using their own sources to increase the passion among existing/new clients for the brand. Customer evangelism is the purchasing intention arising from strong affinity and admiration for the brand in question (Chaudhuri & Holbrook, 2001); it brings about the transfer of information, ideas, and emotions about the brand to others (Doss, 2014).

Although similar to other customer groups actively engaging in word-of-mouth communication such as market mavens, opinion leaders, influencers, and brand advocates, customer evangelists differ from these groups with the translation of their passion and loyalty into action. Customer evangelists are inherently extroverted, recommend the brand to others passionately, and discredit rival brands. Furthermore, they place great trust in the brand and, as a result of this, they consider themselves to be a part of the organization or a community (Arkonsuo et al., 2015; McConnell & Huba, 2007).

Customer evangelism is a psychological concept and stems from the emotional attraction of the client towards the brand (Scarpi, 2010). As it is the case in religious evangelism, customer evangelism is also a transformative experience affecting a minority among the users of goods and services (Becerra & Badrinarayanan, 2013). The varying levels of evangelistic tendencies among clients source from a wide range of psychological and characteristic features of an individual such as personality traits (Doss & Carstens, 2014; Kautish, 2010). At this point, understanding why some customers form deep and permanent bonds with the brand and why they are more motivated to recommend the brand to others provides a competitive advantage to businesses for maintaining sustainable a relationship between the brand and clients.

2 Theoretical Bases of Customer Evangelism

As the concept of customer evangelism consists of psychological and emotional elements, its theoretical bases can be explained with theories of psychology and social psychology. In this section, based on the four-dimensional structure (Quintessence, Word-of-Mouth, Authenticity, Consumer Collectives) proposed to describe customer evangelism in a study titled *Identifying Customer Evangelists* by Collins et al. (2015), each aspect of customer evangelism will be explained through theories of psychology/social psychology and the reasons why customers become evangelists for a brand will be examined.

2.1 Quintessence

The psychological theory to be used for explaining the *Quintessence* dimension of customer evangelism, signifying the sacred/emotional bond formed by the customer with the brand (Belk et al., 1989), is *the theory of attachment* proposed by John Bowlby. Conceptualized by Bowlby in his book titled *Attachment*, published in 1969, the theory of attachment is one of the key theories used to explain the attachment of an individual to something. The theory states that attachment is shaped in accordance with the nature of the relationship formed with the attachment figure (the mother or the caretaker looking after the baby) in infancy (Bowlby, 2012). The first attachment of the individual to the attachment figure during infancy underlies their attachment in future relationships (Ainsworth, 1982). Based on the nature of the attachment in infancy, the individual displays three different styles of attachment behavior. The three styles shaping the dimensions of the theory are secure attachment, avoidance attachment, and anxiety attachment (Hazan & Shaver, 1987). The individual receiving sufficient attention and support from the attachment figure whenever they need in infancy develops secure attachment. A person displaying secure attachment has self-esteem and high self-respect; they behave rationally in their attachment relationships. Avoidance attachment occurs when no emotional bond with the attachment figure was formed during infancy, as a result of the mother refusing to satisfy the needs of the baby or acting in a distant and negligent manner. Due to a lack of confidence, individuals displaying avoidance attachment refrain from establishing attachment relationships with any person or object, refusing emotional attachment. In the case of anxiety attachment, the fear of losing is dominant due to the existence of an attachment figure who was inconsistent in satisfying the needs of the baby during infancy. Not being able to reach their mother when they need during infancy, the individual fears of abandonment and loss throughout their life and, as a result, their attachment is very strong and obsessive in any given context (Ainsworth, 1982; Feeney & Noller, 1990; Hazan & Shaver 1987).

Having an important place in the literature on psychology, the theory of attachment has been also used recently in marketing literature in order to make sense of consumer behavior in various contexts. In this respect, research studies examining the effect of different attachment styles on brand loyalty (Bidmon, 2017; Mende et al., 2013) might be given as examples. Based on these studies, the use of the theory of attachment is recommended to explain the Quintessence dimension of customer evangelism denoting the sacred bond between the client and the brand; different attachment styles are thought to influence customer/brand evangelism as it is the case for brand loyalty. Explaining why certain clients are more likely to show evangelistic tendencies through the theory of attachment would contribute to the existing academic literature with the further conceptualization of customer evangelism, a relatively novel field of research.

2.2 Word-of-Mouth

Propaganda Theory

The first theory to be used to explain *Word-of-Mouth*, the second dimension of customer evangelism, is the propaganda theory. In line with the study of Scarpi (2010) stating that reducing the passion and efforts of evangelist customers for convincing others to become clients of a brand to merely word-of-mouth would be unfair, the concept of propaganda and the propaganda theory are thought to be useful in explaining the behavior of evangelist customers. The theory was conceptualized with the book *Propaganda and Psychological Warfare* penned by Dr. Terence H. Qualter. Like evangelism, propaganda is also borrowed from religion and signifies spreading the Christian faith to the world (Qualter, 1980). Traditionally speaking, propaganda is defined as "the attempt to transmit social and political values in the hope of affecting people's thinking, emotions, and behavior" (Huang; 2015: 422). In a more general sense, propaganda is a series of activities aiming to motivate the addressee in accordance with the emotions, thoughts, and beliefs of the propagandist and to make the addressee adopt a certain lifestyle and change their attitudes (Gambrill, 2012; Walton, 1997).

As far as customer evangelists are concerned, they attempt to convince others of the superiority of the brand in question by spreading positive recommendations and discrediting rival brands, propagandizing with an aim to change the attitudes towards the said brand based on their own goals. The aim and will of changing attitudes of others in line with the propagandist's own opinions behind propagandistic activities (Qualter, 1980) have parallels with the "word-of-mouth" dimension of customer evangelism. Within this context, it is possible to say that the propaganda theory is one of the frameworks that can be used to explain customer evangelism.

Altruism

Another theory to be used to explain the word-of-mouth dimension of customer evangelism is the theory of Altruism. Put forward by Auguste Comte, the theory of Altruism (Scott & Seglow, 2007) is defined as the act committed in the interest of others to one's own detriment (Wilson, 1975), the prioritization of the interests of others over self-interest, and the effort to benefit others (Piliavin & Charng, 1990).

As the theory explains the phenomenon of acting with a consideration of the interest of others, it can also be used to understand the word-of-mouth dimension of customer evangelism. Evangelist customers aim to improve the lives of others by informing them of the product/brand or helping them use the product (Collins et al., 2015; Rothschild et al., 2007). As it is the case for religious evangelism, the primary motivation of customers in the context of customer evangelism is to share the goodness in their own lives with others, improve the lives of others, and introduce the significance brought about by the brand in question to others. Therefore, the theory of altruism can be regarded as one of the fundamental theories underlying customer evangelism.

2.3 Authenticity

Customer evangelists have a true and authentic connection with the product/brand and this dimension of authenticity states that the customer is not motivated with an economic or non-economic incentive as far as their bond with the brand is concerned (Collins et al., 2015). The *self-determination theory* is used to explain the Authenticity dimension of customer evangelism. Conceptualized with the studies by Deci and Ryan in the 1970s, the self-determination theory concerns motivation and personality; it divides motivation into the two categories: autonomous and controlled. While autonomous motivation signifies acting based on the sense of will and having the right to choose, controlled motivation indicates acts steered by pressure. The self-determination theory underlines autonomy and explains the determination of behavior by personal beliefs and value judgments rather than external pressures as well as the sense of choice experienced by the individual (Deci & Ryan, 2004). In this regard, the self-determination theory can be used to explain that the behavior of the evangelist aimed to convince others to become customers is not encouraged by the company and that the evangelist does this consciously, using their own resources.

2.4 Consumer Collectives

Customer evangelists define themselves as a part of consumer communities (Collins et al., 2015). Within the scope of the *consumer collectives* dimension of customer evangelism, *the social identity theory* can be used to explain why evangelist customers are members of consumer communities or why they consider themselves to be a part of such communities. Conceptualized in the early 1970s by Henri Tajfel and John Turner, the social identity theory is an important social psychology theory expounding intergroup relationships and group processes (Abrams & Hogg, 1990). According to the theory, individuals define themselves in accordance with the group to which they belong, comparing their group to other groups. They consider their group to be perfect while underestimating and discrediting other groups (Tajfel, 1982; Turner, 1975; Turner et al., 1987).

Customer evangelism is related to the social identity theory due to the relationship between the consumer and the brand identity (Arkonsuo et al., 2015). A part of the brand or the consumer community consisting of fans of the brand, the customer evangelist perceives the brand as a constituent of their identity and makes efforts to the benefit of the brand.

3 Marketing Concepts Associated with Customer Evangelism

The concept of customer evangelism has drawn considerable attraction within marketing literature in recent years. Due to the advantage of having customer evangelist in the current market conditions in which establishing sustainable customer relations, creating loyal clients, and finding new customers have become increasingly harder, marketing researchers have focused on concepts affecting the process of customer evangelism. Brand satisfaction, consumer-brand identification, brand trust, and brand salience are among the concepts the impacts of which on customer evangelism are analyzed within the academic literature.

From these concepts, customer satisfaction, signifying the degree to which customer expectations are met, was associated with customer evangelism in the literature due to its influence on factors underlying different dimensions of customer evangelism like word-of-mouth and brand loyalty (Anggrarini, 2018; Doss, 2014). Deriving from the social identity theory, the concept of consumer-brand identification denotes the formation of a strong relationship between the consumer and the brand as a result of the perception of the brand by the consumer as a part of their identity. Also preventing the consumer from opting for rival brands, consumer-brand identification was examined in the literature as one of the influential concepts in fostering customer evangelism due to these features. Another marketing concept playing a role in consumer evangelism is brand trust. Brand trust was associated with consumer evangelism since the client trusting in the brand tends to maintain the existing relationship with the brand in question rather than taking the risk of establishing a new relationship with another brand; in this respect, brand trust was found to be influential in customer evangelism (Becerra & Badrinarayanan, 2013; Doss, 2014; Riorini & Widayati, 2015). The concept of "salience" borrowed from social psychology signifies the prominence of one element when compared with others. Used as "brand salience" in marketing, the concept is defined as the accessibility and prominence of a brand in the consumer's mind. Studies show that brand salience affects the tendency of evangelist customers to think of the brand under different circumstances (Anggrarini, 2018; Doss, 2014).

In their study examining the impact of personality traits on customer evangelism, Doss and Cartens (2014) found that extraversion, openness to experience, and neuroticism influence customer evangelism. In particular, the impact of extraversion, i.e. social, talkative and active personality combined with good interpersonal communication skills, on customer evangelism have been analyzed in various research studies (Kautish, 2010; Matzler et al., 2007). Apart from this, there are also studies on the outputs of customer evangelism such as word-of-mouth communication, negative comments about the brand, and customer evangelism on social media (Becerra & Badrinarayanan, 2013; Shaari & Ahmad, 2016).

Conclusion

Businesses focus on understanding the nature of the relationship between the brand and the consumer in order to encourage behavior benefiting the development of the brand like brand loyalty, positive word-of-mouth, and brand advocacy. In this regard, customer evangelists, emerging as a result of the consumer-brand relationship and characterized as a strong bond between the consumer and the brand and the effort for convincing others to become customers of the brand in question, have been drawing more attention from researchers. Customer evangelism includes passion and emotions for the brand. Comprehending the reasons behind the evangelistic tendencies of such customers who are passionately loyal to the brand, share their positive emotions with others and convince them to buy from this brand would provide significant advantages for businesses while finding new clients and increasing their brand success.

As the traits of customer evangelists like being more likely to share more information when compared with other clients, forming stronger emotional bonds, and being less likely to be convinced by the promises of other brand are related to the psychological and characteristic features of the individual, explaining such behavior with psychological theories would prove to be useful to understand customer evangelism. Understanding customer evangelism would help businesses grasp the reasons why the customer becomes an evangelist and, therefore, plan its activities to create more evangelist customers.

The literature on customer evangelism requires more studies and conceptualization. Studies on the concept of customer evangelism would provide businesses with novel ways to get to know their customers and differentiate their clients within the scope of the understanding of "investing the most in the most valuable customer" in their customer relations management.

References

Abrams, D. E. & Hogg, M. A. (1990). *Social Identity Theory: Constructive and Critical Advances.* New York: Springer.

Ainsworth, M. D. S. (1982). Attachment: Retrospect and prospect. In C. M. Parkes & J. S. Hinde (Eds.), *The Place of Attachment in Human Behavior* (pp. 3–30). London: Tavistock Publications.

Anggraini, L. (2018). Understanding brand evangelism and the dimensions involved in a consumer becoming brand evangelist. *Sriwijaya International Journal of Dynamic Economics and Business*, 2(1), pp. 63–84.

Arkonsuo, R. I., Kaljund, K. & Leppiman, A. (2015). Consumer journey from first experience to brand evangelism. *Research in Economics and Business: Central and Eastern Europe*, 6(1).

Becerra, E. P. & Badrinarayanan, V. (2013). The influence of brand trust and brand identification on brand evangelism. *Journal of Product & Brand Management,* 22(5), pp. 371–383.

Belk, R., Wallendorf, M. & Sherry, J. (1989). The sacred and the profane in consumer behaviour: Theodicy on the odyssey. *The Journal of Consumer Research*, 16(1), pp. 1–38.

Bidmon, S. (2017). How does attachment style influence the brand attachment–brand trust and brand loyalty chain in adolescents? *International Journal of Advertising*, 36(1), pp. 164–189.

Bowlby, J. (2012). *Bağlanma.* (Trans. T.V. Soylu). İstanbul: Pinhan Yayıncılık (Original Edition Date, 1969).

Chaudhuri, A. & Holbrook, M. (2001). The chain of effects from brand trust and brand affect to brand performance: The role of brand loyalty. *Journal of Marketing*, 65(2), pp. 81–93.

Collins, N., Gläbe, H., Mizerski, D. & Murphy, J. (2015). Identifying customer evangelists. *In Brand Meaning Management (Review of Marketing Research, Vol. 12),* pp. 175–206, Emerald Group Publishing Limited.

Deci, E. L. & Ryan, R. M. (Eds.). (2004). *Handbook of Self-Determination Research.* Rochester, NY: University Rochester Press.

Demirezen, İ. (2015). *Tüketim Toplumu ve Din*. Istanbul, Turkey: Değerler Eğitimi Merkezi.

Doss, S. K. (2014). Spreading the good word': Toward an understanding of brand evangelism. *Journal of Management and Marketing Research*, 14, pp. 1–16.

Doss, S. K. & Carstens, D. S. (2014). Big five personality traits and brand evangelism. *International Journal of Marketing Studies*, 6(3), p. 13.

Feeney, J. A. & Noller, P. (1990). Attachment style as a predictor of adult romantic relationships. *Journal of Personality and Social Psychology*, 58(2), p. 281.

Gambrill, E. (2012). *Propaganda in the Helping Professions*. New York: Oxford University Press.

Green, M. (1984). What is evangelism? *The Asbury Journal*, 39(2), pp. 34–42.

Hazan, C. & Shaver, P. (1987). Romantic love conceptualized as an attachment process. *Journal of Personality and Social Psychology*, 52(3), p. 511.

Huang, H. (2015). Propaganda as signaling. *Comparative Politics*, 47(4), pp. 419–444.

Kautish, P. (2010). Empirical study on influence of extraversion on consumer passion and brand evangelism with word-of-mouth communication. *Review of Economic and Business Studies (REBS)*, (6), pp. 187–198.

Kawasaki, G. (1992). *Selling the Dream*. New York: HarperBusiness.

Matzler, K., Pichler, E. A. & Hemetsberger, A. (2007). Who is spreading the word? The positive influence of extraversion on consumer passion and brand evangelism. *Marketing Theory and Applications*, 18(1), pp. 25–32.

McConnell, B. & Huba, J. (2007). *Creating Customer Evangelists: How Loyal Customers Become a Volunteer Sales Force.* Chicago: Kaplan Publishing.

Meiners, N. H., Schwarting, U. & Seeberger, B. (2010). The renaissance of word-of-mouth marketing: A 'new' standard in twenty-first century marketing management? *International Journal of Economic Sciences and Applied Research*, 3(2), p. 79.

Mende, M., Bolton, R. N. & Bitner, M. J. (2013). Decoding customer–firm relationships: How attachment styles help explain customers' preferences for closeness, repurchase intentions, and changes in relationship breadth. *Journal of Marketing Research*, 50(1), pp. 125–142.

Piliavin, J. A. & Charng, H. W. (1990). Altruism: A review of recent theory and research. *Annual Review of Sociology*, 16(1), pp. 27–65.

Qualter, T. H. (1980). Propaganda teorisi ve propagandanın gelişimi. *Ankara Üniversitesi SBF Dergisi*, 35(01).

Riorini, S. V. & Widayati, C. C. (2015). Brand relationship and its effect towards brand evangelism to banking service. *International Research Journal of Business Studies*, 8(1).

Rothschild, P. C., Stielstra, G. & Wysong, S. (2007). The pyromarketing model: What venue managers can do to create customer evangelists. *In University Venue Management Conference.* AZ: Phoenix.

Scarpi, D. (2010). Does size matter?: An examination of small and large web-based brand communities. *Journal of Interactive Marketing*, 24(1), pp. 14–21.

Scott, N. & Seglow, J. (2007). *Altruism*. Maidenhead, UK: McGraw-Hill Education.

Shaari, H. & Ahmad, I. S. (2016). Brand evangelism among online brand community members. *International Review of Management and Business Research*, 5(1), p. 80.

Tajfel, H. (1982). Social psychology of intergroup relations. *Annual Review of Psychology*, 33(1), pp. 1–39.

Turner, J. C. (1975). Social comparison and social identity: Some prospects for intergroup behaviour. *European Journal of Social Psychology*, 5, pp. 5–34.

Turner, J. C., Hogg, M. A., Oakes, P. J., Reicher, S. D. & Wetherell, M. S. (1987). *Rediscovering the social group: A self-categorization theory*. Oxford and New York: Basil Blackwell.

Walton, D. (1997). What is propaganda, and what exactly is wrong with it. *Public Affairs Quarterly*, 11(4), pp. 383–413.

Wilson, E. O. (1975). *Sociobiology: The New Synthesis.* Cambridge: Harvard Press.

Ümit BAŞARAN

15 Self-Identity Theory in Consumer Psychology and Behavior

Introduction

Self-concept has a subjective structure regarding the way individuals see themselves. Individuals perceive themselves based on either having or not having certain physical and personality traits, skills and abilities, values, emotions, and social standings. Furthermore, they adhere to certain social groups or avoid being associated with others within the framework of self-concept. In addition to self-concept, definitions such as "self", "identity", and "self-identity" are employed and studied interrelatedly in the academic literature to denote the holistic perceptions of the individuals about themselves. Self-identity signifies the social category labels occurring as certain associations comprising one's self come together. Furthermore, self-concept and self-identity are closely related to structures such as symbolic interactionism, symbolic consumption, self-assessment, self-respect, social identity, the actual self, the ideal self, and the extended self.

Self-concept and self-identity are considered to be significant variables affecting consumer behavior since consumers actualize the definitions and perceptions regarding their selves and their self-identities partly through the products and brands they consume. In other words, they try to create, regulate, alter, and expand their selves and self-identities based on the products they own and consume. Furthermore, they attempt to support their senses of self and self-identities by using the products and brands reflecting their personality traits, images, experiences, and values. Thus, they maintain the continuity of their actual selves or self-identities while striving to attain their ideal selves or self-identities. Besides, they gravitate towards products and brands that would allow them to be accepted to various social groups within the framework of their social identities.

This chapter includes an analysis of the concepts of self and self-identity in the literature of consumer psychology as well as the relationship between the two concepts. Then it attempts to provide an overall perspective regarding the questions of in what sense and how these interrelated concepts affect consumer behavior towards products and brands.

1 Self-Concept and Self-Identity in Consumer Psychology

Self-concept consists of individuals' feelings and perceptions about who they are and comprises their attitudes, beliefs, and emotions concerning themselves (Hawkins & Mothersbaugh, 2010:428). It functions as a directional, explanatory, and individualized structure governing what individuals would be aware of, what they would think about, what kind of emotions they would feel, and for what they would be motivated (Oyserman & Packer, 1996:191). Within this framework, self-concept is defined as "the sum of self-perceptions and self-assessments regarding one's role identities, personality traits, physical attributes, and skills" (Kettle & Haubl, 2011:475). Therefore, terms used to denote individuals' comprehensive perceptions about themselves such as "self", "self-concept", "identity", and "self-identity" are used interrelatedly in the academic literature (Belk, 1988; Stets & Biga, 2003).

One's sense of self consists of a self-focus dimension occurring within the framework of actual and ideal selves and a self-location dimension arising within the scope of public and private selves (Kardes et al., 2011:152). The concept of actual self signifies individuals' perceptual reality regarding what and who they are while the ideal self is composed of individuals' aspirations concerning their ideals and goals about the image they want to attain (Malar et al., 2011:36; Sirgy, 1982:288). Social self-concept denotes consumers' thoughts and beliefs about how others see them whereas ideal social self-concept is shaped based on the image consumers want others to have about them (Hosany & Martin, 2012:686).

While making definitions of self-concept, individuals make use of conceptualizations of self like identities as well as self-evaluations such as self-respect (Gecas, 1982:4). Self-identity signifies the part of one's self related to a certain type of behavior and reflects the labels one uses to define themselves (Biddle et al., 1987:326). Thus, it indicates consumers' category labels concerning what a person in that category looks like, thinks, feels and does (Solomon, 2018:201). The identity theory claims that self-identity emerges as a collection of internalized meanings associated with certain roles one plays within society. Furthermore, self-identity represents how individuals perceive as unique and different from others within the framework of certain roles (Stryker & Burke, 2000:286). In this context, self-identity is based on one's categorization of self as related to a certain role (Stets & Burke, 2000:225). Various disciplines approach the concept of self-identity from three different perspectives (Thoits & Virshup, 1997:106–133) These perspectives can be listed as personal identities consisting of self-definitions in terms of unique and idiosyncratic characteristics, role identities denoting the definition of self as a person who performs a particular social role, and social identities representing the self that one associates with a social group (Pierro et al., 2003:48). In other words, one's self is composed of the combination of a wide range of identities. One's different identities become apparent at different times depending on circumstantial conditions (Wong et al., 2016: 72–73).

Consumers use their material goods as a means to represent their identities, thus constructing, regulating, and maintaining different aspects of their selves such as personal or social self (Wong et al., 2016:72). Major components of extended self can be listed as the consumer's body, internal processes, ideas, experiences, and those people, places, and objects associated with these (Belk, 1988:141). Consumers buy products they consider to be compatible with their selves, values, and social statuses (Saleki et al., 2019:587). Therefore, they regard the products they purchase, use, and consume as materials expanding their selves. The more an identity a consumer has is significant for his definition of self, the more influential it is on purchasing and consumption behavior (Stryker & Burke, 2000:286). Figure 15.1 shows the reasons of consumers behind their consumption. Consumers use products for functional or instrumental reasons to increase the effectiveness of their daily activities and acquire control in their environment. Additionally, they convey crucial messages to others about who they are, using symbolic or expressive functions of the products (Dittmar, 2008:40–41).

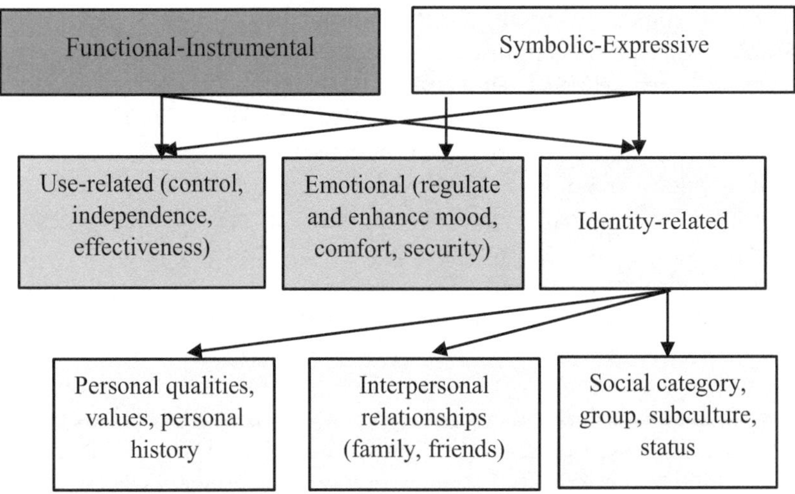

Fig. 15.1: An Integrative Model of the Psychological Functions of Material Possessions. **Source:** Dittmar, 2008

As seen in Figure 15.1 in order to attain their ideal self, consumers tend to opt for products they consider to be helpful in reflecting the positive attributes of their identities or bringing them closer to other individuals they find important (Dittmar, 2008:41). The use of products by consumers for symbolic reasons in a way related to their identities is divided into sub-classifications. Individuals can narrate their personality traits, values, pasts, and experiences through the products they own and consume. Furthermore, these products can be used as indicators of consumers' relationships with people they deem significant, referred to as the primary reference group. Besides this, consumers might regard products as an indicator of their social identity to convey their social standing, material possessions, and statuses to other individuals and to manifest their belonging to social categories like social class and small groups or sub-cultures.

2 The Role of Self-Identity on Consumer Behavior

Consumer self-concepts encompass identities that can also be described as adopted or endowed social category labels related to certain associations (Reed II et al., 2012:314). In the literature of consumer behavior, self-identity is used as an explanatory concept in several strongly related research approaches (Thorbjornsen et al., 2007:765). These can be listed as self- or self-image congruity denoting the consistency between one's self and product or brand image (Ahn, 2019; Sirgy, 1985), symbolic interactionism utilized by products and brands to stimulate consumers' social surroundings (Leigh & Gabel, 1992; Shank & Lulham, 2016), the use of brands and products by consumers to create or expand their selves or self-identities (Belk, 2013), symbolic consumption (Elliott & Wattanasuwan, 1998), and social identity (Wang, 2017; Winterich & Barone, 2011). These studies show that consumers associate products and brands with various features of self or identity such as personality traits, attitudes, roles, or values. Furthermore, they are based on the assumption that consumers use products and brands to construct, regulate, expand, alter, and maintain their selves and identities.

Attitudes towards products and purchasing intentions are profoundly influenced by consumers' self-identity perceptions (Smith et al., 2008:323). For instance, if the consumer sees or wants to see himself as an environmentally-conscious individual with ecological awareness, he is more likely to have positive attitudes and increased purchasing intention towards green products (Barbarossa et al., 2015:155). As far as the harmony between the consumer's sense of self and product/brand image, also known as self-image congruence, is concerned, it has a positive effect on consumer satisfaction and loyalty (Loureiro, et al., 2017:997).

Additionally, within the framework of the symbolic consumption of products by consumers, their function as symbols to communicate with others is related to the use aiming to develop self-identity (Piacentini and Mailer, 2004:252).

Consumers have different motivations regarding the ownership and consumption of products depending on their self-identities. As seen in Table 15.1, Dittmar (2011:749–755) argues that consumer motives for product ownership in line with their identities are constructed within the framework of effectiveness, emotional regulation, actual identity, ideal identity, personal history, symbolic interrelatedness and social identity. In addition, Vignoles et al. (2006: 309) indicates that individuals' motives regarding their self-identities comprise self-efficacy, distinctiveness, continuity, self-esteem, belongingness, and meaning. These components seem to affect consumer perceptions, preferences, attitudes, and behavior towards products and brands (Altintas & Heischmidt, 2018; Shrum et al., 2013).

Tab. 15.1: Identity-Related Functions of Material Goods and Identity Motives. **Source**: Dittmar, 2011

Dittmar's Identity-Related Functions	Vignoles' Identity Motives
Effectiveness Control, independence, autonomy	***Self-efficacy*** *Feel component and capable of influencing environment*
Emotional regulation *Regulate/enhance mood, comfort, security*	
Actual identity *Individuality/differentiation, symbol of personal qualities, values, goals*	***Distinctiveness*** *Distinguish self from other people* ***Continuity*** *Perceive identity as continuous over time*
Ideal identity *Identity repair, moving closer to ideal self, fantasy self*	***Self-esteem*** *See self in positive light*
Personal history *Link to past/childhood, symbol of self-continuity*	***Continuity*** *Perceive identity as continuous over time*
Symbolic interrelatedness *Relationships with specific others, symbolic company*	***Belongingness*** *Be included and accepted within social circles*
Social identity *Social category, group membership, sub-culture, status*	*Also esteem, and distinctiveness for social identity*
	Meaning *Perceive life as ultimately meaningful*

As seen in Table 15.1, consumers with high motives for self-esteem might gravitate towards products allowing them to change their physical appearance. Those with an increased orientation towards actual identities are more likely to use personalized products and brands within the framework of distinctiveness; they might be more willing to buy the works of an artist originating from their region due to the motive for continuity regarding their personal history. Furthermore, owing to the motive for belonging, consumers might opt for luxury products and brands indicating one's social standing that they associate with people and objects they deem significant or they believe to be beneficial for their acceptance in various social groups (Shrum et al., 2013:1181).

Identity types governing consumer behavior vary depending on their referents during their perceptions (Reed II et al, 2012:312). When the perceived identity type is formulated within the framework of a familial (mother, father, child) or professional (manager) role, this can be explained with the affiliation to a self-categorization, using one's consistent behavioral patterns towards consumption and the role identity theory. If it occurs related to characters from comics, cartoons, fiction, or movies, imaginary social structures or interpretations arise through marketers, culture, or popular media. In the case of consumer perceptions of identity being formulated in relation to familiar individuals such as thesis supervisors, siblings, or school counselors, consumer behavior is examined through the lens of the identification theory. This theory is based on the maintenance of the relationship built on individuals included in personal communicative processes and identity definitions. When identity is constructed by brand spokespeople, musicians, artists or popular culture icons, the effort to liken oneself to such individuals with no personal contact is explained using the impression management theory.

Identity, as perceived by consumers, might also be formulated within the framework of group references as relationships with small familiar groups the members of which are known to the individual, such as one's family or a group of master's students. In such a case, within the scope of the reference group theory, consumer behavior is affected by the maintenance of the affiliation to the reference group or the support from other members. If the identity is formulated related to larger groups of which one does not know each member personally such as gender identity (e.g. male, female), ethnic identity, or political identity, consumer behavior is explained, within the scope of the self-categorization theory, with the motive to be included in these groups categorized by a certain member. If consumer identity emerges within the framework of wide-scale social associations such as national identity (e.g. European, American) or human identity, within the scope of the social identity theory, consumer behavior is related to the aspiration to become a component of wide-scale, irregular, and abstract groups and to influence opinions of other individuals in society.

Conclusion

It is a known fact that consumers use products and brands to formulate their self-assessments regarding who they are. Furthermore, they are more likely to opt for products and brands they identify with certain aspects such as their characteristics, physical attributes, values, beliefs, and personalities. They also develop positive attitudes towards products and brands having the image that would allow them to attain the level of self-concept they desire. Due to certain images, features, and benefits they offer, products and brands are perceived by consumers as elements contributing to their communication with their social environment. Therefore, using brands and products, consumers get the chance to be accepted to various social groups or reference groups or to associate themselves with such groups within the framework of their social identities.

Self-concept consists of subjective evaluations and perceptions of consumers concerning themselves whereas self-identity can be described as category labels they perceive in relation to certain roles, characters, individuals, or social groups. Therefore, role identities, individuals one wants to identify oneself with or be similar to, reference groups, gender identities, or ethnic identities might influence the formation of self-identity. During any type of behavior displayed by the consumer, the identity type dominant over purchasing attitudes, preferences, and behaviors depends on which identity is foregrounded within the scope of self-concept. Individuals generally consume products and brands in alignment with their identities with motives such as influencing their environment; attaining emotional order; reflecting their traits, values, and aims upon their environment; increasing their self-respect; or being included in various social categories or groups.

When any category label is embraced by the consumer, factors leading to the salience of the identity in question increase the possibility of identity-based consumer behavior. This self-label adopted by the consumer allows various meanings to be transformed while making it possible to experience products and brands associated with this label. In alignment with the identity they embrace, the consumer starts assessing the individuals and objects around them in terms of their congruity; this affects their emotions, thoughts, and behavior towards products. Within this framework, consumers seem to behave in accordance with their salient identities. Therefore, self-concept and various identity types constituting self-concept are considered by marketers as a significant psychographic variable to understand consumer behavior. Understanding the elements affecting the processes of formulating, regulating, and maintaining self-identity as well as how these processes work is particularly essential for marketing and consumer research.

References

Ahn, J. (2019). Cognitive antecedents and affective consequences of customers' self-concept in brand management: A conceptual model. *International Journal of Contemporary Hospitality Management*, 31(5), pp. 2114–2128.

Altintas, M., & Heischmidt, K. A. (2018). Gender differences in self-identity motives for luxury consumption. *Journal of Behavioral Studies in Business*, 10, pp. 51–78.

Barbarossa, C., Beckmann, S. C., Pelsmacker, P. D., Moons, I., & Gwozdz, W. (2015). A self-identity based model of electric car adoption intention: A cross-cultural comparative study. *Journal of Environmental Psychology*, 42, pp. 149–160.

Belk, R. (1988). Possessions and the extended self. *Journal of Consumer Research*, 15(2), pp. 139–168.

Belk, R. W. (2013). Extended self in a digital world. *Journal of Consumer Research*, 40, pp. 477–500.

Biddle, B. J., Bank, B. J., & Slavings, R. L. (1987). Norms, preferences, identities and retention decisions. *Social Psychology Quarterly*, 50(4), pp. 322–337.

Dittmar, H. (2008). To have is to be? Psychological functions of material possessions. In H. Dittmar (Ed.), *Consumer Culture, Identity and Well-Being*, pp. 25–48, Hove, Sussex: Psychology Press.

Dittmar, H. (2011). Material and consumer identities. In S. S. Schwarts, K. Luyckx & V. L. Vignoles (Eds.), *Handbook of Identity Theory and Research* (pp. 745–769). New York: Springer.

Elliott, R., & Wattanasuwan, K. (1998). Brands as symbolic resources for the construction of identity. *International Journal of Advertising*, 17(2), pp. 131–144.

Gecas, V. (1982). The self-concept. *Annual Reviews*, 8, pp. 1–33.

Hawkins, D. I., & Mothersbaugh, D. L. (2010). *Consumer Behavior: Building Marketing Strategy*. New York: McGraw-Hill/Irwin.

Hosany, S., & Martin, D. (2012). Self-image congruence in consumer behavior. *Journal of Business Research*, 65(5), pp. 685–691.

Kardes, F. R., Cronley, M. L., & Cline, T. W. (2011). *Consumer behavior*. Ohio: South-Western Cengage Learning.

Kettle, K. L., & Haubl, G. (2011). The signature effect: Signing influences consumption-related behavior by priming self-identity. *Journal of Consumer Research*, 38(3), pp. 474–489.

Leigh, J. H., & Gabel, T. G. (1992). Symbolic interactionism: Its effects on consumer behaviour and implications for marketing strategy. *Journal of Services Marketing*, 6(3), pp. 5–16.

Loureiro, S. M. C., Gorgus, T., & Kaufmann, H. R. (2017). Antecedents and outcomes of online brand engagement. *Online Information Review*, 41(7), pp. 985–1005.

Malar, L., Krohmer, H., Hoyer, W. D., & Nyffenegger, B. (2011). Emotional brand attachment and brand personality: The relative importance of the actual and the ideal self. *Journal of Marketing*, 75(4), pp. 35–52.

Oyserman, D., & Packer, M. J. (1996). Social cognition and self-concept: A socially contextualized model of identity. In J. L. Nye & A. M. Brower (Eds.), *What's Social about Social Cognition? Research on Socially Shared Cognition in Small Groups* (pp. 175–201). Thousand Oaks: Sage Publications.

Piacentini, M., & Mailer, G. (2004). Symbolic consumption in teenagers' clothing choices. *Journal of Consumer Behaviour*, 3(3), pp. 251–262.

Pierro, A., Mannetti, L., & Livi, S. (2003). Self-identity and the theory of planned behavior in the prediction of health behavior and leisure activity. *Self and Identity*, 2(1), pp. 47–60.

Reed II, A., Forehand, M. R., Puntoni, S., & Warlop, L. (2012). Identity-based consumer behavior. *International Journal of Research in Marketing*, 29(4), pp. 310–321.

Saleki, R., Quoquab, F., & Mohammad, J. (2019). What drives Malaysian consumers' organic food purchase intention? The role of moral norm, self-identity, environmental concern and price consciousness. *Journal of Agribusiness in Developing and Emerging Economies*, 9(5), pp. 584–603.

Shank, D. B., & Lulham, R. (2016). Symbolic interaction with consumer products: An affect control theory approach. *Sociology Compass*, 10(7), pp. 613–622.

Shrum, L. J., Wong, N., Arif, F., Chugani, S. K., Gunz, A., Lowrey, T. M., Nairn, A., Pandelaere, M., Ross, S. M., Ruvivo, A., Scott, K., & Sundie, J. (2013). Reconceptualizing materialism as identity goal pursuits: Functions, processes, and consequences. *Journal of Business Research*, 66(8), pp. 1179–1185.

Sirgy, M. J. (1982). Self-concept in consumer behavior: A critical review. *Journal of Consumer Research*, 9(3), pp. 287–300.

Sirgy, M. J. (1985). Using self-congruity and ideal congruity to predict purchase motivation. *Journal of Business Research*, 13, pp. 195–206.

Smith, J. R., Terry, D. J., Manstead, A. S. R., Louis, W. R., Kotterman, D., & Wolfs, J. (2008). The attitude–behavior relationship in consumer conduct: The Role of norms, past behavior, and self-identity. *The Journal of Social Psychology*, 148(3), pp. 311–334.

Solomon, M. R. (2018). *Consumer Behavior: Buying, Having, and Being*. Harlow, Essex: Pearson Education Limited.

Stets, J. E., & Biga, C. F. (2003). Bringing identity theory into environmental sociology. *Sociological Theory*, 21(4), pp. 398–423.

Stets, J. E., & Burke, P. J. (2000). Identity theory and social identity theory. *Social Psychology Quarterly*, 63(3), pp. 224–237.

Stryker, S., & Burke, P. J. (2000). The past, present, and future of an identity theory. *Social Psychology Quarterly*, 63(4), pp. 284–297.

Thoits, P. A., & Virshup, L. K. (1997). Me's and we's: Forms and functions of social identities. In R. D. Ashmore & L. Jussim (Eds.), *Self and Identity: Fundamental Issues* (pp. 106–133). Oxford: Oxford University Press.

Thorbjornsen, H., Pedersen, P. E., & Nysveen H. (2007). 'This is who I am': Identity expressiveness and the theory of planned behavior. *Psychology & Marketing*, 24(9), pp. 763–785.

Vignoles, V. L., Regalia, C., Manzi, C., Golledge, J., & Scabini, E. (2006). Beyond self-esteem: Influence of multiple motives on identity construction. *Journal of Personality and Social Psychology*, 90(2), pp. 308–333.

Wang, T. (2017). Social identity dimensions and consumer behavior in social media. *Asia Pacific Management Review*, 22(1), pp. 45–51.

Winterich, K. P., & Barone, M. J. (2011). Warm glow or cold, hard cash? Social identity effects on consumer choice for donation versus discount promotions. *Journal of Marketing Research*, 48(5), pp. 855–868.

Wong, P., Hogg, M. K., & Vanharanta, M. (2016). Couples' narratives of shared-self, possessions and consumption experiences. *Journal of Consumer Behaviour*, 16(1), pp. 72–81.

Hatice AYDIN and Somayyeh BIKARI

16 Evaluation of Cognitive Dissonance Theory

Introduction

A consumer may be affected by a plethora of factors as they engage in consumption behavior. Confining consumption behavior to external factors or explaining it exclusively with external factors is not considered to be a rational approach. The individual is a social being and might display a cognitive dissonance with their inner world. A consumer thinking that they have made their final decision may be influenced by the statements of the person next to them during the act of purchasing. Due to this influence, the consumer might reverse the decision. This change of mind can be explained by the cognitive dissonance theory (Özhan Dedeoğlu, 2002: 77). The theory defines cognitive dissonance as the psychological discomfort following the act of decision making.

The theory of cognitive dissonance was put forward by Leon Festinger, a social psychologist. It is the first theory to recognize motivational results stemming from inconsistencies within the cognitive system (Breker, 2009: 5). The theory, suggests that as dissonance increases, so does psychological tension; as a result, the individual takes action to reduce dissonance. In other words, every disharmony creating psychological tension is unpleasant and the individual seeks ways to rationalize their thoughts (Tanford & Montgomery, 2015: 4). At this point, the way one copes with the said disharmony arouses curiosity.

Both cognitive dissonance and the ways to cope with the dissonance have become subjects of interest for marketing theorists aiming to understand the reasons behind consumer behaviors. Understanding the factors influencing the cognitive dissonance with the inner world of the consumer or the outcomes of the said dissonance within the scope of the marketing literature is also crucial. Taking the outcomes of dissonance into account shows that cognitive dissonance is a phenomenon to be addressed in marketing. Liang (2014: 59) indicated that individuals use the coping strategies of congeniality bias and refutation to alleviate the situation inducing cognitive dissonance. In this sense, it is possible to say that there are many ways to cope with cognitive dissonance.

The present study touches on the concept of cognitive dissonance and evaluates the precursors of cognitive dissonance as well as coping strategies. The general results of the studies revealed that the most frequent precursors of cognitive dissonance are confidence and risk. Adaptive and non-adaptive strategies were found to be the coping strategies against cognitive dissonance. Various suggestions were made based on the results of the study.

1 The Concept of Cognitive Dissonance

Cognitive dissonance is defined as the disharmony between two situations. A contradiction between attitudes, behaviors, and beliefs is observed in the case of such a dissonance (Çalışkan et al., 2017: 138). The concept was coined by the American psychologist Leon Festinger in the 1950s. According to Festinger, cognitive dissonance is the complement of an individual's behaviors, attitudes, and factors of knowledge on their environment. In his book titled "A Theory of Cognitive Dissonance", Festinger (1957: 2) defines cognitive dissonance as disharmony between cognitions. Dissonance between cognitions is defined as dissonant relationships between the individual's knowledge, ideas or beliefs concerning their environment and the behavior of themselves or someone else. This dissonance might evoke emotional distress within the individual. It occurs when the individual experiences a disharmony between their cognitions, emotions, and behavior. Within this context, the concept originates from the field of psychology.

During its initial years, this concept was mostly described as cognition or the act of awareness. However, it has started to be discussed more often in the present context in which the issues of retaining and accurately transmitting information have become more significant. Steele and Liu (1981) defined cognitive dissonance as the state of discomfort experienced by the individual due to disharmony. Sweeney et al. (2000) associated cognitive dissonance with negative emotions like anxiety, apprehension, and regret. In this context, cognitive dissonance denotes a psychological process. Solomon (2017) indicated that seeking consistency and order underlies the theory of cognitive dissonance. In the present day, it is claimed that cognitive dissonance signifies not only the disharmony between cognitions but also the inconsistencies in attitudes, emotions, and behavior (Maertz et al. 2009; McKimmie et al., 2003). Emerging in various forms from past to present, the issue of cognitive dissonance has become a frequent topic of study in marketing in recent years (Liang, 2016; Wilkins, Beckenuyte & Butt, 2016).

In marketing, cognitive dissonance refers to the state of disharmony in purchasing behavior. The individual might be irresolute between two or more options for goods or services. When the individual purchases the good or service in question, they might think that there were better alternatives. In this case, they might experience cognitive dissonance due to the regret about missing the better alternative. In this context, the concept of cognitive dissonance generally denotes the psychological discomfort occurring while choosing one out of many alternatives. However, the consumer might suffer from dissonance regarding not only goods and services but also the means of shopping. This discomfort becomes more evident in online purchases. A wide range of factors like the reliability of the information and website trigger cognitive dissonance among consumers (Eskiler & Altunışık, 2015). When the consumer cannot decide regarding online purchases, believes that they were deprived of the opportunity of shopping from brick-and-mortar stores, thinks that their method of shopping was unwise or feels uncertain, cognitive dissonance increases. However, not every purchasing behavior results in cognitive dissonance. Cognitive dissonance also increases when the purchasing decision is of critical importance for the consumer, the cost is high, the product is perceived to be indispensable by the consumer and the owned product performs poorly (Ranjbarian et al., 2014). Therefore, the decision made at the end might create even more dissonance if the individual's attitudes, values, perceptions, and tendencies contradict. Thus, researching possible situations and contexts in which the dissonance experienced by the consumer can occur is vital.

2 Potential Situations and Context Leading to Cognitive Dissonance

The consumer is a psychological being rather than an economic one. Therefore, it is impossible to explain consumer behavior with a fixed formula (Akyıldız, 2008). The argument that the consumer is a psychological being can be explained by many examples, such as opting for one of the two services offered at the same time, selecting a brand while buying an item or choosing a vacation destination. Certain conditions need to arise for the consumer, a psychological being, to experience cognitive dissonance (Yücel & Çizel, 2019: 107). The three basic conditions for cognitive dissonance are as follows:

- The purchasing decision must be critical for the consumer: As the material or intangible cost the customer is willing to bear in exchange for the good or service to be purchased increases, so does dissonance.
- The good or service to be purchased must be indispensable for the consumer: The absence of alternatives to the product to be purchased might increase cognitive dissonance.
- The purchasing decision must have long-term results: If returns or replacements are difficult, this might increase dissonance while the consumer makes a purchasing decision.

As environmental conditions are chaotic in both physical and social senses, the level of dissonance increases, and it becomes more difficult to make future decisions. The tendency of making future decisions the easy way without straining is a natural outcome of such an environment. In this context, cognitive dissonance is also apparent in the financial sector. The attitudes of individual investors in "cognitive dissonance" are also evaluated (Çetiner et al., 2019). On one hand, investors behave based on their emotions with a motive of avoiding harm or regret, yet on the other hand, they might act irrationally to obtain results quickly. Cases and contexts in which individuals experience cognitive dissonance might occur before, during or after the purchasing behavior.

The dissonance before the purchasing behavior arises in the case where the consumer cannot decide between too many alternatives. A consumer with a more elevated mood might experience cognitive dissonance while making decisions about instantaneous purchases. As for the post-purchase period, dissonance might arise as a result of novel considerations suggesting that the product is not suitable for the desire or need in question. However, it is not possible to say that all purchasing decisions will lead to dissonance (Oliver, 1997). A consumer experiencing cognitive dissonance might need to change their behavior or attitudes.

Regardless of their case or context, evaluating the factors causing cognitive dissonance as well as the outcomes of the said dissonance is vital.

3 Precursors and Outcomes of Cognitive Dissonance

There are numerous factors leading to cognitive dissonance among consumers and cognitive dissonance might also have negative consequences. The precursors and outcomes of cognitive dissonance, therefore, have been the subject of many research studies. Some of these studies are as follows.

Negative word-of-mouth communication was indicated as one of the variables affecting cognitive dissonance (Kim, 2011). Ayazlar and Yüksel (2012) stated that the quality of the website, perceived risk and confidence affect cognitive dissonance and, in turn, the dissonance influences consumer behavior. Saleem et al. (2012) argue that hedonic consumption, impulse purchases, and involvement cause cognitive dissonance. Sharifi and Esfidani (2014) explained that relationship marketing activities reduce post-purchase cognitive dissonance. Liang (2016) revealed that reading positive comments online after the purchase decreases cognitive dissonance among consumers. Çalışkan et al. (2017) found that perceived website service quality among consumers reduces cognitive dissonance. Aydın and Yılmaz (2018) discovered that perceived confidence, value, risk, impulse purchases, and hedonic consumption influence cognitive dissonance. Taşar and Dedeoğlu (2019) indicated that the preceding variables leading to cognitive dissonance are impulse purchases, psychological tension, sales promotions and discounts, indecisiveness, mood and feedback from other people around the consumer.

As seen above, there are numerous non-negligible factors affecting purchasing decisions made by consumers. These factors influence purchasing processes. What is important here is to determine whether the post-decision cognitive process differs from the pre-decision cognitive process. Oliver (1997: 243) states that cognitive dissonance during purchasing processes starts as a simple concern and persists through the following purchasing phases. Oliver explained this process with four phases: Alpha, Beta, Gamma, and Delta. Table 16.1 shows the phases of cognitive dissonance during the purchasing process.

Tab. 16.1: Purchasing Decision Phases and Factors of Dissonance. **Source:** Oliver, 1997

Phase	*Definition*	*Focus of Dissonance*	*Psychological Response*
Alpha	Pre-decision	The alternative is attractive	Decisional conflict
Beta	Post-decision, pre-purchase	The selected alternative is attractive when compared with foregone alternatives	Concern
Gamma	Post-purchase, pre-ownership, Post-ownership, pre-usage/experience	The foregone alternatives are attractive, and the selected alternative performs adequately	Concerns about performance, doubting self (the decision)
Delta	Post-usage	Performance results, future performance	Regret, guilt, (dis) satisfaction

As seen in Table 16.1; the Alpha phase signifies the pre-decision stage, Beta the post-decision and pre-purchase stage, Gamma the post-purchase and pre-experience stage, and Delta the post-usage stage. The focus and outcome of each decisional process are different.

The theory of cognitive dissonance encompassing a plethora of precursors and outcomes denotes a phenomenon that needs to be coped with. The following section provides information about strategies to cope with this phenomenon.

4 Coping Strategies for Cognitive Dissonance

The theory of cognitive dissonance signifies the discomfort resulting from the inconsistency or disharmony between two cognitive situations. It is generally conceived of as the interrogation of the inconsistency between the inner and outer world of an individual. For instance, cognitive dissonance might arise when the consumer cannot decide between two products. In fact, following the purchase, the regret about the product not purchased may cause the individual to question the purchase. The theory of cognitive dissonance comes into play as it consolidates the processes resulting in cognitive outcomes such as beliefs, opinions, and considerations on the act in question (Seker, 2015: 24). When the individual feels that they might have acted wrongly while making their decision and thinks of the features of the selected alternative that might be considered negative, they will make a personal effort, either consciously or unconsciously, to reduce dissonance (Festinger, 1957; Oliver, 1997). Cognitive dissonance also produces behaviors aimed to alleviate the situation creating emotional distress within the individual. In this context, it is possible to say that dissonance is motivational. In other words, there are different ways to act for reducing dissonance. At this point, one needs to employ various coping strategies. Coping strategies might appear in different forms. These forms can be listed as changing, eliminating or reducing the perceived salience of the cognitions, behaviors or emotions leading to dissonance (McKimmie et al., 2003; Maertz et al., 2009). Making use of coping strategies, the individual endeavors to re-establish the harmony between dissonant cognitions, attitudes, behaviors or emotions. For example; regretting a purchase, the consumer might justify their purchasing decision, rationalize it, look for new information, seek support for their actions, attribute the responsibility to an external source, change their behavior or reduce its level of salience, comfort themselves psychologically, avert the situation creating the dissonance or consider other options like returning the product.

Observed in a wide range of forms, coping strategies are fundamentally classified as adaptive and non-adaptive (maladaptive) in the academic literature (Pieters & Zeelenberg, 2007; Dickinson & Holmes, 2008).

Adaptive coping behavior makes use of rational problem-solving mechanisms. With an active coping strategy, the individual might change the behavior leading to dissonance. For instance, a smoker can quit smoking with such a strategy. Doing so, the individual eliminates the situation causing pressure. It might not always be easy to change behavior. In this case, taking into account the difficulty of breaking a harmful habit or the irreversibility of the purchasing behavior, attitudes can be changed. Here, non-adaptive coping strategies come into play. Non-adaptive strategies are based on emotions. They do not include the management of the source of the emotion arising during the negative situation but the use of a defense mechanism. The individual applies the defense mechanism in two ways.

The first way is to ignore the negative cognitions; the second is to deny the relationship between the cognitions. For example, the individual might counteract the harmful effects of smoking by exercising regularly or allege that smoking reduces their stress. In this context, non-adaptive coping strategies can be listed as avoiding the situation leading to discomfort, performing corrective actions by forgetting or sharing the situation with other people, or finding justifications that can make the situation reasonable and acceptable (Taşar & Dedeoğlu, 2019; 121). Another strategy aiming to reduce the dissonance felt by the individual is social support. Social support can be described as the advice given by people using the same product or service. While making a purchasing decision, consumers make use of the social support strategy regarding risk reduction and confidence in recommendations (Kim, 2011). As a form of social support, the communication established by businesses with their consumers has the utmost importance.

Conclusion and Suggestions

The cognitive process governs human behavior. Despite the thoughts, experiences, external factors or emotional influences affecting the individual, making a consumption decision might turn into a significant problem due to cognitive dissonance.

At the beginning of this chapter, owing to its magnitude, the concept of cognitive dissonance was explained in detail. Then, the precursors and outcomes of this context were examined. Upon reflecting on the studies in the academic literature in an integrated manner; perceived risk, confidence and impulse purchases can be indicated as preceding factors. Return requests and negative word-of-mouth are noted as the most frequently discussed output variables.

The chapter also looked at how to cope with cognitive dissonance. In this regard, adaptive and non-adaptive strategies were explained to be the fundamental strategies to cope with dissonance. Furthermore, the social support strategy was also emphasized as a potential coping strategy.

Numerous research studies on cognitive dissonance evaluate the precursors or outcomes of the phenomenon. However, a study encompassing precursors and outcomes as well as coping strategies was not found in the academic literature; the lack of such a study was particularly apparent in the Turkish academic literature. In this regard, the study is considered to be a contribution to the existing literature. More applied studies can be conducted on the basis of this theoretical study.

Increasing the number of qualitative and quantitative studies to decode the cognitive process is thought to be necessary to explain the process in which the consumer makes a purchasing decision.

References

Akyıldız, H. (2008). Tartışılan Boyutlarıyla Homo Economicus. *Süleyman Demirel Üniversitesi İktisadi ve İdari Bilimler Fakültesi Dergisi*, 13(2), pp. 29–40.

Ayazlar, R. A., & Yüksel, A. (2012). Web sitesi kalitesi, risk ve güven: Bilişsel çelişki ve tüketim sonrası davranışlar üzerine etkileri. *Seyahat ve Otel İşletmeciliği Dergisi*, 9(1).

Aydın, E. ve Yılmaz, Ö. (2018). Online Alışverişte Bilişsel Çelişki Davranışlarının İncelenmesi. *Anemon Muş Alparslan Üniversitesi Sosyal Bilimler Dergisi*, 6, pp. 333–339.

Breker, T. (2009). *The Theory of Cognitive Dissonance and Its Application in Marketing: An Overview of Literature and Practical Experiences.* Saarbrücken: VDM Verlag Dr. Müller.

Dickinson, S., & Matthew, H. (2008). Understanding the emotional and coping responses of adolescent individuals exposed to threat appeals. *International Journal of Advertising*, 27(2), pp. 251–278.

Çalışkan, B. Ö. Ö., Yavuz, M., & Akca, M. (2017). Elektronik ortamda alışveriş yapan tüketicilerin algıladıkları web sitesi hizmet kalitesi ve bilişsel çelişkileri arasındaki ilişkide kurumsal itibarin rolü. *Sosyal Bilimler Dergisi*, 4(13), pp. 136–146.

Çetiner, M., Gökcek, H. A., & Turp Gölbaşı, B. (2019). Davranışsal finans açısından bilişsel çelişki, aşırı güven ve taklit ve sürü davranışları boyutlarında bireysel yatırımcı kararları üzerine bir inceleme. https://www.researchgate.net/publication/334573134 Accessed on: 15.02.2020.

Eskiler, E., & Altunişik, R. (2015). Algılanan Değer ve Müşteri Memnuniyetinin Satın Alma Eğilimleri Üzerine Etkisi. *III. Rekreasyon Araştırmaları Kongresi.* pp. 483–493. http://www.anatoliajournal.com/kongre_arsivi/rekreasyon/3.rekreasyon/RAK2015%20BI%CC%87LDI%CC%87RI%CC%87%20KI%CC%87TABIv6.pdf Accessed on 15.04.2020.

Festinger, L. (1957). *A Theory of Cognitive Dissonance*. Stanford: Stanford University.

Kim, Y. S. (2011). Application of the cognitive dissonance theory to the service industry. *Services Marketing Quarterly*, 32(2), pp. 96–112.

Liang, Y. (2014). *The effect of cognitive dissonance on the selection of post-decision online reviews: Congeniality bias and refutational perspectives.* Unpublished PhD Thesis. Michigan State University, USA.

Liang, Y. J. (2016). Reading to make a decision or to reduce cognitive dissonance? The effect of selecting and reading online reviews from a post-decision context. *Computers in Human Behavior*, 64, pp. 463–471.

Maertz, C. P., Hassan, A., & Magnusson, P. (2009). When learning is not enough: A process model of expatriate adjustment as cultural cognitive dissonance reduction. *Organizational Behavior and Human Decision Processes*, 108(1), pp. 66–78.

McKimmie, B. M., Terry, D. J., Hogg, M. A., Manstead, A. S. R., Spears, R., & Doosje, B. (2003). I'm a Hypocrite, but so is Everyone Else: Group Support and the Reduction of Cognitive Dissonance. *Group Dynamics: Theory, Research, and Practice,* 7(3), pp. 214–22

Mowen, J. C. (1995). *Consumer Behavior* (4th ed.). Englewood Cliffs: Prentice Hall.

Oliver R. L. (1997). *Satisfaction: A Behavioral Perspective on the Consumer.* New York: McGraw-Hill.

Özhan Dedeoğlu, A. (2002). Tüketici davranışları alanında kalitatif araştırmaların önemi ve multidisipliner yaklaşımlar. *Dokuz Eylül Üniversitesi İktisadi ve İdari Bilimler Fakültesi Dergisi,* 17(2), pp. 75–92.

Pieters, R., & Zeelenberg, M. (2007). A theory of regret regulation. *Journal of Consumer Psychology*, 17(1), pp. 29–35.

Ranjbarian, B., Safari, A., Karbalaei, R., & Jamshidi, M. (2014). An analysis of the consumer's spiritual intelligence on its post-purchase cognitive dissonance and satisfaction: Consumers of home appliances in Naein City as a case study. *Advances in Environmental Biology*, 8(17), pp. 984–990.

Saleem, M. A., Ali, R. A., & Ahmad, S. (2012). Purchase cognitive dissonance: Impact of product involvement, impulse buying and hedonic consumption tendencies. *Interdiciplinary Journal of Contemporary Research in Business*, 4(5), pp. 1051–1060.

Seker, S. E. (2015). *Motivasyon Teorisi (Motivation Theory)* YBSAnsiklopedi, v. 2, is. 1, pp. 23–27.

Shahin Sharifi, S., & Rahim Esfidani, M. (2014). The impacts of relationship marketing on cognitive dissonance, satisfaction, and loyalty: The mediating role of trust and cognitive dissonance. *International Journal of Retail & Distribution Management*, 42(6), pp. 553–575.

Solomon, M. R. (2017). *Consumer Behavior: Buying, Having, and Being.* 12. Basım, Boston: Pearson.

Steele, C. M., & Liu, T. J. (1981). Making the dissonant act unreflective of self. *Personality and Social Psychology Bulletin*, 7(3), pp. 393–397.

Sweeney, J. C., Hausknecht, D., & Soutar, G. N. (2000). Cognitive dissonance after purchase: A multidimensional scale. *Psychology & Marketing*, 17, pp. 369–385.

Tanford, S., & Montgomery, R. (2015). The effects of social influence and cognitive dissonance on travel purchase decisions. *Journal of Travel Research*, 54(5), pp. 596–610.

Taşar, B., & Dedeoğlu, A.Ö. (2019). Tüketimde Bilişsel Uyumsuzluk ve Öncülleri Üzerine Pilot Araştırma. *Ege Stratejik Araştirmalar Dergisi*, 10(2), pp. 119–128.

Wilkins, S., Beckenuyte, C., & Butt, M. M. (2016). Consumers' behavioural intentions after experiencing deception or cognitive dissonance caused by deceptive packaging, package downsizing or slack filling. *European Journal of Marketing*, 50(1/2), pp. 213–235.

Yücel, E., & Çizel, B. (2019). Bilişsel Uyumsuzluk Ölçeğinin Türkçeye Uyarlanması: Geçerlik ve Güvenirlik Çalışması. *Seyahat ve Otel İşletmeciliği Dergisi*, 16(1), pp. 106–120.

Emre HARORLI

17 Socioemotional Selectivity Theory

Introduction

Age differences have significant theoretical effects on emotive/experiential and negotiation processes. Therefore, psychological studies focus on determining the factors influencing the decision-making process. In this context, it is crucial to understand whether these processes are elemental for senior adults as well.

Arguing that senior adults are motivated to prioritize emotionally-significant objectives, socioemotional selectivity theory (SST) claims that older individuals are driven to extrapolate emotional significance from life. Old age has a rapidly growing potential globally. This potential is vital due to limited support and the increasing pressure on resources. Understanding the objectives behind the consumption of older consumers is crucial for marketers aiming to develop goods and services for them. Thus, older consumers constitute a significant market segment. Additionally, it is essential for practitioners to reveal how senior consumers assess, process, and react to information. This chapter begins with a section defining and conceptualizing SST; then, it discusses the importance of SST within the context of consumer psychology.

1 Socioemotional Selectivity Theory

The growth of the senior population and the decrease in birth rates lead to an increase in the global age average (Pour Mohammad & Drolet, 2019). This increase over the course of many years understandably arrests the attention of researchers studying the potential impacts of this change in the global demographic structure extensively (Strough et al., 2015) and putting forward novel theories as a result. One of these theories is the socioemotional selectivity theory (SST).

Socioemotional selectivity theorists Carstensen et al. (1999) allege that as a result of the limited time perspective, the individuals attach greater importance to emotion-based targets or, in other words, focusing more on emotional satisfaction. Therefore, these individuals become more selective in their social activities. Alternatively stated, senior adults attempt to set more emotionally-significant objectives by seizing the day and deepening existing close relationships. In contrast, young adults try to have more new experiences, to obtain more information, and to widen their social networks (Jiang & Fung, 2019).

The thought of nearing "the end" leads to an increased orientation towards social and emotional targets (Fung et al., 1999). Here, "the end" signifies death, and death is generally associated with chronological old age. However, it would be inaccurate to limit old age to chronological aging because one's chronological age does not reveal any information about one's health, personality, cognitive development, role in social life, and social status. Evaluating old age within the framework of various biological, psychological, and sociological factors makes it easier for researchers to obtain more detailed and more specific results. Regardless of the characteristics selected to assess old age, it is possible to say that aging has biological, physiological, psychological, and sociological impacts on individuals, either positive or negative. For example, studies are showing that senior adults perform more poorly in terms of mnemonic and attention skills such as short or long-term memory and processing speed when compared with young adults. Still, the parts of their brain dealing with information are preserved (Gutchess, 2011). However, it should be noted that aging does not affect memory performance of every senior adult in the same way (Yoon et al., 2009). Furthermore, a chronologically younger individual might also feel depleted biologically (e.g., having a terminal disease) or psychologically (e.g., due to the sudden death of a loved one). In such a situation, one's emotional objectives show similarities with those of older individuals (Mather & Carstensen, 2005), and the question of how one perceives time comes into prominence.

In a study conducted in 1999, Zimbardo and Boyd argue that time or time perspective (TP) affects human behavior. Similarly, SST also claims that the perception of time plays a crucial role in the designation and fulfillment of social goals (Carstensen et al., 1999). For instance, one determines plans and purposes based on a time frame. However, these plans and goals might vary depending on TP. To illustrate, one can say that the willingness to gain knowledge of a topic, make plans, and setting targets are positively correlated with the perceived life span increases (Mather & Carstensen, 2005).

Studied extensively within the scope of gerontological theories, the concept of selectivity is used as an emotional regulation strategy by senior adults (Sims et al., 2015). In time, older adults decline physically, normatively, and cognitively, setting attainable goals for themselves to be able to maintain their comfort and go on with their daily lives (Sands et al., 2018). In other words, senior adults try to avoid negative experiences while preserving and maintaining positive ones (Grossmann et al., 2014). Essentially, as they grow older, individuals attach greater importance to emotions balancing emotive states, averting from regret, and pleasing the individual rather than knowledge-related objectives (Yoon et al., 2009) while formulating their decision-making strategies based on emotions (Carpenter & Yoon, 2015).

2 Consumer Psychology within the Scope of Socioemotional Selectivity Theory

The knowledge, emotions, and social surroundings of consumers are the psychological factors affecting purchasing behavior. Many studies endeavored to determine the effect of age on purchasing decisions by examining the relationship between age and activities like information collection about a good or service, product preferences, attitudes towards a product, and (re)purchasing. Studying senior consumers within the framework of SST is crucial for consumer psychology.

SST concentrates on two categories of social motivation: gaining knowledge or establishing new social relationships, and emotional satisfaction. The motivation to gain knowledge and establish social relationships explain the goal of acquiring in-depth knowledge about one's self and social environment. As for the motivation of emotional satisfaction, it denotes the objective of feeling good about oneself, making emotional inferences about life, deepening social connection, and preserving one's self (Fung et al. 1999; Carstensen, Fung, & Charles, 2003).

The limited physical mobility and/or lower motor skills of senior adults might restrain their access to knowledge (Yoon et al., 2009). Furthermore, as they have extensive experience in many subjects, they do not require redundant knowledge. In other words, the scope of knowledge-seeking narrows, and the number of information sources decreases as one grows older (Pour Mohammad & Drolet, 2019). For instance, senior consumers do not concentrate on collecting information in decision-making as it is mentally or physically challenging. Instead, they prefer constructing smaller consideration sets (buying a familiar product and/or brand at a familiar price) (Carpenter & Yoon, 2015).

In their study examining the impact of scores and comments given by other users on young and senior adults, von Helversen et al. (2018) found that young adults, in particular, rely on average user scores and positive product reviews, whereas senior consumers do not take them quite seriously. However, they also revealed that senior adults are more susceptible to the effect of negative reviews. The researchers believed that the reason behind this was that a rational strategy for senior consumers was having emotional objectives in mind to avoid potential and, in particular, emotional losses.

The impact of one's social environment is crucial in getting information. One's social environment is the primary source of information. Opinions, observations, and knowledge of and cultural exchanges with others are vital for the persistence of information; knowledge transfer occurs through social means to a great extent (Carstensen et al., 1999). However, in the later stages of adulthood, social interaction tends to decrease gradually (Fredrickson & Carstensen, 1990). This decrease limits the access of older adults to new information.

SST argues that older adults prefer social relationships through which they can have more meaningful life and form intense and strong bonds (Carstensen & Mikels, 2005). For instance, in a study conducted with young and older adults, Fredrickson & Carstensen (1990) gave the options of a close family member, a close friend, and the author of a book they read and asked the participants to pick one of these options as their social partner. 65% of the older adults participating in the study were observed to determine a family member as their social partner, whereas this rate was only 35% among young adults. In other words, as people grow older, they become gradually more selective in their choices of social partners and invest in fewer people (English & Carstensen, 2015). Older adults trust more in the information obtained from external sociological sources such as family members, relatives, and close friends, i.e., their nuclear social circle (Fung et al., 1999; Pour Mohammad & Drolet, 2019).

However, according to Hettich et al. (2018), older consumers rely more on mass communication tools, whereas younger consumers value the opinions of their friends and colleagues. They associated these findings with the increase in the time older adults spend in front of the television as a result of their narrowing social circles and the consequent positive attitudes towards the media.

In a study in 2003, Fung and Carstensen (2003) evaluated the reactions from different age groups to emotion-themed and information-themed advertising and revealed that the former had a more permanent place in the memories of older consumers. Similarly, researching age-related motivations through the responses to emotional advertising, Williams and Drolet (2005) handled emotion and information-themed advertising within the framework of chronological age and time perspective, finding that older consumers and younger ones manipulated into thinking that their lifetime is limited liked and remembered emotional advertising more and found emotional advertising avoiding negative emotions particularly more appealing. In other words, older adults value emotionally-convincing messages more than rational or informative ones (Yoon et al., 2009).

Decision-making is a result of the complex and holistic evaluation of cognitive and emotive processes. If the process needs more descriptive information, the individual in question makes decisions by description; but if descriptive information is insufficient and past knowledge and experiences come into the forefront during the process, the individual makes decisions by experience. Older adults are expected to assess the information they gathered while making a decision differently from young adults. For example, young adults process information faster than older adults; as one grows older, the processing and use of emotional knowledge becomes more significant in both routine and non-routine decisions (Peters et al., 2007). Older consumers refer to their past experiences more frequently to formulate their decision-making strategies. Therefore, they try to balance the decline in their cognitive functions as a result of the aging process by using the knowledge and experience obtained throughout the years. For instance, older consumers are better at guessing the prices sold at a store using their past experiences and familiarity (Carpenter & Yoon, 2015).

As one grows older, the processing and use of emotional information in both routine and non-routine decision-making become vital (Peters et al., 2007). Recent psychological studies on decision-making processes underline the significance of emotional processes. While older adults have a difficult time in issues requiring to make complex cognitive decisions, they are observed to make better decisions in cases demanding emotional decision-making (Carpenter & Yoon, 2015). In SST, this is explained by the increased importance attached by older adults to emotional goals and, as a result, better interpretation of complex emotional matters (Carstensen et al., 2003; Peters et al., 2007).

Older consumers are expected to make different purchasing decisions and display different behaviors when compared with young adults because they have are more experienced due to their previous purchases and, therefore, do not dwell on minute details while making complicated preferences (Lambert-Pandraud et al., 2005). For older consumers usually formulating their assessments of products based on their emotions, positive emotions are prioritized. While evaluating the quality of and their satisfaction from the product in question, they are more influenced by emotional factors rather than cognitive ones (Kaur et al., 2018).

Older adults attempt to feel younger by manipulating their TP, dressing, and acting like more youthful people. Venues targeting children and younger people like Disneyland are popular honeymoon destinations for adults as well because they expand their TP and relive their childhood. Similarly, by manipulating the TP of consumers, i.e., by convincing them to think like a younger person or, in contrast, by making them feel that they have limited time, marketers try to change the consumption preferences of consumers (Gutchess, 2011). For example, in advertisements including traffic or occupational accidents, consumers are encouraged to get life insurance by making them think that their life hangs on a thread and their TP is limited; conversely, by promoting warm vacation destinations and hotels in winter attempt to convince consumers to reserve their places early on by evoking the feeling that their TP is extended.

Shopping at a store is a considerable challenge for older consumers (Kuppelwieser, 2016). In particular, crowded venues like supermarkets and shopping malls contain a substantial amount of distractive information confusing older consumers. Mainly unfamiliar places affect the decision-making capacity of older consumers. As a result, they might not find the brand they would like to buy, settling for other brands (Carpenter & Yoon, 2015).

As they grow older, consumers are more likely to repurchase the same brands and become more loyal customers. This is associated with the decline among older consumers in the performance of seeking and evaluating new information (Pour Mohammad & Drolet, 2019). SST argues that older consumers have different motivations, goals, and habits when compared with young adults. Similarly, in contrast to younger consumers, older consumers consider maintaining relationships with familiar providers more important as far as their consumption habits are concerned (Yoon et al., 2009). In their study, Phua et al., (2020) found that older consumers are more likely to opt for long-established and older brands they are familiar with.

Brand loyalty might vary depending on many factors like past experiences with products, habits, nostalgia, and the desire to remain unchanged in terms of potential (Arensberg, 2018). There are certain research studies showing that as they get older, consumers tend to remain loyal to specific products and brands, developing emotional bonds with the brand in question. For example, in a study examining repurchasing behavior, Lambert-Pandraud et al. (2005) found that older consumers consider fewer alternatives while choosing brands, automobile dealers, or models and that they are more likely to buy the products of a brand they used previously. However, older consumers having higher emotional sensitivities also pose certain risks for the brands in question because potential negative experiences might make these consumers opt for different brand alternatives.

In brief, these studies demonstrate that older consumers have high brand loyalty. This has different outcomes in terms of marketing management. The growth of the older consumer segment provides significant advantages, particularly for the future rivals of strong and deeply-rooted brands while presenting severe challenges for new businesses.

Conclusion

Taking the fact that the senior population will reach 2 billion in the medium term into consideration, one can state that older consumers constitute a considerable market segment for many sectors and that they will have significant market potential.

Many marketers consider older adults generally as individuals having difficulties in physical and/or mental activities who are antisocial and unwilling to try new things (Sherman et al., 2001). However, this has started to change gradually. People refuse to age, trying to participate in healthy living activities to look and feel younger (Kim et al., 2007). Programs specially curated for older adults at gyms and spa centers might be considered a result of this increasing demand. Furthermore, each older generation considers the next younger generation to be more knowledgeable, lively, active, and outgoing. Furthermore, the younger generation believes that being open to change is a crucial attitude (Sherman et al., 2001). So, having relatively more experience in using tools like computers, the Internet, cell phones, or social media, the younger generation has easier access to information and is more successful in finding and processing information when compared with the previous generation.

These features demonstrate that the older adult market has an internally heterogeneous structure. Dividing this market into homogeneous sub-groups would allow marketers to gather more accurate and comprehensive data. While categorizing the older adult market; biological, psychological, and sociological age must also be taken into consideration in addition to chronological age.

SST places particular emphasis on the effect of nuclear social circles of older adults. While planning marketing activities, taking the nuclear social circle into account is vital for the success of marketing plans.

Research studies demonstrate that older consumers are significantly loyal to certain businesses and brands. To secure their positions, marketers must pay due attention to their current young consumers.

Different approaches must be developed for the older consumer market, and their unique features and dynamics must be taken into consideration to develop a successful marketing strategy. Understanding the market dynamics created by older adults better would create new opportunities for businesses, leading to an increase in their turnover.

References

Arensberg, M. B. (2018). Population aging: opportunity for business expansion, an invitational paper presented at the Asia-Pacific Economic Cooperation (APEC) International Workshop on Adaptation to Population Aging Issues, July 17, 2017, Ha Noi, Viet Nam. *Journal of Health, Population and Nutrition*, *37*(1), 7. https://doi.org/10.1186/s41043-018-0138-0 Accessed on: 18.03.2020.

Carpenter, S. M., & Yoon, C. (2015). Aging and consumer decision making. In *Aging and Decision Making: Empirical and applied Perspectives* (pp. 351–370). Elsevier Academic Press. https://doi.org/10.1016/B978-0-12-417148-0.00017-0 Accessed on: 18.03.2020.

Carstensen, L. L., Fung, H. H., & Charles, S. T. (2003). Socioemotional selectivity theory and the regulation of emotion in the second half of life. *Motivation and Emotion*, *27*(2), pp. 103–123. https://doi.org/10.1023/A:1024569803230 Accessed on: 18.03.2020.

Carstensen, L. L., Isaacowitz, D. M., & Charles, S. T. (1999). Taking time seriously: A theory of socioemotional selectivity. *American Psychologist*, *54*(3), pp. 165–181. https://doi.org/10.1037/0003-066X.54.3.165 Accessed on: 18.03.2020.

Carstensen, L. L., & Mikels, J. A. (2005). At the intersection of emotion and cognition: Aging and the positivity effect. *Current Directions in Psychological Science*, *14*(3), pp. 117–121. https://doi.org/10.1111/j.0963-7214.2005.00348.x Accessed on: 18.03.2020.

English, T., & Carstensen, L. L. (2015). Emotions and aging. In *International Encyclopedia of the Social & Behavioral Sciences* (2nd Ed.), 7(1998), pp. 490–495. Oxford: Elsevier. https://doi.org/10.1016/B978-0-08-097086-8.25056-3 Accessed on: 18.03.2020.

Fredrickson, B. L., & Carstensen, L. L. (1990). Choosing social partners: How old age and anticipated endings make people more selective. *Psychology and Aging*, *5*(3), pp. 335–347. https://doi.org/10.1037/0882-7974.5.3.335 Accessed on: 18.03.2020.

Fung, H. H., & Carstensen, L. L. (2003). Sending memorable messages to the old: Age differences in preferences and memory for advertisements. *Journal of Personality and Social Psychology*, *85*(1), pp. 163–178. https://doi.org/10.1037/0022-3514.85.1.163 Accessed on: 18.03.2020.

Fung, H. H., Carstensen, L. L., & Lutz, A. M. (1999). Influence of time on social preferences: Implications for life-span development. *Psychology and Aging*, *14*(4), pp. 595–604. https://doi.org/10.1037/0882-7974.14.4.595 Accessed on: 18.03.2020.

Grossmann, I., Karasawa, M., Kan, C., & Kitayama, S. (2014). A cultural perspective on emotional experiences across the life span. *Emotion*, *14*(4), pp. 679–692. https://doi.org/10.1037/a0036041 Accessed on: 18.03.2020.

Gutchess, A. H. (2011). The Aging Consumer: Perspectives from Psychology and Economics. In A. Drolet, N. Schwarz, & C. Yoon (Eds.), *Choice Reviews Online*, 48(06). https://doi.org/10.5860/choice.48-3362 Accessed on: 18.03.2020.

Hettich, D., Hattula, S., & Bornemann, T. (2018). Consumer decision-making of older people: A 45-year review. *Gerontologist*, *58*(6), pp. E349–E368. https://doi.org/10.1093/geront/gnx007 Accessed on: 18.03.2020.

Jiang, D., & Fung, H. H. (2019). Social and Emotional Theories of Aging. In *Work across the Lifespan* (pp. 135–153). Elsevier. https://doi.org/10.1016/B978-0-12-812756-8.00006-2 Accessed on: 18.03.2020.

Kaur, D., Mustika, M. D., & Sjabadhyni, B. (2018). Affect or cognition: Which is more influencing older adult consumers' loyalty? *Heliyon*, *4*(4), e00610. https://doi.org/10.1016/j.heliyon.2018.e00610 Accessed on: 18.03.2020.

Kim, H.-Y., Jolly, L., & Kim, Y.-K. (2007). Future forces transforming apparel retailing in the United States. *Clothing and Textiles Research Journal*, *25*(4), pp. 307–322. https://doi.org/10.1177/0887302X07306851 Accessed on: 18.03.2020.

Kuppelwieser, V. G. (2016). Towards the use of chronological age in research – A cautionary comment. *Journal of Retailing and Consumer Services*, *33*, pp. 17–22. https://doi.org/10.1016/j.jretconser.2016.05.016 Accessed on: 18.03.2020.

Lambert-Pandraud, R., Laurent, G., & Lapersonne, E. (2005). Repeat purchasing of new automobiles by older consumers : Empirical evidence and interpretations. *Journal of Marketing*, *69*(2), pp. 97–113.

Mather, M., & Carstensen, L. L. (2005). Aging and motivated cognition: The positivity effect in attention and memory. *Trends in Cognitive Sciences*, *9*(10), pp. 496–502. https://doi.org/10.1016/j.tics.2005.08.005 Accessed on: 18.03.2020.

Peters, E., Hess, T. M., Västfjäll, D., & Auman, C. (2007). Adult age differences in dual information processes: Implications for the role of affective and deliberative processes in older adults' decision making. *Perspectives on Psychological Science*, *2*(1), pp. 1–23. https://doi.org/10.1111/j.1745-6916.2007.00025.x Accessed on: 18.03.2020.

Phua, P., Kennedy, R., Trinh, G., Page, B., & Hartnett, N. (2020). Examining older consumers' loyalty towards older brands in grocery retailing. *Journal of Retailing and Consumer Services*, *52* (January 2019), p. 101893. https://doi.org/10.1016/j.jretconser.2019.101893 Accessed on: 18.03.2020.

Pour Mohammad, A., & Drolet, A. (2019). The influence of age and time horizon perspective on consumer behavior. *Current Opinion in Psychology*, *26*(1977), pp. 94–97. https://doi.org/10.1016/j.copsyc.2018.07.008 Accessed on: 18.03.2020.

Sands, M., Livingstone, K. M., & Isaacowitz, D. M. (2018). Characterizing age-related positivity effects in situation selection. *International Journal of Behavioral Development*, *42*(4), pp. 396–404. https://doi.org/10.1177/0165025417723086 Accessed on: 18.03.2020.

Sherman, E., Schiffman, L. G., & Mathur, A. (2001). The influence of gender on the new-age elderly's consumption orientation. *Psychology and Marketing*, *18*(10), pp. 1073–1089. https://doi.org/10.1002/mar.1044 Accessed on: 18.03.2020.

Sims, T., Hogan, C. L., & Carstensen, L. L. (2015). Selectivity as an emotion regulation strategy: Lessons from older adults. *Current Opinion in Psychology*, *3*, pp. 80–84. https://doi.org/10.1016/j.copsyc.2015.02.012 Accessed on: 18.03.2020.

Strough, J., Löckenhoff, C. E., & Hess, T. M. (2015). Aging and Decision Making Empirical and Applied Perspectives. In T. M. Hess, J. Strough, & C. E. Löckenhoff (Eds.), *Aging and Decision Making*. Academic Press. https://doi.org/10.1016/c2013-0-05180-8 Accessed on: 18.03.2020.

von Helversen, B., Abramczuk, K., Kopeć, W., & Nielek, R. (2018). Influence of consumer reviews on online purchasing decisions in older and younger adults. *Decision Support Systems*, *113*, pp. 1–10. https://doi.org/10.1016/j.dss.2018.05.006 Accessed on: 18.03.2020.

Williams, P., & Drolet, A. (2005). Age-related differences in responses to emotional advertisements. *Journal of Consumer Research*, *32*(3), pp. 343–354. https://doi.org/10.1086/497545 Accessed on: 18.03.2020.

Yoon, C., Cole, C. A., & Lee, M. P. (2009). Consumer decision making and aging: Current knowledge and future directions. *Journal of Consumer Psychology*, *19*(1), pp. 2–16. https://doi.org/10.1016/j.jcps.2008.12.002 Accessed on: 18.03.2020.

Zimbardo, P. G., & Boyd, J. N. (1999). Putting time in perspective: A valid, reliable individual-differences metric. *Journal of Personality and Social Psychology*, *77*(6), pp. 1271–1288. https://doi.org/10.1037/0022 3514.77.6.1271 Accessed on: 18.03.2020.

Section 3 Practices of Consumer Psychology

Hayrettin ZENGİN

18 Metaphoric Analysis of Consumption Concept in Digital Natives

Introduction

This chapter dealing with various aspects of the psychological dimension of consumption aims to reveal the emotions and thoughts of consumers, going beyond the analysis of their instantaneous and superficial behavior. Consumer behavior towards goods and services are influenced by subconscious emotions and thoughts that are difficult to express rather than instantaneous and superficial ideas (Zaltman, 2003). Uncovering subconscious information by understanding consumer behavior and decisions to steer their actions with the aim of creating added value for consumers is crucial researchers and practitioners. One of the most frequently adopted methods to this end is "metaphors". Metaphors affect the way perceptions are created by bringing out consumer emotions and opinions (Lakoff & Johnson, 2008).

Used for many complex and abstruse concepts, metaphors provide significant convenience for communicating with consumers (Capelli & Jolibert, 2009). Many companies make considerable use of metaphors in their endeavor to understand consumers and produce goods and services satisfying their needs, aiming to increase the chance of consumers buying their products. As technology dominating daily life and decisions in the present day, companies focus on the current and future identities of their consumers along with their potential sales.

In terms of their technological dispositions, users are classified as "digital natives" and "digital immigrants". Digital natives are described as people born in the digital age, therefore having an excellent command of technology. As for digital immigrants, they attempt to keep up with technology without a perfect command of technology use, similar to a person learning a second language and speaking it with a strong accent. As digital natives have never lived in a period without digital media, technology plays a vital role in their daily lives and actions. It is possible to regard digital natives as "digital customers" with disposable income in favor of differentiating themselves from others to draw more attention on social media (Sayar & Yalaz, 2019).

Considering the significant changes in our daily practices brought about by the digital age, understanding how the generation of digital natives makes sense of the multi-dimensional concept of consumption is vital. To this end, this study uses metaphor analysis, one of the methods that might be used to understand and explain "consumption", an abstract and complex concept. This chapter will attempt to reveal the perceptions of the digital generation regarding the concept of consumption through metaphors.

1 The Concept of Metaphor

Interpreting one concept based on another is the basis of metaphors (Lakoff & Johnson, 2008). While making sense of something, one idea is explained through another word by likening it to something else (Palmer & Lundberg, 1995). Therefore, an abstruse and complex concept becomes understandable through the lens of a familiar concept (Erdem & Sarvan, 2001). While explaining a concept, one might utilize either the abstract or concrete meanings of other concepts (Morgan, 1998).

In the case of metaphors, while expressing an unfamiliar concept, one uses similes, comparisons, or narrations through a similar phenomenon (Demir, 2008, cited in Atar, Şener, & Onay, 2016). In this respect, categorized as verbal or visual, metaphors are defined as figurative linguistic devices (Phillips, 2000). In verbal metaphors created through figurative expression, concepts are used in place of one another through words and idioms, with one of the words used in its literal meaning and the other in the connotational sense. This is called an analogy (Boozer, Wyld, & Grant, 1991). In metaphors visually constructed through figurative expression, once again the analogical method is used. Therefore, two objects and images replacing one another are juxtaposed, indirectly allowing the observer to interpret this visualization (Phillips, 2000).

According to Lakoff and Johnson (2008), the processes in which individuals make sense and think of concepts inherently take place through metaphors. Difficult and complex, abstract concepts are not easy for the human mind to interpret. To do this, our minds refer to previous experiences to concretize abstract concepts. In addition to the pivotal role of individual experiences and personality traits in the formation of metaphors (Schmitt, 2005), factors like cultural values, language, religion, and race also influence metaphors (Giannetti, 2014).

As metaphors have a potent impact on one's thoughts (Zaltman, 2003; Thibodeau, 2016), they are frequently used to explain novel and unknown concepts (Lakoff & Johnson, 2008). Metaphors allow us to observe the reality of opinions of individuals (Schmitt, 2005) while creating a wide range of different opinions (Koro-Ljungberg, 2001). In this respect, they are invaluable for scientific research (Delbaere & Slobodzian, 2018).

2 Findings

Taking the economic and sociological significance of consumption transcending the mere fulfillment of needs in the present day, the designation of the interpretations of future consumers and decision-makers regarding this concept is crucial. Determining the consumption preferences in the economic sense and lifestyles in the sociological sense of future target audiences, along with their significations regarding the concept, might provide important data for businesses and decision-makers in their future projections. Within this framework, uncovering the interpretations of the generation of digital natives (individuals under 20 years of age) regarding the phenomenon of consumption is vital.

In this respect, this chapter uses metaphors to reveal the opinions and interpretations of digital natives concerning consumption. To this end, it will attempt to provide answers to the following questions:

1. What metaphors do digital natives have regarding consumption?
2. Under which categories these metaphors can be classified?

For the purposes of the study, digital natives participating in the study were asked to complete the sentence "*Consumption* is *like* ... *because* ...". The meanings of the words "like" and "because are significant in studies employing the metaphorical method. "Like" allows one to present the similarity about the *source* and *subject of the metaphor* while "because" consists of the *reason* and *logical foundation* of the similarity in question (Saban, Koçbeker, & Saban, 2006).

For the research, 289 digital natives filled out forms; 48 of these forms were excluded from the study as they did not include any sources of metaphor, lacked reason (logical foundation), or were inconsequential. In the end, a total of 241 forms were assessed.

Table 18.1 shows the age and gender structure of the digital natives participating in the study. The selection of the individuals born in 2000 and 2001 was deliberate since the historical process takes the year 2000 as the basis while classifying digital natives.

Tab. 18.1: Age and Gender Distribution of Participants. **Source:** Created by Author

Age	f	%	**Gender**	f	%
19	64	27	Female	140	58
20	177	73	Male	101	42
Total	*241*	*100*	*Total*	*241*	*100*

2.1 Analyzing the Data

Using the techniques of "*metaphor analysis*" and "*content analysis*", this section analyzes the "*sources*" and "*logical foundations*" of metaphors. In the initial stage, the forms that do not fulfill the criteria for the metaphor analysis, i.e. those *not including metaphors* and *not having logical foundations*, were discarded. Furthermore, the basic criterion for the analysis was the development of the metaphor by both genders. Metaphors formulated by a single participant or multiple participants of the same gender were excluded from the analysis.

Table 18.2 shows the distribution of the metaphors created by both genders as per the criteria indicated above. A total of 42 metaphors were proposed in the 172 forms evaluated within the scope of the analysis. "*Brand*" has the highest frequency among the metaphors related to consumption. This metaphor is followed by "*Money*". While the metaphors of "*Brand*" and "*Money*" are distributed evenly among the two genders, the third metaphor of "*Automobile*" is indicated predominantly by male participants (7 times by male participants (88%), once by female participants (12%)). As for the sixth metaphor of "*Handbag*", it was mostly uttered by female participants with 5 instances (83%) whereas male participants expressed it only once (17%). It can be stated that gender is an important variable for the creation of the metaphors "*Automobile*" and "*Handbag*".

Tab. 18.2: Metaphors Created by Digital Natives. **Source:** Created by Author

	Metaphor	Female	Male	Total		Metaphor	Female	Male	Total
1	Brand	11	8	19	*22*	Sun	2	1	3
2	Money	5	4	9	*23*	Gasoline	1	2	3
3	Automobile	1	7	8	*24*	Air	2	1	3
4	Love	6	1	7	*25*	Medication	1	2	3
5	Bread	3	4	7	*26*	School	1	2	3
6	Handbag	5	1	6	*27*	Freedom	2	1	3
7	Social media	4	2	6	*28*	Marriage	2	1	3
8	Water	3	2	5	*29*	Coke	2	1	3
9	Lover	1	4	5	*30*	Watching series	1	2	3
10	Starbucks	3	2	5	*31*	Friend	1	2	3
11	Craziness	4	1	5	*32*	Pasta	1	1	2
12	Credit card	2	2	4	*33*	Vaccination	1	1	2
13	Potato chips	3	1	4	*34*	TV	1	1	2
14	Sleep	2	2	4	*35*	Ending	1	1	2

Tab. 18.2: Continued

	Metaphor	Female	Male	Total		Metaphor	Female	Male	Total
15	Entertainment	3	1	4	*36*	Child	1	1	2
16	Shopping mall	2	2	4	*37*	Cycle	1	1	2
17	Cigarettes	1	3	4	*38*	Colony	1	1	2
18	Chocolate	3	1	4	*39*	Salt	1	1	2
19	iPhone	2	2	4	*40*	Book / Novel	1	1	2
20	Alcohol	1	2	3	*41*	Grocery store	1	1	2
21	Life	2	1	3	*42*	Mother	1	1	2
						Total	*93*	*79*	*172*

2.2 Conceptual Categories and Analysis

This section makes conceptual categorizations of the metaphors created by the generation defined as digital natives 20 and under 20 years of age regarding the concept of consumption based on common characteristics. Being expressed by participants of both genders was the basic criterion for this categorization. The examination of the reasons and logical foundations of metaphors lead to their classification into five conceptual categories. These conceptual categorizations and their shares in percentages are shown in Table 18.3.

The model developed by Miles and Huberman is used to determine the reliability of the studies employing the metaphorical method to interpret various concepts. The model suggests that the researcher must take the consensus rate calculated with the formula $\Delta = C \div (C +) \times 100$ (Δ: reliability coefficient, C: number of agreements, ∂: number of disagreements). To achieve internal consistency, an agreement between coders is sought and a threshold of 80% agreement is necessary (Miles & Huberman, 1994 cited in Baltacı, 2017).

Within this framework, *expert opinions* were also collected to determine the reliability of the research. Three professors from the Department of Marketing within the Faculty of Business were consulted to confirm whether the metaphors included in the conceptual categories were representatives of their categories. The professors were first given two lists comprised of the metaphors and conceptual categories as well as the explanations of the categories. Then, they were asked to match the metaphors with conceptual categories. The consensus rates of the professors were calculated as 86%, 89%, and 93%, therefore satisfying the conditions for agreement (reliability) regarding the distribution of the metaphors into the conceptual categories.

Tab. 18.3: Conceptual Categories and Percentages of Metaphors. **Source:** Created by Author

Conceptual categories	**Number of metaphors**	**%**	**Σ**
Category 1: Consumption as a necessity	13	30	30
Category 2: Consumption as a regrettable concept	12	29	59
Category 3: Consumption as an elating concept	7	17	76
Category 4: Consumption as an addictive concept	6	14	90
Category 5: Consumption as an indicator of wealth	4	10	100
Total	*42*	*100*	

Category 1: Consumption as a Necessity

Approaches using the luxury dimension of consumption in particular as a data source concern the fact that goods and services are consumed mostly due to their wide-range significances and definitions rather than their basic functions. This statement about consumption does not mean, however, that goods and services do not have basic functions. The association of consumption with needs is thought to be effective in the perception of consumption *as a necessity*. The large number of metaphors associated with the perception of consumption *as a necessity* begs an assessment of the concept of needs within the framework of Maslow's hierarchy of needs. Needs can be defined as strong drives necessary for survival, leading to happiness when met and causing discomfort when not met. The said drives are thought to have a considerable share in the place of the concept in the minds of consumers.

Table 18.4 shows the metaphors comprising the category of *consumption as a necessity* and their distribution in terms of gender. 13 out of 42 metaphors created by participants of both genders evaluated in the study (30%) are in this category. The metaphors of *Money*, *Bread*, *Handbag*, and *Water* within this category are the ones with the highest frequencies. The top five metaphors can be evaluated within the scope of vital necessities, except for the metaphor of *Handbag*. One reason for the high ranking of the metaphor of *Handbag* might be the perception among women that it is an essential item.

- *Consumption is like money because it is impossible to live without money. (Age: 19, Gender: Male)*
- *Consumption is like a handbag because it organizes my life. I cannot imagine my life without a bag. I feel naked without it. I do not even know where to put my hands without it. (Age: 20, Gender: Female)*

- *Consumption is like the sun because there is no life without the sun. (Age: 20, Gender: Female)*
- *Consumption is like gasoline because a car will not work without gasoline. (Age: 20, Gender: Male)*
- *Consumption is like pasta because it seems like a life without pas*te will be impossible after the coronavirus (Age: 19, Gender: Male)

The metaphors of *Vaccine* and *Pasta* are thought to stem from the fact that people stocked pasta and research for a vaccine was a hot topic in the agenda following the declaration by the World Health Organization of the disease called COVID-19 caused by the coronavirus as a pandemic. Tab.

Tab. 18.4: Consumption as a Necessity. **Source:** Created by Author

	Metaphor	**Female**	**Male**	**Total**		**Metaphor**	**Female**	**Male**	**Total**
1	Money	5	4	9	**8**	Air	2	1	3
2	Bread	3	4	7	**9**	Medication	1	2	3
3	Handbag	5	1	6	***10***	School	1	2	3
4	Water	3	2	5	***11***	Freedom	2	1	3
5	Life	2	1	3	***12***	Pasta	1	1	3
6	Sun	2	1	3	***13***	Vaccination	2	1	3
7	Gasoline	1	2	3		*Total*	*29*	*23*	*52*

Category 2: Consumption as a Regrettable Concept

The Turkish Language Association defines 'regret as a feeling of disappointment as a result of the undesired and inappropriate consequences of one's actions' (TDK, 20.02.2020). Regret causes significant emotional discomfort due to its negative nature. One can state that unconscious and unnecessary shopping is the leading cause of regret within the context of consumption. Table 18.5 shows the metaphors created under the category of *"Consumption as a regrettable concept"*.

- *Consumption is like a credit card because you do not think of the payments while using it, but you regret spending money when the credit card bill arrives. (Age: 20, Gender: Male)*
- *Consumption is like potato chips because when you eat them, they are delicious but then you wonder if they were worth all the calories. (Age: 20, Gender: Female)*
- *Consumption is like marriage because it is difficult to choose a spouse, you make efforts to charm them and dream of them but when you eventually get what you want, you feel a sense of emptiness. (Age: 20, Gender: Female)*

- *Consumption is like sleep because you can sleep for a while, continuously wanting to sleep more. In the end, you realize that you slept for hours. When you wake up, you become upset with yourself because of all the hours you just wasted. (Age: 19, Gender: Male)*

Tab. 18.5: Consumption as a Regrettable Act. **Source:** Created by Author

	Metaphor	Female	Male	Total		Metaphor	Female	Male	Total
1	Credit card	2	2	4	*7*	TV	1	1	2
2	Potato chips	3	1	4	*8*	Ending	1	1	2
3	Sleep	2	2	4	*9*	Child	1	1	2
4	Marriage	2	1	3	*10*	Cycle	1	1	2
5	Coke	2	1	3	*11*	Colony	1	1	2
6	Watching series	1	2	3	*12*	Salt	1	1	2
						Total	*18*	*1*	*33*

Category 3: Consumption as an Elating Concept

The relationship between wealth or money and happiness has been a popular research topic among economic theorists. The data gathered so far confirm the traditional economic statement that money can indeed buy happiness. According to the United Nations (UN) Happiness Report of 2019 (Helliwell, Layard, & Sachs, 2019), the top three countries in terms of happiness are Finland, Denmark, and Norway. The per capita income over US$ 50,000 in these countries confirms the traditional economic statement concerning the relationship between money and happiness.

Money, thus consumption (spending), and the access to goods and services desired (demanded) to satisfy limitless wants are among the crucial factors of one's happiness. In this context, the fact that the metaphors created by the participants are related to "happiness" implicitly confirms the traditional economic statement. Table 18.6 shows the metaphors created in relation to the category of consumption as an elating concept.

The fact that the metaphors created regarding the concept of consumption are associated with *happiness*, in addition to the prominence of the metaphor of *Love*, is thought to be related to the life stages of participants during which they tend to rely more on emotional decisions.

- *Consumption is like love because love makes one hold on to life, sweeping one off one's feet. It is like a journey in a sea of happiness. (Age: 20, Gender: Female)*
- *Consumption is like a shopping mall because you lose track of time while in a mall. You even happily forget yourself. (Age: 20, Gender: Female)*
- *Consumption is like a friend because it is always with us, we always need them, it is our source of happiness. (Age: 20, Gender: Male)*

Tab. 18.6: Consumption as an Elating Concept. **Source:** Created by Author

	Metaphor	**Female**	**Male**	**Total**
1	Love	6	1	7
2	Lover	1	4	5
3	Entertainment	3	1	4
4	Shopping mall	2	2	4
5	Friend	1	2	3
6	Book / Novel	1	1	2
7	Grocery store	1	1	2
	Total	*15*	*12*	*27*

Category 4: Consumption as an Addictive Concept

The loss of rationality and control in consumption has had economic, social, and psychological consequences, leading to the assessment of the concept by different scientific disciplines. Particularly in marketing, new concepts like oniomania, shopping sprees, excessive consumption, and addiction to consumption have become popular research topics, parallelly to post-modern consumer behavior (Altunışık, Bora, & Sarıkaya, 2010). Experienced by all groups of individuals regardless of gender, social status, and age, addiction to consumption leads people to spend excessively with the impulse of buying unnecessary items without any control. The short-term happiness brought by this kind of buying turns into long-term guilt and anxiety. Table 18.7 shows the metaphors created within the category of "Consumption as an addictive concept".

- *Consumption is like social media because you initially enjoy social media but then you realize that you spent hours on these outlets, you feel regretful. You say you would not use them again, but you cannot keep this promise. This leads to regret again. (Age: 20, Gender: Male)*
- *Consumption is like chocolate because it makes you happy at the first bite, making you want to eat more. But when you think of all the calories, you regret*

eating it. Then again, you want and eat chocolate again. You cannot quit. (Age: 19, Gender: Female)

- *Consumption is like a mother because our mothers are everywhere in our lives, we cannot do anything without her; in a way, we are addicted to her. Having someone thinking of everything initially feels good, but then we cannot do anything without her. (Age: 20, Gender: Female)*

Tab. 18.7: Consumption as an Addictive Concept. **Source:** Created by Author

	Metaphor	Female	Male	Total
1	Social media	4	2	6
2	Craziness	4	1	5
3	Cigarettes	1	3	4
4	Chocolate	3	1	4
5	Alcohol	1	2	3
6	Mother	1	1	2
	Total	*14*	*10*	*24*

Category 5: Consumption as an Indicator of Wealth

As far as the societal aspect of consumption is concerned, the function of consumption in the regulation of relationships between individuals plays a crucial role particularly in the designation of social statuses. Regardless of gender, people attempt to determine their social statuses and societal standings through the goods and services they consume. They opt for luxury items and status symbols to appear to be more respectable, popular, and wealthy. In a study on the perception of the concept of luxury representing different socio-economic statuses using the data from the statistical regional unit classification of the Turkish Statistical Institute, "*wealth*" was the most prevalent concept associated with luxury in all regions and among all income groups (Kurnaz, 2019: 98–99).

The present study emphasizes that the metaphor of "wealth" created in relation to the concept of consumption underlines the increased status and elevated identity brought about by consumption. Table 18.8 shows the metaphors created within the perception of consumption as an indicator of wealth and identity.

- *Consumption is like a brand because people wearing brands are so cool. I also think that everyone looks at me when I wear designer brands. (Age: 19, Gender: Female)*

- *Consumption is like Starbucks because even their cups are cool. If you find a corner to sit at Starbucks, you are so cool. (Age: 19, Gender: Male)*

Tab. 18.8: Consumption as an Indicator of Wealth. **Source:** Created by Author

	Metaphor	Female	Male	Total
1	Brand	11	8	19
2	Automobile	1	7	8
3	Starbucks	3	2	5
4	iPhone	2	2	4
	Total	*17*	*19*	*36*

Conclusion

The present study aimed to formulate certain conceptual categories by revealing the associations among the generation of digital natives, referred to as such as they were born in the technological age, regarding the phenomenon of consumption through metaphors. It is not possible to holistically explain the interpretation of a multi-dimensional and complex concept like consumption with a single metaphor. Therefore, one requires a wide range of metaphors encompassing different mentalities in order to understand and interpret the concept of consumption better.

Interpretations of consumption among digital natives are influenced by a plethora of factors. To minimize these differences, only participants aged 19 and 20 were admitted to the study. Based on the assumption that gender is an important factor in the interpretation of consumption, a balance between male and female participants was aimed. The study classified the metaphors created by digital natives under five conceptual categories. The conceptual category of *consumption as a necessity* in which the concept is defined as the fulfillment of vital needs has a share of 30% when compared with other categories. Besides this category of *consumption as a necessity*, ranking the highest among others, the remaining categories can be classified as negative or positive. The conceptual categories of *consumption as a regrettable concept* and *consumption as an addictive concept* might be categorized as negative whereas the categories of *consumption as an elating concept* and *consumption as an indicator of wealth* can be considered to be positive. In other words, besides the association with fundamental needs, consumption was associated with negative and positive concepts in a balanced manner.

The present study examining the psychological aspects of consumption contributed to a deeper understanding of the complex concept of consumption through metaphors. Therefore, consumption was analyzed through the perspective of future consumers and decision-makers, i.e. digital natives. The study might also shed light on future studies examining multiple generations through various metaphorical techniques to determine mental perspectives regarding consumption.

References

Altunışık, R., Bora, B. & Sarıkaya, N. (2010). Alışveriş çılgınlığı: tüketici gözüyle alışveriş çılgınlığı olgusunun incelenmesi üzerine bir nitel araştırma. *15. Ulusal Pazarlama Kongresi Bildiri Kitabı*, pp. 50–59.

Atar, G. M., Şener, G. & Onay, A. (2016). Aşkın metafor hali: sevgililer günü kapsamında kadın ve erkek dergilerindeki reklamlarda aşkın sunumu. *Global Media Journal*, 6 (12), pp. 411–433.

Baltacı, A. (2017). Nitel veri analizinde Miles-Huberman modeli. *Ahi Evran Üniversitesi Sosyal Bilimler Enstitüsü Dergisi*, 3 (1). pp. 1–15.

Boozer, R. W., Wyld, D. C. & Grant, J. (1991). Using metaphor to create more effective sales messages. *The Journal of Consumer Marketing*, 7 (1).

Capelli, S. & Jolibert, A. (2009). Metaphor's validity in marketing research. *Psychology and Marketing*. 26 (12). pp. 1079–1090.

Delbaere, M. & Slobodzian, A. D. (2018). Marketing's metaphors have expired: An argument for a new dominant metaphor. *Marketing Theory*. pp. 1–11. DOI: 10.1177/1470593118796697 Accessed on: 22.02.2020.

Erdem F. & Sarvan, F. (2001). Akademik örgütlerde rehberlik ilişkilerinin metaforlarla analizi. *Yönetim Araştırmaları Dergisi*, 1, pp. 1–10.

Giannetti, L. (2014). Savoring power, consuming the times: the metaphors of food inmedieval and renaissance Italian literature by Palma. *Renaissance Quarterly*, 67 (1), pp. 328–329.

Helliwell, J., Layard, R. & Sachs, J. (2019). *World happiness report 2019*. New York: Sustainable Development Solutions Network. pp. 1–136. https://s3.amazonaws.com/happiness-report/2019/WHR19.pdf Accessed on: 22.02.2020.

Koro-Ljungberg, M. (2001). Metaphors as a way to explore qualitative data. *Qualitative Studies in Education*. 14 (3), pp. 367–379.

Kurnaz, A. (2019). *Lüks ve Satın Alma Niyeti: Kavramlar, Teoriler, Ilişkiler ve Uygulama*. Gazi Kitabevi, Ankara.

Lakoff, G. & Johnson, M. (2008). *Metaphors We Live by*. Chicago: The University of Chicago Press.

Morgan, G. (1998). *Yönetim ve Örgüt Teorilerinde Metafor*. Gündüz Bulut (Ed.). Mess Yayınevi, İstanbul.

Palmer, I. & Lundberg, C. C. (1995). Metaphors of hospitality organizations. *Cornel Hotel and Restaurant Administration Quarterly*, 36 (3), pp. 80–85.

Phillips, B. J. (2000). The impact of verbal anchoring on consumer response to image ads. *Journal of Advertising*, 29 (1), pp. 15–24. DOI:10.1080/00913367.2000.10673600 Accessed on: 22.02.2020.

Saban, A., Koçbeker, B. N. & Saban, A. (2006). Öğretmen adaylarının öğretmen kavramına ilişkin algılarının metafor analizi yoluyla incelenmesi. *Kuram ve Uygulamada Eğitim Bilimleri*, 6 (2). Pp. 461–522.

Sayar, K. & Yalaz, B. (2019). *Ağ*. İstanbul: Kapı yayınları.

Schmitt, R. (2005). Systematic metaphor analysis as a method of qualitative research. *The Qualitative Report*, 10(2). pp. 358–394.

Thibodeau, P. H. (2016). Extended metaphors are the home runs of persuasion: Don't fumble the phrase. *Metaphor and Symbol*, 31 (2), pp. 53–72.

TDK, (The Turkish Language Association) (2020). 'Pişman olmak = Regret', https://sozluk.gov.tr/?kelime=nedamet%20duymak%20(veya%20getirmek) Accessed on: 22.02.2020.

Zaltman, G. (2003). *Tüketici Nasıl Düşünür.* A. Semih Koç (Ed.). 2nd ed. İstanbul: MediaCat Yayınları.

Volkan TEMİZKAN

19 Does the Principle of Least Effort Affect the Intention to Continue Using a Mobile Shopping Application?

Introduction

Marketing experts have always wanted to understand the emotions and opinions of their target audiences. This effort has brought about a crossover between marketing and psychology. The endeavor to comprehend consumer behavior better underlies the intersection between the two disciplines. This is beneficial for both the business and the consumer. Through the efforts in this respect, the consumer is likely to save time, energy, and money. In fact, saving time and minimizing the required amount of effort is one of the most significant benefits, because individuals tend to opt for the way in which they are the least likely to encounter resistance. Claiming that people choose the least difficult way of achieving a goal, Guillaume Ferrero (1894) named this theoretical framework "the principle of least effort". After Ferrero, George Kingsley Zipf (1949) evaluated this theory within the framework of human behavior. According to Zipf, individuals want to choose the easiest way, among other alternatives, to accomplish their tasks.

While elaborating on the theory, Zipf gives the example of a carpenter who places the tools he uses closer to him, minimizing the efforts he puts in to do his work. Today, always kept by one's side, smartphones are the most frequently used devices. This frequent use will lead consumers to opt for applications requiring the least amount of effort. Mobile applications are software developed for mobile devices. Although these software products have similarities with desktop applications in terms of design and development processes, their development environments, contents, hardware and the technology used differ from the afore-mentioned (Grotnes, 2009). Applications for mobile shopping are generally offered by businesses providing B2C or C2C sales services (Islam et. al., 2010). Mobile shopping denotes the transactions consumers make using their mobile devices (Ko et al., 2009).

Technological advancements, particularly those in mobile Internet technologies, have enabled consumers to make almost every possible online transaction from their smartphones. Online shopping is among the most popular transactions made using smartphones. In mobile commerce, mobile applications are preferred by consumers to websites because they are considered to be more convenient, faster, and easier to monitor (Natarajan et. al., 2018). Therefore, the difficulties in using mobile shopping applications must be eliminated to provide the simplest purchasing experience to the consumer. However, it is a known fact that even for the simplest money transfers like wire transfers or EFT, customers lose time while navigating through various menus in mobile banking applications (Poggenpohl, 2019). As far as mobile shopping is concerned, even a single second wasted during the loading time can reduce conversions by up to 20% (Matinyan, 2019). Such a context has also created a shift in the criteria for success. Offering user-friendly (UF) mobile applications providing positive user experience (UX) for consumers shopping and browsing from small-sized smartphone screens has become one of the most significant criteria. Here, being user-friendly is a prerequisite for a positive user experience.

The purpose of this research study is to examine the factors affecting the intention of consumers adopting the principle of least effort to continue using a mobile shopping application. Based on the model formulated at the end of the literature review, the study aims to see whether the variables of "being user-friendly" and "providing a positive user experience" affect the intention of consumers to keep using the mobile shopping application in question. Furthermore, the literature review did not show any other studies examining the three concepts comprising the basic variables of the present study. For this reason, the fundamental objective of the study is to make a causal analysis of the variables of being user-friendly and providing a positive user experience as precursors of the intention to keep using the said application.

1 Theoretical Framework

1.1 Mobile User Experience (MEX)

ISO 9241-210 defines user experience as a person's perceptions and responses that result from the use and/or anticipated use of a product, system or service (ISO 9241-210: 2009). Hassenzahl and Tractinsky (2006) stated that the three most important components affecting user experience are the user, the system, and the content. In various models proposed in the literature, the concept of experience was examined from three perspectives: product-centered, interaction-centered, and user-centered (Forlizzi & Battarbee, 2004).

The consumer tends to repeat behavioral patterns to which they are accustomed psychologically. In favor of simplicity, the consumer wants to use web pages intuitively as it is the case in desktop interfaces with a computer. Therefore, first impressions matter; 79% of online buyers do not use a website again if they had a negative user experience (Matinyan, 2019). Additionally, they do not have the time or patience to fill out forms and payment details (Kowalski, 2019). If the site takes too long to load, the consumer cannot find the product they are looking for, or the payment process seems as if it is not going to end; the consumer feels time pressure and leaves the site disappointed without buying the products they added to their basket.

1.2 User-Friendly Mobile Application

The meaning of being user-friendly is wider than the mere concept of usability. High-quality content, ease of use, speed, and frequency of updating are four significant factors encouraging consumers to visit the said website again (Rosen & Purinton, 2004). 76% of users believe that the ease of use is the most important feature for a website (Kowalski, 2019). Designing web content is similar to designing a physical landscape in several ways. Computer interaction is an intense cognition encompassing perceptions and preferences. The interaction in this context signifies not only the perception of the landscape and appearance by the user but also the usage and experience of the platform.

Research studies show that application design, functionality, user interface structure and graphics, user interface input and output, the content of the application, and the way it is presented affect the perception of the application in question as user-friendly (Hoehle & Venkatesh, 2015:454).

1.3 Continued Intent to Use

The two most frequently used models to explain the reasons behind the adoption or rejection of information technologies (IT) by users are the Technology Acceptance Model (TAM) and the Planned Behavior Model (PBM). Specifically focusing on the estimation of the acceptableness of an information system, the Technology Acceptance Model was developed in 1986 based on the Reasoned Action Approach proposed by Fishbein and Azjen in 1975. It assumes that the use of an information system is determined by behavioral intent. However, behavioral intent depends on the attitude of the individual towards the use of the system as well as their perception regarding its benefits (Fishbein & Ajzen, 1975; Ajzen & Fishbein, 1980). Intention to display behavior is a factor indicating the extent to which one puts in the effort to do so. The more the user intends to display the said behavior, the more likely they are to behave in that way.

The number of studies on mobile user experience and the impact of user-friendliness on the intention to keep using the mobile application concerned increases gradually. Rauschenberger et al. (2013: 40) defines 'usability as familiarity while describing user experience as the impact of the product on the end-user'. Garrett (2006) argued that when one has a pleasurable experience with a product, they would be more willing to purchase the next product from the same company. Ji et al. (2006) described usability as the indispensable quality of software systems. According to Chiew and Salim (2003), usability is one of the most important factors determining the success of a website. In their study, Hoehle and Venkatesh (2015: 454) proposed a scale, attempting to conceptualize mobile application usability through a 10-step procedure. Their scale might be used to define the functions and design features of the mobile application in question. Ghose and Park (2013) indicated that users are less willing to buy niche products when they use devices with smaller screens to browse websites.

2 Methodology

2.1 Hypotheses, Research Model, and Sample Selection

Marketing experts agree on the necessity of offering a user-friendly application in order to provide a good user experience. Based on the assumption that a comfortable and practical shopping experience would contribute to the intention to keep using the application, the first hypothesis (H_1) was formulated as follows:

H_1: The user-friendliness of a mobile shopping application has a positive impact on the intention to continue using the application concerned.

The first impression and the shopping experience of the consumer are of vital importance. Designs must easily direct the user to the content and product categories they look for or to the menu they last checked, therefore eliminating confusion. Therefore, the resulting positive experience would affect the intention of the user to keep using the application. This was indicated in the second hypothesis (H_2) as follows:

H_2: The positive user experience provided by a mobile shopping application has a positive impact on the intention to continue using the application concerned.

The conveniences during the processes in which the user signs up, signs in, searches for products, filters search results, collects information, makes comparisons, adds products to basket, and pays for the products on a user-friendly application would contribute to positive user experience. If the mandatory registration section is removed in the payment page, sales were found to increase by 45% (Kowalski, 2019). Therefore, the third hypothesis of the study (H_3) was designated as follows:

H_3: The user-friendliness of a mobile shopping application has a positive impact on a positive user experience.

Based on these hypotheses, Figure 19.1 shows the research model.

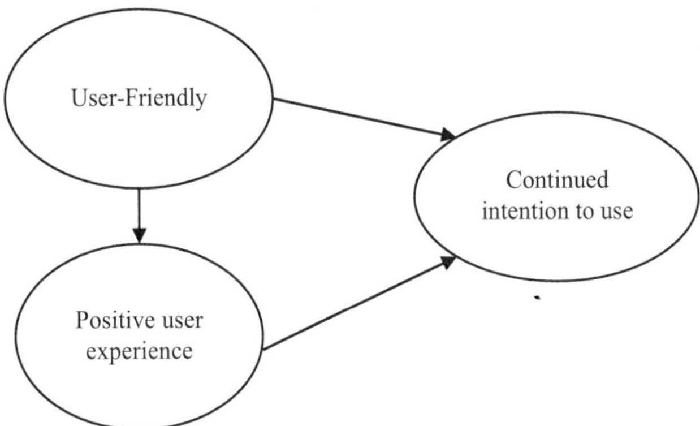

Fig. 19.1: Research Model. **Source:** Created by Author

While designating statements on user-friendliness, the scales proposed by McKinney et al. (2002), Waite and Harrison (2002), and Hoehle and Venkatesh (2015). For statements regarding user experience, the scales developed by Ji et al. (2006) and Waite and Harrison (2002) were employed. Finally, the scales proposed by Bhattacherjee (2001), Venkatesh and Goyal (2010), and Hoehle and Venkatesh (2015) were used while formulating the statements on the continued intention to use. The statements in the survey form were prepared using a 5-point Likert scale. After translating the scales consisting of three dimensions and 21 statements from English, a pilot study was conducted through face-to-face questionnaires following necessary adaptations. The method of convenience sampling was employed, using questionnaires as the data collection tool. The online questionnaire created within the scope of the study was distributed among 285 individuals stating that they have shopped using the mobile application concerned between 27 June – 30 July 2019. After discarding the forms filled incorrectly and erroneously, a total of 274 forms were assessed. The data gathered from the assessment were processed using SPSS 22.00 and the software package of AMOS 20.00. Structural Equation Modeling (SEM) was used to reveal scale validity. An explanatory factor analysis (EFA) was made for the structural validity analysis. To find discriminant validity, a confirmatory factor analysis (CFA) was made.

3 Research Findings and Analysis

Table 19.1 shows the demographic features of the participants.

Tab. 19.1: Demographic Features. **Source:** Created by Author

Gender	f	%	Age	f	%
Female	107	39.5	18–30	209	77.1
Male	164	60.5	31–43	40	14.8
			44–56	19	7.0
			57–69	3	1.1
Total	*271*	*100*	*Total*	*271*	*100*
Education Level	**f**	**%**	**Income**	**f**	**%**
Primary school	3	1.1	0–3000	183	67.5
High School	19	7.0	3001–6000	54	19.9
Associate degree	114	42.1	6001–9000	23	8.5
Bachelor's degree	95	35.1	9001–12000	6	2.2
(Post)graduate	40	14.8	12000+	5	1.8
Total	*271*	*100*	*Total*	*271*	*100*

39.5% of the 271 participants are women and the rest of them are men. The age distribution shows that 77.1% of the participants are between 18 and 30 years of age. As far as income levels are concerned, 67.5% of participants have an income between 0 and 3000 Turkish liras. The factors determined at the end of the EFA are shown in Table 19.2.

Tab. 19.2: Results of the Exploratory Factor Analysis. **Source:** Created by Author

Structures	Statements	Exploratory Factor Loads
1st Factor User-friendliness (α= .96; KMO= .876; p=0.000; Explained Variance: 32.41)		
UF1	On a user-friendly and well-designed mobile application, I must be able to sign up and sign in conveniently.	0.723
UF2	On a user-friendly and well-designed mobile application, I must be able to search and compare products easily.	0.767
UF3	On a user-friendly and well-designed mobile application, I must be able to filter products conveniently.	0.788
UF4	On a user-friendly and well-designed mobile application, I must be able to see the ratings and comments about a product right away.	0.670

Tab. 19.2: Continued

Structures	Statements	Exploratory Factor Loads
2nd Factor: Positive user experience (α= .95; KMO= .876; p=0.000; Explained Variance: 28.80)		
UX2	On a user-friendly and well-designed mobile application, I must be able to find information about products, stocks, promotions, and warranty conditions.	0.717
UX3	On a user-friendly and well-designed mobile application, I must be offered discounts, promotions, and offers about the products I am interested in.	0.816
UX5	On a user-friendly and well-designed mobile application, I must be able to choose between different payment options (e.g. credit card, EFT, wire transfer, cash on delivery).	0.759
UX7	On a user-friendly and well-designed mobile application, I must be able to track my orders and view my order history.	0.685
UX8	On a user-friendly and well-designed mobile application, I must be able to get answers from channels like live support or call centers.	0.711
3rd Factor: Continued intention to use (α= .95; KMO= .750; p=0.000; Explained Variance: 27.47)		
IN1	I consider continuing to use user-friendly applications providing a positive experience.	0.824
IN2	I am more likely to continue using user-friendly applications providing a positive experience.	0.879
IN3	I believe I will keep using user-friendly applications providing a positive experience.	0.893

The explained variance of the scale was calculated as 88% while its Cronbach's Alpha value was found to be α=0.97. The result of the Kaiser-Meyer-Olkin (KMO) test being 0.95>0.70 indicates that the sample size is sufficient, and the result of Bartlett's Test of Sphericity being 0.00<0.01 shows that the statements are consistent with one another.

At the end of the factor analysis, the variables of UF5, DO6, UF7, UX1, UX4, UX6, IN4, IN5, and IN6 were excluded as they disrupted the factor structure or were included in multiple factors. The analysis was repeated after the exclusion of the said items; in the end, 12 statements the factor loads of which range between 67 and 89 were included in the scale. These results show that the scales included in the study have valid structures. Then, confirmatory factor analysis was made on the factors determined with the exploratory factor analysis to see if they are compatible with the factor structures designated with the hypotheses. After testing the measurement model for the latent variables within the structural model, the structural model will be tested when a suitable measurement model is obtained. The measurement model in the Structural Equation Model (SEM) is the confirmatory factor model (Schumacker & Lomax, 2010: 184).

Upon examining the results of the CFA for the measurement model at the level of $p < 0.05$, the standardized regression coefficients of the user-friendliness dimension were valued between 0.909 and 0.947 whereas the standardized regression coefficients of the positive user experience dimension vary between 0.799 and 0.953. Furthermore, the standardized regression coefficients of the third dimension of continued intent to use range between 0.901 and 0.974. These coefficients representing the correlation coefficient obtained from the findings (λ) seem to be at the desired levels. The goodness of fit indices of the model are shown in Table 19.3.

Tab. 19.3: The Goodness of Fit Indices for the Confirmatory Factor Analysis. **Source:** Created by Author

Model goodness of fit indices	Results	Recommended value
X^2/df	2.72	≤ 5
GFI	0.92	≥ 0.8
AGFI	0.88	≥ 0.8
CFI	0.98	≥ 0.9
TLI	0.97	≥ 0.9
RMSEA	0.08	≤ 0.08

The findings suggest that the model corresponds to the data gathered to a satisfactory extent (Doll et al., 1994, Mishra & Datta, 2011). Therefore, it is possible to state that the structures of "user-friendliness, positive user experience, and the continued intent to use" are represented well with the items listed in Table 3. As a result of the satisfactory goodness of fit levels of the CFA model, each structure was analyzed for reliability and validity. To test the reliability of these three structures, the values of average variance extracted (AVE), composite reliability (CR), and Cronbach's Alpha (α) were calculated. Table 19.4 shows these values.

Tab. 19.4: Reliability Test Results among Structures. **Source:** Created by Author

Structure	**CR**	**AVE**
User-friendliness	0.957	0.818
Positive user experience	0.963	0.867
Continued intent to use	0.953	0.871
CR>70, AVE>50, CR>AVE; AVE= Σλ2 / Σλ2+Σε; CR=(Σλ)2 /(Σλ)2+ Σε		

As seen from the table, the structural model is a good fit since the AVE and CR values are above the critical threshold (Hair et al., 2009); the reliability conditions for the variables of the model were also satisfied. Taking all these outcomes into account, path analysis for the structural model was deemed possible owing to the satisfactory results from the CFA.

3.1 Structural Equation Modeling

EFA and CFA eliminated problematic statements while testing and confirming the reliability of the scales. Therefore, the literature review set the foundation for testing the relationships between the variables of the model. The research model in which the variables are evaluated as a whole is shown in Figure 19.2.

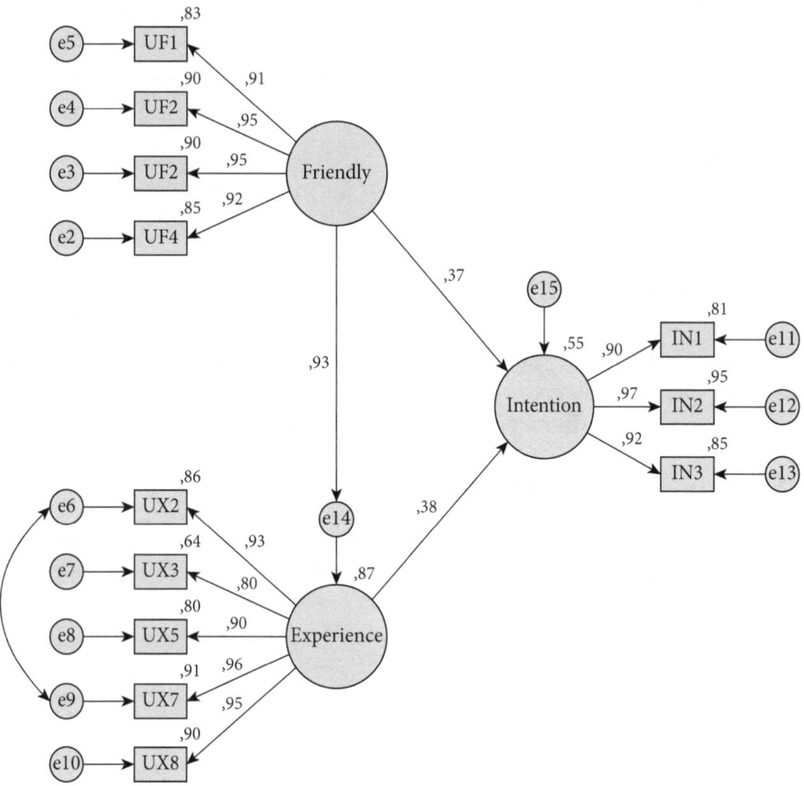

Fig. 19.2: The Structural Model with Standardized Results. **Source:** Created by Author. Note: p<0.001; * p<0.01; ** p<0.05;" p>0,05 (not significant)

Tab. 19.5: The Goodness of Fit Indices for the Research Model. **Source:** Created by Author

Model goodness of fit indices	Results	Recommended value
X^2/df	2.32	≤ 5
GFI	0.93	≥0.8
AGFI	0.89	≥0.8
CFI	0.98	≥0.9
TLI	0.98	≥0.9
RMSEA	0.07	≤0.08

Table 19.5 shows that the goodness of fit values for the structural model are within the desired range and that the model is a good fit. Figure 19.2 indicates that upon examining the regression coefficients, user-friendliness has a positive (β=0.93) and significant ($p<0.05$) impact on positive user experience. Similarly, user-friendliness (β=0.37) and positive user experience (β=0.38) have a positive and significant ($p<0.05$) impact on the continued intent to use. The examination of the R^2 values reveals that user-friendliness explains the majority (87%) of positive user experience. The collective explanatory rate of the variables of user-friendliness and positive user experience is 55% for the continued intent to use. In this respect, the three hypotheses (H1, H2, and H3) of the study were confirmed.

Conclusion

Some mobile shopping applications are used by millions, whereas others are launched without sufficient testing due to unplanned investments. Such a mistake leads users to uninstall the application in question minutes after they install it. The suggested model underlines two principal factors to be emphasized as far as the continued intent to use a mobile application. The two factors are crucial for both developers and service providers. To design mobile applications favored by consumers, the conditions of user-friendliness and positive user experience must be satisfied. These features would allow the creation of applications with higher acceptability and greater success.

The constant online presence demanded by the present-day conditions has had significant outcomes regarding consumer behavior and psychology. The consumer is no longer able to buy a product without checking the price online or make a decision without reading user comments. Furthermore, they are also bothered by the possibility of finding the product for a better price online. As a result, the increasing fear of paying more than necessary for a product (i.e. being overcharged) has led to the proliferation of online shopping, a more realistic setting. With a motivation for saving money while buying goods and services, the consumer is encouraged to use online platforms; this allows them to compare goods and services with a few clicks. Therefore, they want to download mobile applications on which they can browse, compare, and purchase goods and services whenever and wherever they are. This due to the tendency of the human mind to opt for the easiest and fastest way of doing something. At the same time, the individual seeks familiarity and security. A familiar and known place poses fewer risks for the user. Thus, they tend to choose applications with which they had a positive experience. The repetition of this transforms the use of the said mobile shopping application into a habit, or even to an addiction in some cases. Therefore, existing businesses that are about to be launched to the market wanting to obtain competitive advantage need to pay more attention to the design of user-friendly applications providing positive user experience. At this point, it is possible to state that positive experience is the key to maintain the consumer intent to keep using the app in question. Future studies might focus on the impact of prices and trust on the intent to keep using the application concerned.

References

Ajzen, I., & Fishbein, M. (1980). *Understanding Attitudes and Predicting Social Behavior*. Prentice Hall, Engle-wood Cliffs, NJ, USA.

Bhattacherjee, A. (2001). Understanding information systems continuance: An expectation-confirmation model. *MIS Quarterly*, 25(3), pp. 351–370.

Chiew, T. K., & Salim, S. S. (2003). Web use: Website usability evaluation tool. *Malaysian Journal of Computer Science*, 16(1), pp. 47–57.

Doll W.j., Xia, W., & Torkzadeh, G. (1994). A confirmatory factor analysis of the end-user computing satisfaction instrument. *MIS Quarterly*. December.

Ferrero, G. (1894). L'inertie mentale et la loi du moindre effort. *Revue Philosophique de la France et de l'Étranger*, 37, pp. 169–182.

Fishbein, M., & Ajzen, I. (1975). *Belief, Attitude, Intention and Behavior: An Introduction to Theory and Research*. Massachusetts: Addison-Wesley.

Forlizzi, J., & Battarbee, K. (2004). Understanding experience in interactive systems. In *Proceedings of the 5th conference on Designing interactive systems: Processes, practices, methods, and techniques* (pp. 261–268). August, ACM.

Garrett, J. J. (2006). Customer loyalty and the elements of user experience. *Design Management Review*, 17(1), pp. 35–39.

Ghose, A., & Park, S. H. (2013). The negative impact of mobile devices on niche product consumption. *International Conference on Information Systems (ICIS 2013): Reshaping Society Through Information Systems Design*, 5, pp. 4113–4120.

Grotnes, E. (2009) Standardization as open innovation: Two cases from the mobile industry. *Information Technology and People*, 22(4), pp. 367–381.

Hair, J. F., Black, W. C., Babin, B. J., & Anderson, R. E. (2009). *Multivariate Data Analysis*. Upper Saddle River: Prentice Hall.

Hassenzahl, M., & Tractinsky, N. (2006). User experience – a research agenda. *Behaviour & Information Technology*, 25(2), pp. 91–97.

Hoehle, H., & Venkatesh, V. (2015). Mobile application usability: Conceptualization and instrument development. *MIS Quarterly*, 39(2).

ISO 9241-210, International Organisation for Standardisation (2009). Ergonomics of human system Interaction-Part 210: *Human-Centred Design for Interactive Systems* (1), https://www.iso.org/standard/52075.html Accessed on 15.03.2020.

Islam, R., Islam, R., & Mazumder, T. (2010). Mobile application and its global impact. *International Journal of Engineering & Technology* (IJEST), 10(6), pp. 72–78.

Ji, Y. G., Park, J. H., Lee, C., & Yun, M. H. (2006). A usability checklist for the usability evaluation of mobile phone user interface. *International Journal of Human-Computer Interaction*, 20(3), pp. 207–231.

Ko, E., Kim, E. Y., & Lee, E. K. (2009). Modeling consumer adoption of mobile shopping for fashion products in Korea. *Psychology & Marketing*, 26(7), pp. 669–687.

Kowalski, P. (2019). Focus on mobile: UX that boosts revenue. https://www.thinkwithgoogle.com/intl/en-cee/insights-trends/ux-design/focus-mobile-ux-boosts-revenue/ Accessed on: 15.03.2020.

Matinyan, H. (2019). Mobile First: Four tips for the best mobile experience and increasing conversions. https://www.thinkwithgoogle.com/intl/en-cee/insights-trends/ux-design/mobile-first-four-tips-best-mobile-experience-and-increasing-conversions/ Accessed on: 15.03.2020.

McKinney, V., Yoon, K., & Zahedi, F. M. (2002). The measurement of web-customer satisfaction: An expectation and disconfirmation approach. *Information Systems Research*, 13(3), pp. 296–315.

Mishra, P., & Datta, B. (2011). Perpetual asset management of customer-based brand equity-The PAM evaluator. *Current Research Journal of Social Sciences*, 3(1).

Natarajan, T., Balasubramanian, S. A., & Kasilingam, D. L. (2018). The moderating role of device type and age of users on the intention to use mobile shopping applications. *Technology in Society*, 53, pp. 79–90.

Poggenpohl, J. (2019). Tracking BMW's road to a faster mobile experience, https://www.thinkwithgoogle.com Accessed: 20.12.2019.

Rauschenberger, M., Schrepp, M., Cota, M. P., Olschner, S., & Thomaschewski, J. (2013). Efficient measurement of the user experience of interactive products. How to use the user experience questionnaire (UEQ)? Example: Spanish language version. *International Journal of Artificial Intelligence and Interactive Multimedia*, 2(1), pp. 39–45.

Rosen, D. E., & Purinton, E. (2004). Website design: Viewing the web as a cognitive landscape. *Journal of Business Research*, 57(7), pp. 787–794.

Schumacker, R. E., & Lomax, R. G. (2010). *A Beginner's Guide to Structural Equation Modeling* (3rd Edition). New York: Routledge/Taylor & Francis Group.

Venkatesh, V., & Goyal, S. (2010). Expectation disconfirmation and technology adoption: Polynomial modeling and response surface analysis. *MIS Quarterly*, 34(2), pp. 281–303.

Waite, K., & Harrison, T. (2002). Consumer expectations of online information provided by bank websites. *Journal of Financial Services Marketing*, 6(4), pp. 309–322.

Zipf, G. (1949). *Human Behavior and the Principle of Least-Effort*. Cambridge: AddisonWesley.

Aysel KURNAZ

20 Bibliometric Analysis of the Journal of Consumer Psychology

Introduction

Digitalization of certain domains owing to technological advancements, along with the increase in the number of scientific publications, brings about great conveniences regarding the access to academic publications. These conveniences encourage researchers to conduct more in-depth studies in their respective fields. The bibliometric method facilitates the work of researchers significantly as it exhibits the latest developments in scientific disciplines, fundamentals of the discipline in terms of both publications and authors, and tendencies regarding the areas of study in the course of history. Furthermore, it enables one to evaluate the scientific production and performance within the scope of the said discipline of research institutes, universities, and countries in addition to authors and publications (Huang, Ho, & Chuang, 2006).

International scientific citation indices such as the Social Science Citation Index (SSCI) and the Social & Behavioral Sciences play a crucial role as they provide data for bibliometric studies. The databases named the Web of Science Core Collection and Scopus are the most frequently used sources to access the indices (Güzeller & Çeliker, 2017). To provide knowledge of consumer psychology and to clarify the basic dynamics of the field, a study was conducted to find out about the respectable scientific journals dealing with the discipline in question. At this stage, the web page of the Scimago Journal & Country Rank (SJR) (2018) developed based on the information in the Scopus database was examined. SJR lists journals in order of scientific performance, therefore displaying the scientific impact and significance of journals. When 'Business, Management and Accounting' is selected as the subject area and 'Marketing' as the subject category on SJR's web page, the Journal of Consumer Psychology (JCP) ranks 13th based on the data from 2018. It is included at the Q1 level, representing a quartile of the most significant journals, within the same subject area. Considering all these characteristics, JCP, the only publication having the same name as its area of interest, was selected as the research subject.

Published since 1992, JCP is an important scientific journal allowing readers to keep up with the latest developments on consumer psychology by combining the disciplines of marketing and psychology. It is a quarterly journal in English. It is published by John Wiley & Sons on behalf of the Society for Consumer Psychology.

Within the scope of the present study aiming to examine the articles published in JCP between 1992 and 2020 using the biometric method; authors and articles contributing to the scientific production of the field the most, the scientific success of countries, the number of citations within the publications, and the important people and resources of the area were provided. Additionally, the study also attempts to explain the dynamic trends within the subject area.

1 The Method of Bibliometric Analysis

Bibliometric analysis is a statistical method used to evaluate the qualitative and quantitative scope and productivity (Ellegaard & Wallin, 2015) of scientific studies published in a certain period, concerning a specific area of study or publication (Van Raan, 2005). Meticulous data collection is vital for bibliometric analyses as the literature concerned is analyzed systematically (Moed, 2006). The bibliometric method is used frequently by researchers since it comprises information helping them evaluate the performances of subject-specific studies as well as the authors conducting such studies (Du, Wei, Brown, Wang, & Shi, 2013).

Literature research structured to examine the domain of a discipline constrains researchers due to certain limitations of access to resources/data as well as the wide temporal scope despite the existence of effective traditional methods such as systematic analysis or meta-analysis (Aria & Cuccurullo, 2017). Furthermore, the subjectivity of traditional methods also proves a disadvantage. At this point, bibliometric analysis, unlike traditional methods, allows one to evaluate the contributions of author publications and their contributions, institutions, and outlets (Hall, 2011) while facilitating a wide-range examination of the dynamics of the subject area (Zupic & Cater, 2015). As it consists of the statistical analysis of subject-specific scientific publications, bibliometric analysis is thought to prevent potential subjectivity during the assessment of studies (Van Raan, 2004). Since it offers a more objective approach to subject-specific evaluations, it is considered to be a complementary method as an alternative to traditional methods (Zupic & Cater, 2015).

Allowing one to capture a detailed outlook of the scientific area in question (Zupic & Cater, 2015) and, therefore, revealing its evolutionary footsteps (Zhang, Chen, Wang, & de Pablos, 2016), bibliometric methods can be categorized as evaluative and relational approaches (Jiang, Ritchie, & Benckendorff, 2017). Evaluative approaches make use of citation analysis (citation index). The main component of citation analysis is the process in which researchers refer to work and studies of another author and give references to these studies (Lluch, Velasco, Lopez, & Haba, 2009). Within the scope of citation analysis, methods measuring productivity and citation impact such as the Hirsch index (h-index) (2005) and g-index (Egghe, 2006) are used to demonstrate the influence of academic studies (Hall, 2011). The h-index is developed by Jorge E. Hirsch (2005) and states that there are h papers cited at least h times. As for the g-index proposed by Leo Egghe (2006), it assesses the success of publications based on the cumulative contribution by each publication. Furthermore, citation analysis might be used to detect the basic sources of reference within the subject area, important authors, prominent journals, and trending topics. Thus, being one of the methods employed in bibliometric studies, citation analysis allows one to evaluate the quality of scientific publications as well as their contribution to the discipline (Zhang et al., 2016). As for relational approaches, they enable the formulation of relationship networks and patterns (Jiang et al., 2017).

2 Findings

Research data consist of 1033 articles published in JCP between 1992 and 2020 (including January) and scanned in the Scopus database. The R-Studio software and the Bibliometrix R-package was used to conduct a bibliometric analysis on the publications obtained from the Scopus database.

This study examines JCP with the bibliometric method under the title of 'citation analysis' using an evaluative approach; however, it excludes the relational approach. The analysis of the scientific texts published in JCP was made under the two categories of 'descriptive analysis' and 'citation analysis'. The section about the descriptive analysis includes the basic information about the journal and publications, the annual number of published articles, information about the impact factor of the journal, and prominent authors, institutions, and countries. The section concludes with an assessment of the most frequently used concepts included in the keywords given for articles.

As for the section about the citation analysis, it examines the number of publications and citations to the articles in the journal. It deals with the most commonly cited references and journals among the publications. The chapter assesses the information regarding the impacts of the most cited publications and the most prominent authors in JCP based on the indices explained above. It also handles the publications and the number of times their work has been cited for the top 10 authors.

2.1 Descriptive Analysis

The Journal of Consumer Psychology has published the articles of 1416 authors; 125 of these authors are authors of single-authored articles while the remaining 1291 are authors of multi-authored articles. The average number of citations per article is 43, and the average number of authors per study is 1.37. More details are provided in Table 20.1.

Tab. 20.1: Main Information. **Source:** Created by Author

Description	Results
Documents	1033
Documents types	Article
Author's Keywords (DE)	1487
Period	1992–2020
Average citations per documents	43.29
Authors	1416
Author appearances	2524
Authors of single-authored documents	125
Authors of multi-authored documents	1291
Documents per author	0.73
Authors per document	1.37
Co-authors per documents	2.44
Collaboration index	1.49

Published four times a year since 1992, the annual distributions of articles in JCP are shown in Table 20.2. As the journal was published two times only in 1994, this year has the least number of publications with 8 articles. Furthermore, since only one issue was examined in 2020, the number of articles is limited to 12. The years with the highest numbers of publications are 2009 (63), 2012 (61), and 2019 (59), respectively.

Among all the articles published between 1992 and 2020, the 20 authors contributing to the journal the most are shown in Table 20.3. N. Schwarz is on the top of the list with 24 publications, followed by F.R. Kardes who published 19 articles. Schwarz is currently a professor of Psychology and Marketing at the University of Southern California while Kardes is a professor of Marketing at the University of Cincinnati. The 20 most productive authors created 22% of all the content published in the journal with 230 publications.

Upon looking at the countries from which authors published in the journal come, the US was at the top of the list with 74%, followed by Canada with 6%.

80% of all authors come from these two countries (see Table 20.4). However, the rate of collaborations of American authors with others from different countries is quite low with 15%. With a rate of 92% for joint publications, 11 out of 12 publications of Chinese authors are co-authored. While the rates of the top 3 countries in terms of co-publication are below 50%, this rate is higher for the remainder of the top 10 countries.

Tab. 20.2: Annual Scientific Production. **Source**: Created by Author

Year	Articles	Year	Articles	Year	Articles
1992	19	2002	41	2012	61
1993	19	2003	33	2013	55
1994	8	2004	41	2014	47
1995	16	2005	35	2015	46
1996	17	2006	39	2016	53
1997	20	2007	35	2017	46
1998	15	2008	38	2018	46
1999	19	2009	63	2019	59
2000	20	2010	49	2020	12
2001	34	2011	47		

Tab. 20.3: Most Relevant Authors. **Source:** Created by Author

Authors	Articles	Source	Articles
SCHWARZ, N.	24	SIMONSON, I.	11
KARDES, F.R.	19	WYER, JR. R.S.	10
DAHL, D.W.	14	ARIELY, D.	9
KRISHNA, A.	14	BARONE, M.J.	9
IACOBUCCI, D.	12	CRONLEY, M.L.	9
SHAVITT, S.	12	JOHAR, G.V.	9
FITZSIMONS, G.J.	11	NOSEWORTHY, T.J.	9
JOHN, D.R.	11	TORELLI, C.J.	9
MAHESWARAN, D.	11	BETTMAN, J.R.	8
POSAVAC, S.S.	11	DUHACHEK, A.	8

Parallelly to the 80% share of the US and Canada in terms of published articles, the top 20 participating institutions are universities in the US and Canada, as seen in Table 20.5. The University of Michigan is the top contributor with 84 articles. The journal being based in the US might have affected these outcomes.

Tab. 20.4: Corresponding Author's Country (Top 10). Source: Created by Author

Country	Articles	%	SCP*	MCP**	MCP (%)
USA	588	74	500	88	15
Canada	49	6	28	21	43
Netherlands	23	2.9	16	7	30
Hong Kong	21	2.6	8	13	62
China	12	1.5	1	11	92
France	12	1.5	2	10	83
Israel	12	1.5	6	6	50
Korea	11	1.3	5	6	55
Germany	10	1.2	5	5	50
Singapore	9	1.1	2	7	78

*Note: *SCP: single country publications **MCP: multiple country publications*

Tab. 20.5: Top 20 Most Relevant Affiliations. **Source:** Created by Author

Source	Articles	Source	Articles
University of Michigan	84	University of Southern California	33
New York University	53	University of British Columbia	30
University of Minnesota	49	University of Cincinnati	29
Duke University	46	University of Illinois	27
Northwestern University	41	Vanderbilt University	27
University of Pennsylvania	38	Cornell University	21
Columbia University	35	University of Arizona	20
Indiana University	35	University of Florida	20
University of California	35	University of Washington	20
Stanford University	34	Arizona State University	19

The most frequent words in the titles published in the journal within the said period (frequency) are shown in Table 20.6. The titles give certain indications about the content and general subject of the articles. The five most commonly used words are 'consumer' (267), 'brand' (145), 'effect' (118), 'product' (103), and 'behavior' (93). The word 'consumer', in particular, was used significantly more than other words. The table also includes the phrases including the keywords in question. For instance, the data for the word 'brand', includes all entries including the word such as 'self-brand', 'consumer/customer brand', 'brand switching', or 'performance branded'.

Tab. 20.6: Top 20 Most Relevant Words. **Source:** Created by Author

Keywords	Frequency	Keywords	Frequency
Consumer	267	Decision	57
Brand	145	Advertising	56
Effect	118	Attitude	56
Product	103	Evaluation	56
Behavior	93	Social	55
Role	90	Consumption	54
Influence	81	Preference	54
Process	62	Perception	52
Choice	60	Theory	49
Judgment	59	Impact	44

2.2 Citation Analysis

Productivity levels of publications and authors were assessed within the scope of the citation analysis using various indices. The bibliometric indicators of h-index and g-index aim to reveal the impact of research outcomes in scientific publications in a quantitative manner (Jalal, 2019). Table 20.7 shows the h-index of the journal in question as 101. This means that there are 101 articles in the journal that have been cited at least 101 times. Its g-index is 165. Therefore, the most cited articles make cumulative contributions, leading to an increase in the overall impact. The total number of citations to the articles in the journal is 44721.

Tab. 20.7: Source Impact. **Source:** Created by Author

Source	h_index	g_index	Total citations	Start
JOURNAL OF CONSUMER PSYCHOLOGY	101	165	44721	1992

As far as the success of authors in terms of citations is concerned (see Table 20.8), Schwarz (h-index: 13, g-index: 24) authored the most articles. Considering the h-index values, the top five authors are Schwarz, Kardes, Dahl, Shavitt, and Iacobucci while in terms of the g-index values, Krishna is also included in this list. Upon examining the total number of citations to an author, Iacobucci seems to have the highest impact with 2335 citations. This author was followed by Schwarz (1567), Kardes (919), Dahl (817), Maheswaran (672), and Posavac (649).

Tab. 20.8: Author Impact. **Source:** Created by Author

Author	h_index	g_index	Total citations	Articles
SCHWARZ, N.	13	24	1567	24
KARDES, F.R.	13	19	919	19
DAHL, D.W.	12	14	817	14
KRISHNA, A.	8	14	398	14
IACOBUCCI, D.	10	12	2335	12
SHAVITT, S.	11	12	629	12
FITZSIMONS, G.J.	8	11	411	11
JOHN, D.R.	7	11	358	11
MAHESWARAN, D.	10	11	672	11
POSAVAC, S.S.	8	11	649	11

The top 10 most cited articles among all the publications in JCP reveal information about the authors dominating the discipline. Table 20.9 shows that the study by Baron and Kenny published in 1986 is on the top of the list with 48 citations. This study is a seminal resource shaping the subject area. It is followed by Belk's study published in 1988 with 26 citations and the study by Petty, Cacioppo, and Schumann published in 1983. Two studies by Schwarz published in 1983 (23) and 2004 (21) are among the significant studies in the relevant literature. An examination of the journals in which the top 10 articles were published shows that the Journal of Consumer Research is an important publication.

The 2004 study by Schwarz titled 'Metacognitive Experiences in Consumer Judgment and Decision Making' is on the top of the list of most cited articles published in the journal examined within the scope of the present study. Other studies published in the journal were cited 31 times by other studies whereas this study was cited 683 times in total. This displays the importance of the study for both the discipline and the journal.

The analysis results show that the top 10 cited sources (Table 20.11) are parallel with the journals in which the most cited studies are published (see Table 20.10). Similarly, the top three journals are 'The Journal of Consumer Research', 'The Journal of Personality and Social Psychology', and ''The Journal of Consumer Psychology' examined in this study.

Tab. 20.9: Top 10 Most Local Cited References. **Source:** Created by Author

Cited references	Citations
Baron, R.M., Kenny, D.A. (1986), The Moderator-Mediator Variable Distinction in Social Psychological Research: Conceptual, Strategic, and Statistical Considerations, Journal of Personality and Social Psychology, 51, pp. 1173–1182	48
Belk, R.W. (1988), Possessions and The Extended Self, Journal of Consumer Research, 15, pp. 139–168	26
Petty, R.E., Cacioppo, J.T., Schumann, D. (1983), Central and Peripheral Routes to Advertising Effectiveness: The Moderating Role of Involvement, Journal of Consumer Research, 10, pp. 135–146	26
Friestad, M., Wright, P. (1994), The Persuasion Knowledge Model: How People Cope with Persuasion Attempts, Journal of Consumer Research, 21, pp. 1–31	24
Schwarz, N., Clore, G.L. (1983), Mood, Misattribution, and Judgments of Well-Being: Informative and Directive Functions of Affective States, Journal of Personality and Social Psychology, 45, pp. 513–523	23
Simonson, I. (1989), Choice Based on Reasons: The Case of Attraction and Compromise Effects, Journal of Consumer Research, 16, Pp. 158–174	23
Fournier, S. (1998), Consumers and Their Brands: Developing Relationship Theory in Consumer Research, Journal of Consumer Research, 24, pp. 343–373	21
Preacher, K.J., Hayes, A.F. (2008), Asymptotic and Resampling Strategies for Assessing and Comparing Indirect Effects in Multiple Mediator Models, Behavior Research Methods, 40, pp. 879–891	21
Schwarz, N. (2004), Metacognitive Experiences in Consumer Judgment and Decision Making, Journal Of Consumer Psychology, 14, pp. 332–348	21
Kahneman, D., Tversky, A. (1979), Prospect Theory: An Analysis of Decision under Risk, Econometrica, 47, pp. 263–291	20

Tab. 20.10: Top 10 Most Local Cited Documents. **Source:** Created by Author

Document	DOI	Local citations	Global citations
SCHWARZ, N. 2004	10.1207/S15327663JCP1404_2	31	683
TROPE, Y. 2007	10.1016/S1057-7408(07)70013-X	24	540
WYER, J.R. R.S. 2008	10.1016/J.JCPS.2008.09.002	23	90
DIJKSTERHUIS, A. 2005	10.1207/S15327663JCP1503_3	21	249
HAN, S. 2007	10.1016/S1057-7408(07)70023-2	19	281
FEDORIKHIN, A. 2008	10.1016/J.JCPS.2008.09.006	17	124
THOMSON, M. 2005	10.1207/S15327663JCP1501_10	16	891
OYSERMAN, D. 2009	10.1016/J.JCPS.2009.05.008	16	216
KARDES, F.R. 2004	10.1207/S15327663JCP1403_6	15	229
ZEELENBERG, M. 2007	10.1207/S15327663JCP1701_3	15	404

Tab. 20.11: Top 10 Most Local Cited Sources. **Source:** Created by Author

Sources	Articles
Journal of Consumer Research	5945
Journal of Personality and Social Psychology	4229
Journal of Consumer Psychology	2632
Journal of Marketing Research	2232
Journal of Marketing	1087
Psychological Review	847
Journal of Experimental Social Psychology	811
Psychological Science	786
Psychological Bulletin	742
Personality and Social Psychology Bulletin	709

Conclusion

Bibliometric analysis is one of the methods of assessing the productivity of subject-specific publications by revealing the evolutionary development of a scientific domain or journal within a certain period. As it allows one to evaluate scientific publications from a broader perspective and in a more objective manner, it is preferred to other traditional methods by many researchers. This study analyzed the data concerning the descriptive and citation analysis of a journal using the bibliometric method.

At the end of the bibliometric analysis conducted on the 1033 scientific articles published in the Journal of Consumer Psychology between 1992 and 2020, it was revealed that the most prominent authors with the most number of publications and the most significant impact levels are N. Schwarz, F.R. Kardes, D.W. Dahl, A. Krishna, D. Iacobucci, and S. Shavitt. Around three-quarters of the articles published in the journal were submitted by authors from American institutions. 85% of the publications sent from American institutions are single-authored documents. Similarly, the top 20 contributing institutions are universities based in the US and Canada. A total of 696 articles submitted by these universities were published in the journal. The University of Michigan was found to be the top contributor. The findings of the analysis demonstrate the dominant impact of the US as far as country evaluations are concerned. The journal being based in the US is thought to affect these results. Additionally, there is a parallelism between the institutions of journal editors and members of the scientific advisory committee and the prominent institutions in the journal. The study also examined the most frequently used keywords based on the titles of articles published in JCP. It was revealed that the concepts of 'consumer', 'brand', 'effect', 'product', and 'behavior' might be considered as the most extensively studied topics (John & Park, 2016; Kardes, Posavac, & Cronley, 2004; Kim, Park, & Schwarz, 2010; Krishna & Schwarz, 2014; Noseworthy, Wang, & Islam, 2012; Schmitt, Brakus, & Zarantonello, 2015; Torelli & Rodas, 2017). These findings show the dynamic subject trends within the discipline.

The citation analyses revealed that Schwarz, a prominent researcher of psychology and marketing, comes to the forefront with their contributions to both the discipline and the journal. An examination of the studies published in JCP demonstrates that the most cited studies in the field of consumer psychology are conducted by Baron and Kennedy (1986), Belk (1988), and Petty, Cacioppo and Schumann (1983). The most significant periodicals for the discipline were found to be the Journal of Consumer Research and the Journal of Personality and Social Psychology. The outcomes of the present study attempt to demonstrate the level of scientific productivity in the field of consumer psychology as far as the journal in question is concerned. The findings are thought to be important indications for the planning of the publication policy of the journal. Furthermore, they are expected to benefit the development of a point of view regarding the discipline for researchers.

References

Aria, M. & Cuccurullo, C. (2017). Bibliometrix: An R-tool for comprehensive science mapping analysis. *Journal of Informetrics,* 11, pp. 959–975.

Baron, R. M. & Kenny, D. A. (1986). The moderator-mediator variable distinction in social psychological research: Conceptual, strategic, and statistical considerations. *Journal of Personality and Social Psychology*, 51, pp. 1173–1182.

Belk, R.W. (1988). Possessions and the extended self. *Journal of Consumer Research*, 15, pp. 139–168.

Du, H. B., Wei, L. X., Brown, M. A., Wang, Y. Y. & Shi, Z. (2013). A bibliometric analysis of recent energy efficiency literature: An expanding and shifting focus'. *Energy Efficiency*, 6(1), pp. 177–190.

Egghe, L. (2006). Theory and practise of the g-index. *Scientometrics*, 69(1), pp. 131–152, https://doi.org/10.1007/s11192-006-0144-7 Accessed on: 10.02.2020.

Ellegaard, O. & Wallin, J. A. (2015). The bibliometric analysis of scholarly production: How great is the impact? *Scientometrics,* https://doi.org/10.1007/s11192-015-1645-z PMID: 26594073 Accessed on: 10.02.2020.

Güzeller, C. O. & Çeliker, N. (2017). Gastronomy from past to today: A bibliometrical analysis. *Journal of Tourism and Gastronomy Studies,* 5(2), pp. 88–102.

Hall, C. M. (2011). Publish and perish? Bibliometric analysis, journal ranking and the assessment of research quality in tourism. *Tourism Management*, 32(1), pp. 16–27.

Hirsch, J. E. (2005). An index to quantify an individual's scientific research output. *Proceedings of the National academy of Sciences of the United States of America*, 102(46), pp. 16569–16572, https://doi.org/10.1073/pnas.0507655102 Accessed on: 10.02.2020.

Huang, Y. L., Ho, Y. S. & Chuang, K. Y. (2006). Bibliometric analysis of nursing research in Taiwan 1991–2004. *Journal of Nursing Research*, 14(1), pp. 75–81.

Jalal, S. M. (2019). Co-authorship and co-occurrences analysis using BibliometrixR package: A case study of India and Bangladesh. *Annals of Library and Information Studie,* 66, pp. 57–64.

Jiang, Y., Ritchie, B. W. & Benckendorff, P. (2017). Bibliometric visualization: An application in tourism crisis and disaster management research. *Current Issues in Tourism*, https://doi.org/10.1080/13683500.2017.1408574 Accessed on: 10.02.2020.

John, D. R. & Park, J. K. (2016). Mindsets matter: Implications for branding research and practice. *Journal of Consumer Psychology*, 26(1), pp. 153–160.

Kardes, F. R., Posavac, S. S. & Cronley, M. L. (2004). Consumer inference: A review of processes, bases, and judgment contexts. *Journal of Consumer Psychology*, 14(3), pp. 230–256.

Kim, H., Park, K. & Schwarz, N. (2010). Will this trip really be exciting? The role of incidental emotions in product evaluation. *Journal of Consumer Psychology,* 36(6), pp. 983–991.

Krishna, A. & Schwarz, N. (2014). Sensory marketing, embodiment, and grounded cognition: Implications for consumer behavior. *Journal of Consumer Psychology,* 24(2), pp. 1–10.

Lluch, J. O., Velasco, E., Lopez, M. & Haba, J. (2009). Coauthorship and citation networks in Spanish history of science research. *Scientometrics*, 80(2), pp. 373–383. https://link.springer.com/article/10.1007/s11192-008-2089-5 Accessed on: 10.02.2020.

Moed, H. F. (2006). *Citation Analysis in Research Evaluation.* Vol. 9. Berlin: Springer.

Noseworthy T. J., Wang, J. & Islam, T. (2012). How context shapes category inferences and attribute preference for new ambiguous products. *Journal of Consumer Psychology,* 22(4), pp. 529–544.

Petty, R. E., Cacioppo, J. T. & Schumann, D. (1983). Central and peripheral routes to advertising effectiveness: The moderating role of involvement. *Journal of Consumer Research*, 10, pp. 135–146.

Schmitt, B., Brakus, J. J. & Zarantonello, L. (2015). From experiential psychology to consumer experience. *Journal of Consumer Psychology,* 25(1), pp. 166–171.

Scimago Journal & Country Rank (SJR). (2018). https://www.scimagojr.com/journalrank.php?area=1400&category=1406 Accessed on: 25.02.2020.

Torelli, C. J. & Rodas, M. A. (2017). Tightness–looseness: Implications for consumer and branding research. *Journal of Consumer Psychology,* 27(3), pp. 398–404.

Van Raan, A. F. J. (2004). Measuring science. In. H. F. Moed, W. Glanzel & U. Schmoch (Eds.), *Handbook of Quantitative Science and Technology Research* (pp. 19–50). Netherlands: Springer.

Van Raan, A. F. J. (2005). For your citations only? Hot topics in bibliometric analysis. *Measurement: Interdisciplinary Research and Perspectives*, 3(1), pp. 50–62.

Zhang, X., Chen, H., Wang, W. & de Pablos, P. O. (2016). What is the role of IT in innovation? A bibliometric analysis of research development in IT innovation. *Behaviour & Information Technology*, 35(12), pp. 1130–1143. https://doi.org/10.1080/0144929X.2016.1212403 Accessed on: 10.02.2020.

Zupic, I. & Cater, T. (2015). Bibliometric methods in management and organization. *Organizational Research Methods*, 18(3), pp. 429–472.

List of Figures

List of Tables